Making Multilevel Public Management Work

Stories of Success and Failure
from Europe and North America

PUBLIC ADMINISTRATION AND PUBLIC POLICY
A Comprehensive Publication Program

EDITOR-IN-CHIEF

DAVID H. ROSENBLOOM
Distinguished Professor of Public Administration
American University, Washington, DC

Founding Editor

JACK RABIN

RECENTLY PUBLISHED BOOKS

Available Electronically
PublicADMINISTRATION*netBASE*
http://www.crcnetbase.com/page/public_administration_ebooks

Making Multilevel Public Management Work

Stories of Success and Failure from Europe and North America

Edited by Denita Cepiku
David K. Jesuit • Ian Roberge

CRC Press
Taylor & Francis Group
Boca Raton London New York

CRC Press is an imprint of the
Taylor & Francis Group, an **Informa** business

CRC Press
Taylor & Francis Group
6000 Broken Sound Parkway NW, Suite 300
Boca Raton, FL 33487-2742

Printed on acid-free paper
Version Date: 20130401

International Standard Book Number-13: 978-1-4665-1380-8 (Hardback)

Visit the Taylor & Francis Web site at
http://www.taylorandfrancis.com

and the CRC Press Web site at
http://www.crcpress.com

Contents

SECTION III CONCLUSION: CONTESTING MULTILEVEL PUBLIC MANAGEMENT

Introduction

This book is the result of the collaboration among scholars working on public management issues as part of a small network, the Transnational Initiative on Governance Research and Education (TIGRE Net), which has been meeting since 2009. The objective of this volume, which relies on several case studies from Europe and North America, is to consider practices of multilevel public management, identifying the conditions for success and those under which such governance arrangements fail.

Public management increasingly takes place in multilevel settings, because most countries are decentralized to one degree or another, and most problems transcend and cut across administrative and geographical borders. This evolution has affected public management practices in many ways; identifying and analyzing experiences of coordination among different orders of government is increasingly important for both practitioners and researchers. Yet multilevel governance and public management have developed as separate streams of literature, rarely talking to each other. Consequently, this volume provides an original contribution, showing that much can be revealed by the cross-fertilization of the two traditions. By bringing together examples from Europe and North America, between regions and states, it draws conclusions on practices of public management in multilevel governance settings. The book has also been strengthened by the participation of researchers from various disciplines, including public management, political science and international relations, economics, and administrative law. The interdisciplinary nature of the scholarship provides a complete and compelling portrait of multilevel public management as practiced and studied on two continents.

The focus of this book, thus, is on how to make multilevel public management work. The analyses are driven by curiosity about public management practices in the context of multilevel governance. Using an inductive logic, authors study a particular case or a few selected cases and try to highlight lessons learned and implications. From the multiplicity of cases, it becomes possible to identify trends and concerns. The book does not attempt to provide or to build a multilevel public management theory. As Rouillard and Nadeau emphasize in the conclusion, much theoretical and conceptual work remains when it comes to the study of multilevel governance. We thought it important, however, to first describe, trace, analyze, and explain current practices.

Among the factors that many authors find essential to making multilevel public management work are coordination and collaboration—to avoid gaps and conflicts—and, just as importantly, new skills and leadership capacities. An excessive focus on creating networks instead of managing them is too often observed. Once a collaborative venue or partnership is established (between different orders of government, with the private sector, with citizens), public managers are naively convinced that the benefits of collaboration will naturally flow and make policies and decisions more effective. The case studies—best and bad practices, to use a known terminology—show that networks as organizational forms are difficult to manage, as complex in some circumstances as the underlying problems they are meant to address. Therefore, the public sector is in need of finding the right leadership skills, institutional design, and network management mechanisms to avoid deadlock and manage conflict effectively.

Though the case study approach is not necessarily novel and, in fact, is fairly common in the public management field, it is worthwhile here to highlight its particular strengths, and some of its limitations. McNabb defines case research as "a research method, in which qualitative or descriptive data collection and analysis techniques are used to enable a researcher or researchers to add to the knowledge base of a discipline" (2010, 4). There are, clearly, many insights to be gained from an in-depth analysis of a single case or a small number of cases. This approach allows the researcher to identify the specific dynamics at play in a particular situation. These micro- and meso-level dynamics, which are so important to the practice and study of public management, become much harder to identify and explain through large N-type analysis. Consideration of the micro and meso levels through case studies allows the researcher to identify the rule-in-use above and beyond the rule-in-form (Sproule-Jones 1993), as applied within an established constitutional and institutional framework. Though rule-in-form is important and must be considered when studying multilevel governance, rule-in-use generally reflects the on-the-ground reality for practitioners. This book's chapters provide a rich description of the case(s) under study. It is from these narratives that practices can be discovered.

There are drawbacks to a case study approach, however. Most notably, the cases in this book may not reflect generalized practices. As noted above, this book does not attempt to build a theory of multilevel public management, or even to draw broad inferences and rules from the cases under consideration. The issue of generalizability is partly mitigated by considering cases in various jurisdictions in Europe and North America. The conclusions offered are, to a certain extent, limited by the cases considered, yet the evidence is still quite convincing.

This book focuses on cases from Europe (most notably Italy) and North America (both Canada and the United States). While there is no pretention to be either exhaustive or fully representative with these case studies, the reader is given the chance to compare practices across regions and states. Chapters focus either on a single case or, when appropriate, use a comparative approach to look at selected cases. Though the term *multilevel governance* largely was born to describe the European experiment, Italy is not one of the traditional case studies. Yet it is an interesting one for practitioners and researchers who can learn from the country's federalizing process within the overarching European Union (EU) framework. Analyses of Canada and the United States are more common, especially in the literature dealing with federalism and intergovernmental relations. When needed, contributors refer to this literature. Taken together, the three main countries under consideration, with different multilevel governance systems, provide contrasting examples of existing practices. The cases, as such, which also draw from a variety of policy fields, should be of interest to a broad readership, especially practitioners, whether they are interested in multilevel governance or public management or practices in a specific country or in a particular policy area.

The rest of this introduction is divided into three parts. The first section defines the concept of multilevel governance, with particular attention paid to how it relates to public management. The second section highlights the main findings from the presented cases. The third part presents the structure of the book.

Multilevel Public Management

In order to put the book's various contributions into context, a definition of multi-level public management is required, paying particular attention to the already established concept of multilevel governance.

There are multiple definitions of multilevel governance, which admittedly can lead to some confusion. Peters and Pierre's definition is proposed both here and in the conclusion. As they state, multilevel governance "refers to negotiated, non-hierarchical exchanges between institutions at the transnational, national, regional and local levels (...) [and] to a vertical 'layering' of governance processes at these different levels" (Peters and Pierre 2001, 131). There are many components of multilevel governance that should be stressed. The first and most important is that it refers to the interaction among various levels of authority from the transnational to the local. The interaction is non-hierarchical in the sense that each level retains its authority and autonomy and does not become subservient to another. Second, multilevel governance has distinct conceptual advantages. Most notably, the shift from government to governance highlights the networked-nature of the approach, where authority is not only spread vertically but is also shared horizontally with private sector and other non-governmental actors. Third, multilevel governance is management and policy focused, elements that are often overlooked. As noted above, management and policy problems increasingly transcend borders; they cannot be resolved unless there is coordination and collaboration among public sector actors, private and non-governmental actors, across levels of authority.

Multilevel governance is generally used within three areas of scholarship. First, the term is often associated with EU studies where, to a large extent, it was pioneered and popularized by Hooghe and Marks (2001). As a midway point between intergovernmentalism and functionalism, multilevel governance is said to accurately describe the EU as it evolved following the Maastricht Treaty of 1992. Second, multilevel governance has been used to denote a space for international policymaking (Coleman and Perl 1999). Roberge (2004), for instance, has applied it to his discussion of the fight against money laundering and terrorist financing. Third, multilevel governance has often been used when focusing on the regional and local levels of governance, and their interaction with other levels of authority (Lazar and Leuprecht 2007). Within this variant, the concept has also been used to study the place of regions within the EU (European Commission 2001; Wozniak Boyle 2006), as well as in Canada (Horak and Young 2012), where municipalities are not a constitutionally distinct level of governance within the federal system and so are often not captured by federalism studies.

Federal states represent a basic form of multilevel governance arrangements. Federalism studies tend to focus particularly on the jurisdictional division of powers and mechanisms for intergovernmental relations within a country. In contrast, multilevel governance sheds light on vertical and horizontal networks that stretch across levels of authority, above and below the level of the state. Multilevel governance has, at times, been represented largely as an extension of federalism (Painter 2001). It is, however, supposed to go beyond traditional considerations of intergovernmental relations. A federal state, by definition, represents a multilevel system, so that multilevel governance includes but is not limited to the study of federations. The state and the national government represent but one level of a multilevel governance system. Multilevel governance is, therefore, applicable in different settings such as in Europe, with the EU and varied national and subnational governance arrangements, and in North America where the three federations, Canada, the United States, and Mexico, must also operate within the rules of the North American Free Trade Agreement (NAFTA), presented at times as an external constitution (Clarkson 1998).

Multilevel governance is useful in that it can be fused with other theories and approaches. Multilevel governance puts particular emphasis on vertical and horizontal interactions among actors whether from the public, private, or not-for-profit sectors. It is suited as such to working with what is generally referred to as "new public governance" in the field of public management (Osborne 2010), or the policy network or even the actor coalition approach (Sabatier and Jenkins-Smith 1993). Multilevel governance is also coherent with some of the traditional approaches such as public choice, or even the institutional analysis and development framework (Boettke and Coyne 2005). As noted earlier, multilevel public management works only when good cooperation and collaboration exist among actors. Public management quite rightly puts the emphasis on creating and sustaining networks, but how to ensure that such networks remain effective is quite a challenge, especially when that network goes from the transnational to the local.

Despite all of the efforts that have gone into the construction of the multi-level governance concept, there remain many areas for further study. A healthy skepticism still exists, as evidenced by Rouillard and Nadeau's conclusion to this volume, in relation to the very pertinence of multilevel governance as a concept. Again, there is no attempt in this book to theorize multilevel governance anew. Rather, the approach taken is to focus on public management practices in situations of multilevel governance, an area where little to no work has been conducted. How and what is needed to make multilevel public management work? What are the variables necessary for facilitating multilevel public management successes, and what are the conditions that might lead to failure? How are management and policy issues treated in a context of multilevel governance? What does it mean for practitioners to work within a multilevel system? What are some of the benefits and challenges of working in a multilevel environment? What are the important lessons from multilevel public management experiences? Directly or peripherally, the chapters in this book all address these questions.

Contributors to this volume were given the necessary leeway to treat multi-level public management as they saw fit. The book contains chapters within the three streams of multilevel governance literature. For instance, McKeen-Edwards' chapter focuses on the European level of policy making, while Scotti's chapter is more transnational in scope, and Bauroth's chapter clearly focuses on decision making at the local level. Admittedly, there are some chapters, such as that written by Roberge, which would also fit nicely in a book dealing specifically with federalism. Some of the management and policy issues presented, such as fiscal federalism in Italy, as discussed by Mussari and Giordano, will also be well known to readers familiar with the literature on federalism. Through it all, many conclusions about multilevel public management practices emerge. The key ones are presented below.

Key Findings

There are many useful and thought-provoking conclusions to be drawn from our case studies. Five themes appear recurrently in the book. We note them in this section.

First, multilevel public management requires that practitioners and researchers consider constitutional and institutional rules, rules-in-form as well as rules-in-use. Cepiku's chapter as well as Mussari and Giordano's chapter most presciently present this conundrum. Though Italy's constitution refers to the country as a federation, vertical and horizontal public management practices are not fully worked out. These two chapters show that Italy's federalization process is struggling to shift the allocation of resources from historical and incremental determinants to performance-based criteria (i.e., greater autonomy linked to better performances [Cepiku's chapter], and the move from incremental to standard/efficient cost spending [Mussari and Giordano's chapter]). This performance orientation of multilevel systems, however, has brought about undesired (and sometimes unforeseen) effects of competition, and has not necessarily been very effective in reducing territorial gaps. Negative effects include the ineffectiveness of one-to-one central–local bargaining and the weakening of horizontal coordination. How asymmetry is managed remains a key feature of a multilevel system. The issue is not simply one of unforeseen consequences. Rather, actors operating in multilevel public management environments consider and respond to different factors, opportunities, and constraints, including established practices and customs, institutional legacies, and pressure from citizens.

Second, chapters in the book acknowledge the imperativeness of effective coordination and collaboration, as well as managed relationships among and across orders of government, with citizens, with neighboring countries, and in various policy sectors. Interactions among actors shape vertical and horizontal management and result from both institutional constraints and varying interests and resources. The reason why it is so difficult to make multilevel public management work is that there are so many points of entry and exit, and friction, among actors, each defending their interests and with unequal resources. Coordination and collaboration to ensure effective and efficient public management are complicated. There are many obstacles to surmount. Coordination and collaboration or the lack thereof—for example, in networks or other participatory decision-making venues—seem to be a key determinant of multilevel public management's success or failure. Scotti's chapter compares two projects involving various jurisdictions: one project succeeded based on sound collaborative practices (the IPA Adriatic CBC Programme), while another failed due to the lack of collaboration (the Lyons-Turin-Milan-Trieste-Koper-Ljubljana-Budapest high-speed rail line). Scotti places particular emphasis on the need to find mechanisms to manage disagreement.

Another key issue deserving careful consideration is the role of the central government in a multilevel context. As Cepiku's chapter shows, this can range from a technical function based on the provision of information, knowledge, and expertise, to a more political role aimed at successfully negotiating particular conditions in which some forms of collaboration may prove detrimental to some of the actors. Indeed, Roberge concludes in his chapter that the central government is rarely a neutral actor or an arbiter. It also has its own interests to promote, which further complicates policy and decision making.

Third, mental processes, knowledge, and ideas affect multilevel public management. The role of ideas in the social sciences is now well established, yet it is how they play out through the system that really matters. Conteh analyzes innovation policy in Canada. He argues that changes in the global environment are associated with new public management imperatives, such as the need for the public sector to help in fostering innovation. Conteh's chapter, in many respects, highlights a success story in terms of adaptation. Williams, in turn, offers a more problematic portrait in his study of Canada's Department of Finance and its response to environmental policy. Williams' observations on the lack of departmental capacity go a long way to explain, above and beyond the politics, why the Canadian government has such difficulty in moving forward on green initiatives. In Conteh's chapter, actors adapt to a changing reality, while in Williams' case the Department of Finance appears resistant to changing its worldview.

The fourth finding relates to legitimacy. Multilevel public management complicates matters of legitimacy for many reasons. Who decides is not always clear, and the lines of accountability are often blurred. Actors take credit for successes, but blame is easily shifted. Two of the chapters in this book posit that legitimacy is enhanced by broad and inclusive participation. Greitens, Strachan, and Welton demonstrate the importance of public participation in the management of the Great Lakes. McKeen-Edwards analyzes the EU's efforts to foster user input into financial services sector policy making, traditionally a very closed policy area. The institutionalization of the process has helped to take user input into consideration, though success has proven to be circumscribed. There is something unusual about having an expert committee dealing with consumer concerns. Legitimacy of processes and of decisions poses important challenges in the context of multilevel public management. Rouillard and Nadeau in the conclusion posit that this is one of the most significant problems with multilevel governance.

Finally, politics is inherent to multilevel public management. Though at first glance such an observation is not surprising, implications are generally far-reaching. Roberge places particular emphasis on this reality in his chapter on the Canadian financial services sector. He suggests that politics has impeded a valid and needed policy debate on the supervision and regulation of the securities industry, possibly leaving the country vulnerable to market upheavals. Bauroth's chapter on responses to the 2009 Red River flood, especially in North Dakota, leads one to the same type of reflection. Despite clearly laid out processes, politics hindered the adoption and implementation of a sound policy. Public management is often perceived as rational and technocratic. Ultimately, though, politics plays an important role in the outcome. Such a situation is exacerbated in multilevel settings where institutions, actors, and interests diverge widely with multiple points of contact. Multilevel public management is, undoubtedly, messy.

The question remains: What is needed to make multilevel public management work? The multilevel public management institutional framework clearly shapes actors' actions and options, which in turn, through rule-in-use, feeds back into the institutional dimension. The rather circular process is affected by politics, actors' interests, and resources. Clearly, the key factors are found at the micro and meso levels where actors must collaborate and coordinate, manage networks and relationships, and simply make things happen. Multilevel public management works, as demonstrated by Scotti, Conteh, McKeen-Edwards, and Greitens, Strachan, and Welton, when the institutional framework is conducive to and facilitates actors' interactions, thus enhancing, through participation, legitimacy. An important feature of the institutional framework appears to be the creation of a mechanism, or space, to manage conflicts. Bauroth's chapter shows how frustrating and difficult it can be for practitioners to manage, straddle, and work through various interests and perspectives. Cepiku, Mussari and Giordano, Roberge, and Williams demonstrate that multilevel public management does not work as well when the institutional framework is ill-defined and actors' interests impede the proper functioning of networks. Federalism is a variable to consider here in that, in the three states studied, the federal system does not necessarily provide an apolitical or technocratic avenue by which to resolve differences. Multilevel public management works best when appropriate networks are established and managed, and legitimacy is sought through inclusion, all within the institutional framework.

Structure of This Book

This book is structured along two major axes. Section I brings together the chapters that focus on the institutional and legal components of multilevel public management. Within this section, Cepiku and Mussari and Giordanno, as well as Scotti peripherally, consider the particularities of the Italian case. Italy's transformation to a federation is tied both to enhancing the efficiency and efficacy of the state, as well as to better redistributing resources across the country's regions. The chapters in many ways reflect some of the core themes of the established federalism literature, whereby theory and best practices confront tough political choices, self-interested entities, and the inability to cooperate and collaborate.

The EU is, unquestionably, an interesting experiment from the perspective of multilevel public management. The Commission in particular is often accused of being a bloated bureaucracy. The extent to which the EU as a whole, its institutions, and its policies are legitimate has long been challenged, and the Commission has been sensitive to such criticisms. All of this raises an interesting question: Can legitimacy in a multilevel public management system be institutionalized? McKeen-Edwards considers this question in her attempt to disentangle mechanisms put in place by the European Commission in the financial services sector.

Conteh's chapter, also found in this section, provides a nice contrast, showing that vertical and horizontal multilevel governance can be made to work, through sound management and the elaboration and implementation of shared objectives.

Section II of the book focuses more intensely on the role of actors in multilevel public management. Through their analyses of very different policy fields, Roberge and Bauroth question whether politics in multilevel systems can be surmounted to ensure the adoption of an optimal policy. Roberge posits that political dynamics can dwarf the policy process. Bauroth's example from North Dakota demonstrates that a good process is certainly not a guarantee of a satisfying outcome.

As noted above, Williams focuses on management and policy capacity in the Canadian Department of Finance in regard to environmental issues. The finance department is a central agency that, along with the Treasury Board, acts as a guardian for the federal government. Finance's inability to support environmental policy making results from a lack of political will, knowledge, and capacity. The analysis, in many respects, is striking.

Beyond its emphasis on legitimacy and participation, Greitens, Strachan, and Welton present and describe the complex dynamics at play in multilevel public management. Remediation of the Great Lakes Areas of Concern requires the collaboration of public, private, and other non-governmental actors across levels of authority. Their conclusion, which reflects the need for an open and inclusive political process, is a critical finding. From an environmental policy perspective, and unlike Williams' somewhat discouraging analysis, Greitens, Strachan, and Welton give hope that positive and constructive change can take place through increased participation. The observation is not new, but the empirical evidence is most telling.

The book's conclusion (Section III) will surely surprise the reader and requires explanation. The project has focused on how multilevel public management works, its conditions for success and failure, and the lessons that can be learned from various cases. The book is far from a "how-to" guide, or even a list of best practices. That being said, authors provide practical insights into multilevel public management. Theoretical construction is largely left to others. Yet the concept of multilevel governance/public management remains mired in some confusion. Though often presented as a theory, it resembles much more a simple descriptive instrument. The term first emerged in the late 1990s when the EU was defined as a system of multilevel governance. The reality that it describes, however, has existed throughout history. Could multilevel governance not be applied to the Roman Empire with its loose governance arrangements over large swaths of territory, or even to medieval Europe with its diverse layers of authority from the Catholic Church to kingdoms to local lords and private armies? Multilevel governance poses all sorts of theoretical and practical headaches that are too often ignored. Rouillard and Nadeau, thus, were asked to critically assess the concept of multilevel governance, especially as it relates to public management. Their analysis should make practitioners and researchers think twice about how they use the multilevel governance concept. Indeed, the conclusion offers a more critical perspective on multilevel governance than what is provided elsewhere in the book in order to encourage a reflection on the concept's scholarly and practical prospects. At the very least, multilevel public management forces us to think of the institutional framework, actors, networks and relationships, matters of resource allocation, practices of cooperation and collaboration, and about how to ensure participation and legitimacy when decision making appears ever more distant from the citizen, both among and across levels of authority.

Multilevel public management creates multiple opportunities and challenges. This book opens the debate on what is needed to make it work.

References

Boettke, Peter J., and Christopher J. Coyne. 2005. Methodological individualism, spontaneous order and the research program of the Workshop in Political Theory and Policy Analysis. *Journal of Economic Behavior and Organization* 57: 145–158.

Clarkson, Stephen. 1998. *Fearful Asymmetries: The Challenge of Analyzing Continental Systems in a Globalizing World*. Orono, ME: Canadian-American Centre, University of Maine.

Coleman, William D., and Anthony Perl. 1999. Internationalized policy environment and policy network analysis. *Political Studies* XLVII (4): 691–709.

European Commission. 2001. *Multilevel Governance: Linking and Networking the Various Regional and Local Levels*. Report by Working Group. Retrieved 5 July 2012 from http://ec.europa.eu/governance/areas/group10/report_en.pdf.

Hooghe, Liesbet, and Gary Marks. 2001. *Multilevel Governance and European Integration*. Lanham: Rowman and Littlefield.

Horak, Martin, and Robert Young. 2012. *Sites of Governance: Multilevel Governance and Policymaking in Canada's Big Cities*. Montréal/Kingston: McGill-Queen's University Press.

Lazar, Harvey, and Christian Leuprecht. 2007. *Spheres of Governance: Comparative Studies of Cities in Multilevel Governance Systems*. Montréal/Kingston: McGill-Queen's University Press.

McNabb, David E. 2010. *Case Research in Public Management*. Armonk, NY: M.E. Sharpe.

Osborne, Stephen P. 2010. *The New Public Governance: Emerging Perspectives on the Theory and Practice of Public Governance*. Abingdon, UK: Routledge.

Painter, M. 2001. Multi-level governance and the emergence of collaborative federal institutions in Australia. *Policy and Politics* 29 (2): 137–150.

Peters, Guy B., and Jon Pierre. 2001 Development in intergovernmental relations: Towards multilevel governance. *Policy and Politics* 29 (2): 131–135.

Roberge, Ian. 2004. Le Canada et le régime international de lutte contre le blanchiment de capitaux et le financement du terrorisme. *International Journal* LIX (3): 635–654.

Sabatier, Paul A., and Hank Jenkins-Smith. 1993. *Policy Change and Learning: An Advocacy Coalition Framework*. Boulder, CO: Westview Press.

Sproule-Jones, Mark. 1993. *Governments at Work: Canadian Parliamentary Federalism and Its Public Policy Effects*. Toronto: University of Toronto Press.

Wozniak Boyle, Jennifer R. 2006. *Conditional Leadership: The European Commission and European Regional Policy*. Lanham, MD: Lexington Books.

Contributors

Nicholas Bauroth
Department of Criminal Justice and
    Political Science
North Dakota State University
Fargo, North Dakota

Denita Cepiku
Department of Business, Government
    and Philosophy
University of Rome "Tor Vergata"
Rome, Italy

Charles Conteh
Department of Political Science
Brock University
St. Catharines, Ontario, Canada

Filippo Giordano
Department of Management and
    Technology
Bocconi University
Milan, Italy

Thomas J. Greitens
Department of Political Science
Central Michigan University
Mount Pleasant, Michigan

David K. Jesuit
School of Public Service and Global
    Citizenship
Central Michigan University
Mount Pleasant, Michigan

Heather McKeen-Edwards
Department of Political Science
Bishop's University
Sherbrooke, Québec City, Canada

Riccardo Mussari
Department of Business and Law
University of Siena
Siena, Italy

Geneviève Nadeau
Department of Political Science
University of Ottawa
Ottawa, Ontario, Canada

Ian Roberge
Department of Political Science
Glendon College, York University
Toronto, Ontario, Canada

Christian Rouillard
Department of Political Science
University of Ottawa
Ottawa, Ontario, Canada

Elisa Scotti
Department of Political Science,
    Communication and International
    Relations
University of Macerata
Macerata, Italy

J. Cherie Strachan
Department of Political Science
Central Michigan University
Mount Pleasant, Michigan

Craig S. Welton
Department of Political Science
Central Michigan University
Mount Pleasant, Michigan

Russell Alan Williams
Department of Political Science
Memorial University
St. John's, Newfoundland, Canada

INSTITUTIONAL AND LEGAL CONSTRAINTS

Chapter 1

A Network Approach to Asymmetric Federalism: The Italian Case Study

Denita Cepiku

Contents

Introduction and Research Aims

This chapter deals with two general trends that are emerging at the international level: decentralization and asymmetry.

Be it federalism, regionalism, institutional or just administrative decentralization, the public sector in almost every Organisation for Economic Co-operation and Development (OECD) country is increasingly adopting the subsidiarity principle, bringing policy design and implementation closer to its citizens' needs. A second, related trend has to do with asymmetry or differentiation of public policies and public services. In many policy fields centralized procedures have been supplanted in favor of differentiation and coordination. Examples include the introduction of new public expenditure management mechanisms, such as spending reviews (e.g., in the United Kingdom, Canada, and France), and the decentralization of public employment management practices, among others.

A combination of cultural, economic, social, and political factors have in all federations produced asymmetrical variations in the power and influence of different constituent units. In the past decade, the issue of asymmetrical relationships within federations has attracted considerable attention from scholars, and there is a burgeoning literature on this subject (Watts 2005). However, while the legal, financial, and democratic issues related to these asymmetrical relationships have been explored, the public management and public governance aspects have been largely ignored. Following the emergence of new drivers—public sector reforms and globalization, among others—these aspects are now of central relevance.

The demand for asymmetry is here to stay and is increasingly affecting central–regional government relations, although in a different way compared to the past. Asymmetry is no longer based on cultural, historical, or linguistic differences but is proclaimed on the promise of better performance for citizens. Asymmetry is necessary, and there is a case for "managed asymmetry" as a way of preserving the unity of a country (Agranoff 2005) while maximizing its benefits. As Milne put it, "if there is a theatre anywhere in the world that also speaks to these issues, it is undoubtedly contemporary Europe" (2005, p. 8).

Because the determinants of asymmetric federalism seem to be different from the historical ones—that is, the ones informing the masterpiece of Charles D. Tarlton some 40 years ago—and because the type of asymmetric arrangements can range from constitutional to optional, we need to turn our attention from legal aspects to the conditions that are necessary to ensure national unity and real equity among regions and individuals. Thus the time is ripe for public management scholars to join the debate on the governance of asymmetric federalism. In particular, public management research can provide insight into the conditions that allow some key issues with asymmetric federalism to be addressed effectively, such as national unity, identity and solidarity, equity and uniformity, legitimacy, accountability and clarity, and efficiency and effectiveness.

In this chapter, the evolution of the concept of asymmetric federalism is analyzed, highlighting the strong public management and public governance foundations of recent arrangements. Presented is an investigation into whether asymmetry contributes to or undermines internal harmony and effectiveness, whether it is a divisive force instead of a unifying force, and most importantly, which conditions may be required for each possible outcome. Key issues concerning the potential benefits and risks of asymmetry are also examined.

Italy, with its federalizing process and the emergence of asymmetry, provides an interesting case study for understanding these issues. The additional functions (and resultant autonomy) that some pilot regions have asked to assume amount to over €16 billion in public expenditures that have shifted from the central to the regional level. Furthermore, the International Monetary Fund (IMF) has recommended that federalism be implemented at variable speeds, given the regional differences in administrative capacity (International Monetary Fund 2011). Moreover, the current financial crisis and the implementation of fiscal recovery plans in most OECD countries inevitably require effective coordination and capacity among different orders of government.

The chapter proposes a collaborative model of asymmetry, as opposed to the traditional (poorly performing) model, which is primarily based on bilateral arrangements between regions and the central government. It takes into account the issue of territorial differences in Italy, the type of policies that can reduce the development gap (equality versus equity, uniformity versus asymmetry), their feasibility, expected benefits, and possible risks. Particular attention is paid to the public management conditions that allow handling these risks and to the central governance mechanisms that can enable virtuous circles in the regions that are lagging behind.

Conceptual Framework for Asymmetric Federalism

It should first be stated that federalism is the acknowledgement of some kind of asymmetry. Second, asymmetry does not represent a problem or a negative phenomenon. Nonetheless, asymmetric federalism raises issues that, if not adequately addressed, can bring about negative consequences.

Asymmetric federalism means federalism based on unequal powers and relationships in political, administrative, and fiscal arrangements among the units within a federation (Congleton 2006). In other words, "*symmetry* refers to the extent to which component states share in the conditions and thereby the concerns more or less common to the federal system as a whole," while "the concept of *asymmetry* expresses the extent to which component states do not share in these common features" (Tarlton 1965, 861). This definition provides two important clues for understanding asymmetry. First, it may refer to the original conditions of the

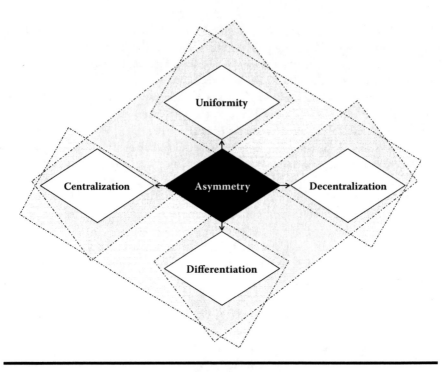

Figure 1.1   Asymmetry and classical categorizations.

different units (historical, economic, social, ethnic, and cultural) that have led to asymmetry, as well as to the outcome of the federalizing process (i.e., the actual relations between governments) (Watts 2005). Second, Tarlton uses the word "extent," which means that different degrees of asymmetry are possible. Decentralization at its extreme (i.e., independence) is the point at which the maximum degree of asymmetry is reached. In contrast, full centralization means uniformity of arrangements. However, two remarks are worth making. First, decentralization can be either asymmetric or symmetric. Second, deep centralization and uniformity do not necessarily ensure real equity (or uniformity of outcomes). That being said, asymmetry is considered to be a way of bypassing both trade-offs and debates (centralization versus decentralization; equity versus differentiation) (Cecchetti 2010) (Figure 1.1).

Federalism accommodates asymmetry by ensuring powers of self-rule at the level of constituent units; it is accepted that different units may employ that power in different ways and toward different ends (Graefe 2005). "The whole point of a federation is to allow the federated states to design and implement the policies and programs that most effectively address the specific challenges that confront them" (Maclure 2005). Asymmetry is a powerful representation of the idea that federalism is more than just the pooling of resources, values, and ideals; it is also based on the diversity of its constituent elements (Pelletier 2005).

Nonetheless, asymmetric federalism should not be confused with either the variety of laws and public policies emanating from the different federal entities or with the "natural" diversity that results from inherent differences (social contexts, demographics, geography, or resources) among regions (Pelletier 2005). Instead, it entails a genuine consideration of diversity in the organization of political and constitutional relations, relating to regional jurisdictions, powers, responsibilities, and missions. In this regard, asymmetry can be considered as the expression of a refined version of the classic centralization–decentralization categorization (Pelletier 2005) or "a very uneasy compromise" (Brown 2005).

A relevant distinction can be made between de jure asymmetry—embedded in constitutional and legal processes, where constituent units are treated differently under the law—and de facto asymmetry, which refers to the actual practices or relationships arising from the impact of cultural, social, and economic differences among constituent units within a federation. De facto asymmetry is typical of relations within virtually all federations and may be transitional or permanent (Watts 2005).

De jure asymmetry may be embodied in:

■ Constitutional provisions or different intergovernmental policies and formal agreements*
■ The allocation of fiscal resources and financial transfers
■ Representation within federal institutions such as the federal second legislative chamber (Watts 2005)

Each of these arenas of asymmetry raises different issues that need to be analyzed and governed using various disciplinary perspectives (see Figure 1.2). It is worth noting that public management issues have received far less attention than the others. Furthermore, the proliferation of examples of asymmetry in national public policy, arising from regional choices to opt out, has made asymmetry in law less relevant, considering that these choices are available to all regions (Smith 2005).†

Whether exhibited in the constitution or in public policy, the rationale of asymmetry is rooted in the validity of treating unequals unequally, while the principle at work in symmetry is to deal equally with alleged equals (Smith 2005). Nonetheless, an underlying reluctance to develop a more differentiated conception of equality has been noted (Maclure 2005).

---

* There have been two approaches to establishing de jure asymmetry in the distribution of powers within federal systems. One has been to increase the jurisdiction of particular member states. A second approach, found in constitutional provisions or formal intergovernmental agreements, has been to retain a formal symmetry for all member states in the allocation of autonomy or jurisdiction but to embody within that framework provisions that enable an optional asymmetrical exercise of those powers by all states (Watts 2005).

† The main example here is Canada and the choices made by Québec to opt out. Smith (2005) notes that these choices are available to all provinces, thus making this kind of asymmetry one of outcome or fact rather than law.

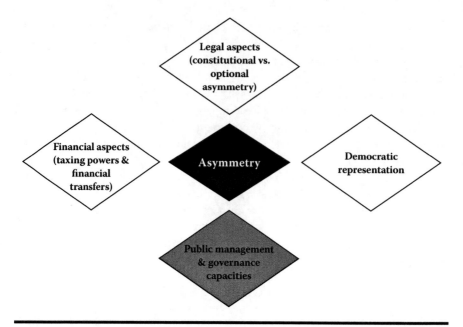

Figure 1.2 Key aspects of asymmetric federalism.

Asymmetry was first recognized in regard to different relationships among U.S. southern states (Tarlton 1965; Agranoff 2005). Nowadays, federations such as Germany and Australia place a high value on uniformity while countries such as Switzerland or the United States deal with diversity by providing for greater decentralization. In political unions such as Spain and the United Kingdom, asymmetry of powers is applied more generally rather than being the exception (Brown 2005). Other examples of significant asymmetry are found in Canada (the 9-1-1 system), Belgium, India, Malaysia, and Russia (Watts 2005).

Asymmetric federalism exists whenever governments at the same level of geographic responsibility have different regulatory and fiscal powers (Congleton 2006). Recent examples of asymmetry have also used differences in management and governance capacities to characterize relationships among governments. The main drivers of this kind of asymmetry include the election of governments seeking a flexible federalism, a greater differentiation of competitive patterns among regions as a consequence of globalization, the increasing tolerance for asymmetry due to the recent new public management/public governance reforms, and the coexistence of chronic deficits and continuing budget surpluses in different regions (Brown 2005).

Five dominant differences in management and capacity have been identified by the OECD (Charbit and Michalun 2009): information asymmetries among orders of government; capacity (in terms of human, knowledge, or infrastructural resources); revenue (namely, the difference between subnational revenues and the required expenditures for subnational authorities to meet their responsibilities);

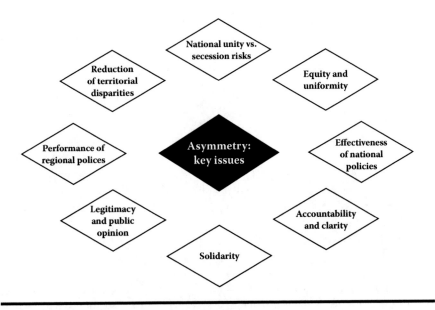

Figure 1.3   Key issues with asymmetric federalism.

administration (when administrative borders do not correspond to functional economic areas at the subnational level); and policy (when ministries take purely vertical approaches to cross-sectoral policy).

The literature on federalism has investigated extensively the politics of asymmetry (such as the distribution of political power), its legal (Croisat 1999; D'Atena 2006; Petroski 2007; Lupo et al. 2010) and financial aspects (taxing powers and financial transfers), along with de jure asymmetric systems of intergovernmental financial transfers that have been employed to make the de facto financial capacities of the member states less asymmetrical (Watts 2005). In contrast, the preconditions for and consequences of differentiation in terms of public management and governance are still much in need of research. A better understanding of these aspects would help the definition of mechanisms and strategies to deal with some key issues of asymmetric federalism (see Figure 1.3).

The sparse literature does, however, offer some suggestions, though most of these are based on the assumption that asymmetry is adopted to accommodate historical differences (cultural, linguistic, etc.) rather than to reflect differentiated managerial and technical capacities. Consequently, asymmetric federalism tends to gain legitimacy in a way that is path dependent.

These differences can no longer be dealt with by an exclusively top-down approach based on the central government's intervention, but instead require the development of horizontal collaborative relations among the different regions. Of primary concern is what incentives should be provided to regions that are more capable and are performing better than others, in order to make them collaborate with the regions that are lagging behind. A more traditional approach that makes collaboration compulsory for regions asking for additional powers and autonomy could be employed. However, as the literature on networks has well highlighted, these arrangements tend to be ineffective.

Charles Tarlton raised the issue of unity in his pivotal 1965 article, questioning to what extent federalism can be expected to sustain the stimulus to and the need for unity in the face of the pressures of separatism. Pelletier (2005) suggests that, far from weakening national unity and contributing to the breakup of countries, the adoption of asymmetric policies allows federated entities to coexist in harmony, reducing unwarranted tensions and counterproductive confrontations, and even eliminating the demands for secession. The realization of this scenario, however, requires increased coordination and coercion from the central government (Tarlton 1965, 874).

Another key issue is equity (a concept that is different from equality). Equity may refer to starting conditions (asymmetrical beginnings that have led to special statute regions in many countries), to outcomes (real equity) or to an intermediate condition (i.e., equity of opportunity, which links asymmetry to capacities) (Brown 2005). The latter is becoming increasingly relevant in many countries, including Italy, not only in response to the unsatisfactory results of special regions, but also as an arrangement much more in line with a complex and continuously changing environment.

From a legitimacy point of view, equity of opportunity is hard to criticize (Gibson 2005). Nonetheless, the legitimacy gained either from equity of opportunity or from path dependency will need equity of outcomes in order to materialize at both the regional and central levels.

Other issues include clarity and predictability and the risks of creating a dangerous state of confusion in federative relations (Pelletier 2005).

Historical Sketch of Plural Italy: From Unification to the Federalizing Process

Can Italy be considered a federal country? This question sparks lively debate between those representing the law (a revision of the Italian Constitution states that it is a federal country) and those representing economic, managerial, or political science perspectives. The debate is reminiscent of the one on formal *ex ante* uniformity and equity of outcomes. In a sense, the federal argument is not essential to the debate over asymmetry. Given the research aims of this chapter, which are more substantial than formal, a broad definition of federal countries has been adopted: a constitution is federal if "two levels of government rule the same land and people. Each level has at least one area of action in which it is autonomous. There is some guarantee of the autonomy of each government in its own sphere"

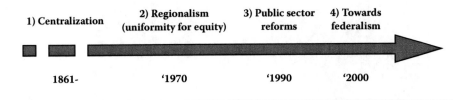

1) Centralization	2) Regionalism (uniformity for equity)	3) Public sector reforms	4) Towards federalism
1861-	'1970	'1990	'2000

Figure 1.4 Key stages in the history of state and administration in Italy.

(Riker 1964, 11). It can be said that Italy is a regional state with strong federalizing trends in place. (Political thought over the past decade and legislation approved in 2001 list local governments, regions, and the central government as equal components of the Republic.) In summary, Italy is not nominally a federal state although the policy intentions in this regard are strong and the legislation has been approved.

The history of state and administration in Italy includes four stages, which are significant for our analysis of asymmetry and public management conditions (see Figure 1.4).

One hundred and fifty years after unification, the Italian public sector is relatively young when compared to the administrative systems of other European countries, such as France, Spain, and the United Kingdom. Pre-unitary Italy included highly differentiated regions: the Sardinia realm, the Two Sicilies realm, the Vatican State, the Lombardo–Veneto realm, and the Tuscany, Parma, and Modena dukedom (part of the Sardinia realm in 1860). Pre-federal Italy included elements of both centralized France and regional Germany, with performance being disproportionately heterogeneous across regions.

Prior to political and administrative unification, the Italian states, with the exception of Lombardo–Veneto, were coalescing around the French administrative model. In the years immediately following unification, there were many discussions about which administrative model to adopt at the national level. The two main options were the Lombardo–Veneto model, based on a contingency approach emphasizing local specificities and considered to be highly successful, and the French-inspired Piedmont (Napoleonic) model, based on principles of organizational uniformity. The Piedmont model was selected hesitantly, considering the bureaucratic fragility of the southern administrative systems and the decentralization experienced under Bourbon rule (Meneguzzo 2008).

Thus, the influence of pre-unification administrative systems remains, and the Italian state and public administration are the result of the cross-fertilization of different administrative cultures:

1. Bureaucratic Napoleonic traditions (Piemonte and Sardinia)
2. The Rechtsstaat tradition (Austro–Hungarian derived, and applied in Lombardia and Veneto)
3. The weak-state models more similar to the Vatican State and the Two-Sicilies realm (South Italy)

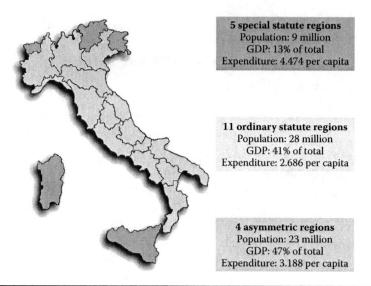

5 special statute regions
Population: 9 million
GDP: 13% of total
Expenditure: 4.474 per capita

11 ordinary statute regions
Population: 28 million
GDP: 41% of total
Expenditure: 2.686 per capita

4 asymmetric regions
Population: 23 million
GDP: 47% of total
Expenditure: 3.188 per capita

Figure 1.5   Ordinary, special statute, and asymmetric regions in Italy.

These administrative cultures illustrate differing visions of institutional and organizational models, and a diversity of relationships between government and citizens/civil society.

The unification process was based on a strongly centralized model of state, intended to enforce national identity. The new model aimed to centralize political accountability and unify policy making and executive activities. In the aftermath of unification, the central government gained authority at the local level in almost every field with the exceptions of defense and justice. The focus of the authoritarian fascist regime (1922–43) remained the enforcement of nationalism without any room for regional differences.

The recognition of special status for some regions did not escape the top-down approach based on uniformity, with the special statutes being approved by a state constitutional law (Gianfrancesco 2010) (Figure 1.5).[*]

A second relevant stage began in the 1970s when three important reforms were introduced in Italy (the Giannini reforms): the reform of the healthcare system, the reform of the fiscal system, and the creation of regional governments. The decentralization trend was enforced in 1977 and again in 1997–98. It is worth noting that regionalism in the 1970s was also strongly based on uniformity in the (unsuccessful) struggle to ensure equity.

---

[*] Four special statute regions were introduced by the constituent assembly in 1948. Sicily and Sardinia were characterized by strong separatist movements; Valle d'Aosta and Trentino-Alto Adige were included for the protection of their francophone and germanic linguistic minorities, respectively. In 1963, the special status of Friuli-Venezia Giulia was recognized, acknowledging its cross-border nature and less-developed economy.

The 1990s marked the introduction of the most radical public management reforms in Italy. In the 1980s some rich and dynamic regions first called for greater autonomy, no longer based on disadvantages or on historical reasons. The Bassanini law n. 59/1997 enforced the asymmetry trend (in terms of functions transferred from the regions to the local governments) as a means to achieve substantial equity. This was confirmed by the constitutional reforms of 1999 and 2000 and enforced by the introduction of direct elections of the presidents of the regions (1999) and the role of regional statutes.

Only recently, thus, has an asymmetric approach to federalism formally emerged. As often happens, this was first manifested in the law, with a constitutional revision in 2001 acknowledging the possibility for regions to claim additional functions.

It is reasonable today to call into question the effectiveness of uniformity in reducing the gap between the different regions in Italy. The huge cultural and economic differences of pre-unified Italy persist, and modernization and managerial reforms have proceeded at different speeds. Furthermore, the experience of special regions is not encouraging. Thus, can asymmetry succeed where unification failed?

Implications and Consequences of Asymmetric Federalism in Italy

In Italy, regions are classified in the following two ways:

- A formal classification, based on the distinction that the Constitution makes between special-statute and ordinary-statute regions. This special status, given to some border regions, was the price that the nascent Republic had to pay to ensure their loyalty. Today, the differentiation remains in only financial and dimensional terms (if we exclude Sicily) and is no longer motivated by historical origins.
- A substantial classification, based on an observed gap between regions (northern and southern) in terms of administrative capacity and performance (Tables 1.1 and 1.2). This north–south gap exists independently from the attribution of special status, as in the case of Sicily.

Formal Asymmetry Motivated by Politics, Language, and History

In Italy there is asymmetry between the seventeen ordinary regions and the five special regions. This experience with asymmetry, as in other countries, is the first test before introducing a more sophisticated form of asymmetry based on performance.

A key example of historical asymmetry comes from Spain (the four faster-route autonomous communities). Its foray into asymmetric federalism was motivated by

BOX 1.1: THE FEDERALIZING PROCESS IN ITALY

The regional level of government has been included in the Italian Constitution since 1948. Nonetheless, it was only in the 1970s that these governments were created and only several years after made effective with the devolution of functions related to the healthcare sector.

In the 1990s, the devolution of resources and tasks to the subnational levels of government was part of the public sector reform process designed to improve the quality of public services, making local public managers more responsible and differentiating public policies in a heterogeneous territory. Since the beginning, the federalizing process has been characterized by secessionist demands from the northern regions, the only ones able (in financial and capacity terms) to take on relevant functions from the center (Bordignon 2011). The process should also be viewed in combination with decentralization in other European countries (Spain, United Kingdom, and Belgium) and the development of the European Union, all of which have increased territorial competition.

During the 1990s, relevant reforms included changes to the electoral systems with the direct elections of regional presidents and mayors, the increase of own revenues of local governments, the reduction of central transfers, new competencies, and greater autonomy to local governments. This process culminated in Decree 56/2000 on regional financial equalization, which aimed to combine autonomy, responsibility, and territorial equalization.

During the 2000s, these innovative elements dwindled as the political forces in power promoted policies that ran counter to the previous reforms while the opposition feared the loss of support from the south. Meanwhile, the economic crisis and budget constraints have intensified central controls and decreased the autonomy of the subnational levels of government.

The delegated law n. 42 of 2009 is the result of a difficult political compromise solution, one that is full of contradictions and attempts to link high levels of territorial solidarity with expenditure efficiency and greater financial controls over local governments. While the contents of the law are considered by federalist experts to be quite unpretentious (concerning financial allocation and equalization mechanisms, with the functions remaining basically unchanged), it has become a divisive symbol of Italian society and has received great attention and prompted rhetoric in the mass media.

The Monti government has not expressed itself on the federalism issue. Two possible options are available: (1) a stop in the federalizing process notwithstanding the reforms of the Constitution and the recent laws and (2) a rethinking of the federalism model, granting greater autonomy to advanced regions able to carry out additional functions (asymmetric federalism). This second model can accommodate north–south differences in the tax base, in the quality of services, and in varying local preferences for the desirable degree of decentralization. Furthermore, asymmetry can offer the benefits of disciplined pluralism with no ideological preconceptions, small-scale experimentation, and richness of ideas and experiences (Kay 2003).

both politics and history and was meant to be transitional. Efforts at standardization occurred from 1992 to 1995. The system remains flexible and undetermined as no competence is a priori excluded from being transferred to the regions (Agranoff 2005; El Pais 2010; Cepiku 2011). An evaluation of the first type of asymmetry in Spain revealed a positive impact in terms not only of maintaining national unity during its process of transformation to a democratic state, but also of bringing government closer to the citizens. In addition, in recent years, relations between the central government and the autonomous communities improved, becoming less conflicted. Unsatisfactory results have to do with the scale of public employment (which increased by 42.5 percent in 10 years) and the loss of opportunity to reorganize the central government in order to avoid overlapping and duplication with regional governments. Finally, the allocation of tasks among orders of government is not clear, and the local governments have often been excluded from some key decisions in the repartition of functions (Blanco Valdès 2004; Cepiku 2011).

Canada also provides an interesting learning experience with its 2004 health accord and the shift from the shared-cost programs of the post-war era to a new multilevel governance model that involves a greater formal acceptance of asymmetry in terms of provincial variation in program design (Graefe 2005).

If we are to evaluate asymmetry of the first type in Italy, an initial conclusion can be reached by observing the failure to reduce the territorial gap through uniformity (Table 1.1). Statistics (such as the ISTAT [national statistical institute] poverty index, data from the Ministry of Health or the Ministry of Economy and Finance) describe a country in which regions that deliver public services and policies comparable to Scandinavian countries coexist alongside regions with high poverty rates. Greater regional costs and expenditures do not correspond to higher levels of quality. For instance, the cost of raising a child in Calabria is 394 euros; in Lazio, 260 euros; in Lombardy, 226 euros; in Veneto, 240 euros. An Italian reader knows well that the former regions have lower performance rates, in terms of competencies and education levels achieved. The gap in healthcare is even more significant, with the expenditure per inhabitant ranging from 30 to 51 euros in Puglia, Marche, and Piedmont, to 439 and 384 euros in Sicily and Lazio, respectively (Italian Ministry of Finance data[*]).

---

[*] See also Tucci, C. 2010. Region-by-region map of expenditure for school, health and security, Il Sole 24 Ore. http://www.ilsole24ore.com/art/SoleOnLine4/Norme%20e%20 Tributi/2010/02/ragioneria-stato-distribuzione-regionale-spesa-statale.shtml?uuid= 31190d0e-14aa-11df-949a-6432fdfe4ee9#

Table 1.1 An Overview of the Three Italies

Regions	Population (2010)	GDP per Capita (2009; in €)	Public Expenditure (2010; million €)	Public Expenditure per Capita (2010; €)
Special Statute Regions				
Valle D'Aosta	127,866	34,099	1,506	11,758
Trento PA	1,028,260[a]	30,116	8,538[a]	9,082
Bolzano PA	1,028,260[a]	35,318	8,538[a]	7,486
Friuli V.Giulia	1,234,079	28,001	7,371	5,969
Sicilia	5,042,992	16,834	23,820	4,720
Sardegna	1,672,404	19,609	9,108	5,441
Asymmetric Federalism Regions				
Piemonte	4,446,230	27,187	16,334	3,669
Lombardia	9,826,141	32,401	35,202	3,566
Veneto	4,912,438	28,937	15,106	3,067
Emilia Romagna	4,395,569	31,044	13,940	3,158
Ordinary Regions				
Liguria	1,615,986	26,905	6,906	4,273
Toscana	3,730,130	27,887	12,803	3,423
Umbria	900,790	23,626	3,134	3,468
Marche	1,559,542	25,609	5,082	3,253
Lazio	5,681,868	29,255	32,668	5,726
Abruzzo	1,338,898	21,241	6,221	4,640
Molise	320,229	20,377	1,703	5,322
Campania	5,824,662	16,686	23,272	3,992
Puglia	4,084,035	17,139	15,229	3,726
Basilicata	588,879	18,058	2,523	4,289

Table 1.1 (continued) An Overview of the Three Italies

Regions	Population (2010)	GDP per Capita (2009; in €)	Public Expenditure (2010; million €)	Public Expenditure per Capita (2010; €)
Calabria	2,009,330	16,534	8,400	4,178
Italy	60,340,328	25,365	–	4,115

Source: Italian Ministry of Finance–RGS (January 2012–2010 data) and Istituto Nazionale di Statistica (February 2012–2009 data).

[a] 8,538 refers to Trentino-Alto-Adige, including Trento and Bolzano autonomous provinces.

This situation is pointing toward a more advanced form of differentiation based on performances.

Moving toward Performance-Based Asymmetry

The shift from asymmetry that is historically determined by cultural, linguistic, and political differences to asymmetry based on the management and governance capacities of the regions (i.e., the post-2001 asymmetry introduced in Italy by constitutional reform, with the revision of Article 116, third paragraph) is even more relevant in times of global crisis.

According to Article 116, third paragraph of the Italian Constitution, asymmetry may be requested by any region following consultation with local governments. A state law must then be approved by a qualified majority. Possible differentiation areas include the regional government's organizational structure and management, additional legislative and regulatory competences of the region, differentiated administrative decentralization of functions to local governments, and greater financial autonomy. Potential benefits include better efficiency in light of significant social and economical territorial differences; resolution of distributive conflicts and acknowledgement of differentiated preferences toward decentralization; vertical "competition" among the central, regional, and local governments; experimentation with different institutional and managerial approaches and learning; and enhanced responsibility and fiscal discipline.

Three regions—Lombardia (2006), Veneto (2007), and Piemonte (2008)—have put forward requests for greater responsibilities with reference to some specific policy areas (Figure 1.6). These are regions whose economic systems grow faster than the rest of Italy. Their reasons are mainly economic and include greater responsiveness to local needs and preferences, excellence developed in certain areas, positive externalities for the whole country, and greater efficiency as compared to delivery by the central government.

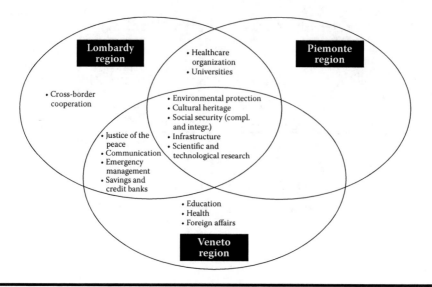

Figure 1.6   Additional functions demanded by asymmetric regions.

These demands for greater autonomy and additional functions have not yet been approved by the central government. The "necessary financial resources" for implementing asymmetric federalism, mentioned in Article 14 of law 42/2009, have yet to be identified along with the main governance mechanisms. Funding asymmetric federalism is a central issue for its implementation: on the one hand, to cover its costs completely by regional own revenues is an unrealistic and discriminatory option; on the other hand, co-participation quotas are complex to determine, while private funding may produce undesired consequences.

Asymmetric federalism has significant financial implications, with over €16 billion to be transferred to the relevant regions if Article 116 of the Constitution is implemented (Figure 1.7, Table 1.2).

The transfer of responsibility for the justice of the peace system is an interesting case. Several northern regions have a special interest in assuming this function, for both economic reasons (in order to provide the businesses that have invested in the territory with a better justice system) and political reasons (in order to achieve positive results on the topic of federalism before elections take place). While some regions are more oriented toward assuming purely administrative and managerial tasks, Lombardy approved a resolution in 2007 asking for the acknowledgement of a regional model for the selection, appointment, and training of peace judges[*] (Quintavalle 2012).

Key issues surrounding asymmetric federalism include the following.

---

[*] See Resolution N. VIII/0367, Lombardia Region, VIII Legislature. Available from http://www.regione.veneto.it/NR/rdonlyres/FFBC9DF3-BE13-48EA-8B99-ADEF336B23C5/0/xstamperiaDocumentonelleregioni.pdf

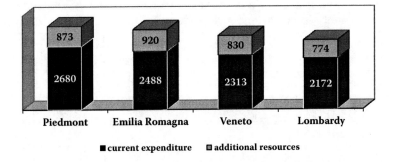

Figure 1.7 The financial impact of asymmetric federalism on regional budgets (expenditure per inhabitant, data in €). (From Cestari, A. 2011. *Towards Asymmetric Federalism: The Impact on Regional Budgets.* **CNA Emilia Romagna–Assemblea regionale.)**

The Political Issue

Shall asymmetric federalism be transitory or permanent? The shift from the need to preserve cultural values to the importance of gaining autonomy to enhance performance would seem to suggest that asymmetry is a permanent way of dealing with federalism. Also, will differentiation give rise to greater political asymmetry?

The Democratic Issue

The legitimacy of asymmetry will depend both on the way that the decision to grant greater autonomy has been adopted and on the results produced by an asymmetric system. Regarding the former, several authors have asked for formal representation of the regions in Parliament (D'Atena 2006; Bifulco and Lupo 2010). This is a rather difficult reform to accomplish in the short term, although it is highly desirable. An alternative would be to enhance horizontal cooperation between regions and to open up the decision-making process that grants additional autonomy to all regions. Without such reforms, a bilateral discussion between the central government and the asymmetric regions may be viewed as illegitimate, and the risk is that relevant supra-regional issues may remain outside of the debate.

The Public Governance Issue

First, does the central government have the capacity to assess and monitor the management capacity of the asymmetric regions over time? This means being able to answer the following question: Are these regions able to reach higher levels of efficiency and effectiveness for the additional functions, and are they able to sustain these levels over time? The Italian state has yet to build this capacity and to develop institutional measurement and management mechanisms for the decision to grant

Table 1.2 An Estimate of the Resources to Be Transferred Following the Implementation of Asymmetric Federalism (2009 Data, in € millions)

Function	Emilia Romagna	Lombardia	Piemonte	Veneto
Education	1972	4729	2257	2436
Healthcare	21	166	23	23
Cultural heritage	53	93	56	64
Scientific and technological research	44	112	43	37
Environmental protection	17	50	36	101
Communication	8	30	11	16
Infrastructure	736	763	506	303
Territorial development	2	1	1	88
Public works	13	30	31	64
Energy	0	0	0	0
Social security (complementary and integrative)	14	39	17	11
Foreign affairs	1	3	1	2
Justice of the peace	9	19	7	10
Emergency management	145	163	301	100
Total per region	3035	6198	3290	3255
Total	*15,778*			

Source: Il Sole 24 Ore, 20 December 2010.

(or not) further autonomy. The demands for additional functions from three Italian regions are still awaiting an answer on this point.

Second, will the central government enact capacity-building policies for the other regions? Inter-regional learning and capacity enhancement programs are needed. It would be too unrealistic to view these policies as the exclusive domain of the central government. Instead, the asymmetric regions should play an explicit role in improving the capacities and performances of the other regions if the unity forces are to prevail over the separatist ones, as Tarlton stated some decades ago.

The Equity Issue

This issue is directly linked to the previous point: Arrangements are needed to ensure that while asymmetry allows the more capable regions to develop at a faster pace, it does not result in a greater territorial gap, with the less-developed regions lagging behind. Instead, asymmetry will gain legitimacy and acceptance from the public only if it contributes to better outcomes for all Italian citizens. What prerequisites are needed to create a virtuous cycle in the less-developed regions? How can the central government ensure that the regions with greater autonomy (and resources) will create positive momentum for improvements in the other regions?

Federal leadership, in its steering role, must assure harmonization through national standards, while also refusing or limiting the demand for asymmetry whenever the risk of disaggregating forces appears.

A Proposal: A Network Model of Asymmetric Federalism

In light of the considerations discussed in the previous paragraph, a network model of asymmetry emerges, which can address the asymmetry demands more effectively than the traditional bilateral–contractual model. The need to evolve toward a network model is also supported by Italy's experience with its special statute regions (Figure 1.8).

The network model of asymmetry (Figure 1.9) has several characteristics that allow for the coexistence of different degrees of autonomy with virtuous circles of development. Its main feature is the prevalence of collaboration over competition; collaborative relations between the different types of regions are the pillars of this model. This collaboration should be flexible and oriented toward the areas of excellence of asymmetric regions rather than toward formal elements of the

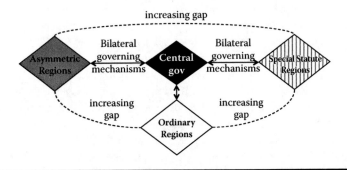

Figure 1.8   The traditional model of asymmetry.

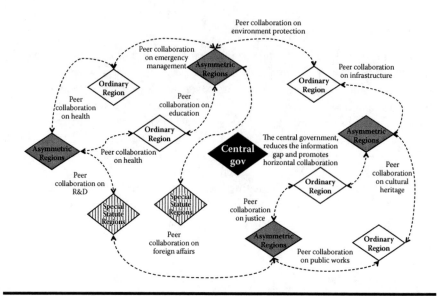

Figure 1.9 A networked model of asymmetry. (*Note*: Asymmetry in this figure refers to performance-based asymmetry. Thus, asymmetric regions represent those having higher management capability and performance records. The special statute regions include both high- and underperforming regions.)

regional statutes. For instance, if the Lombardy region is willing to take on the justice function because it has developed particular competencies over time, it should also take on the task of encouraging the development of these skills in the less-developed regions.

A special point deserves to be made regarding the role of the central government and the horizontal relationships between the regions in the two asymmetry models. Regarding the former, while in the traditional model the central government is solely responsible for equalizing the capacity differences between the different regions (with scarce success as past experience has demonstrated), in the network model of asymmetry this effort is shared. In this manner, both equity and effectiveness are safeguarded: equity, as the effort is better shared; and effectiveness, because the regions best able to take on particular functions are called to help those most in need. This does not mean that the presence of the central government is less relevant. On the contrary, it has the crucial and more complex role of circulating information, monitoring the outcomes of regional policies and funding disparities. In other words, the central government should act as a network leader.

Insofar as the relationships between the regions are concerned, two mechanisms have been widely discussed in the juridical literature on federalism: first, the introduction of a chamber of Parliament representing the regions (the bill waiting for parliamentary approval*); and second, the reform of an existing cooperation instrument—the regional conferences (introduced in 1983). The first instrument, although highly desirable, can be implemented only in the longer term and as part of a wider reform of the electoral system. The regional conferences, either general or sectoral, exist in several countries (examples are the Canadian Council of Ministers of Education or the Canadian Council of Resource and Environment Ministers; in the United States, such regional conferences form the basis of a cooperative model of federalism; in Switzerland, they represent the place where many intercantonal issues are dealt with). In Italy, several authors have called for reforms to make these conferences effective instruments for implementing federalism (see Bifulco 2005). Decree n. 281/1997 enlarged the competencies of the state–regions and of the state–cities conferences. The former are the main venue for participation by the regions in central government decision-making processes and mitigate the lack of a parliamentary chamber for regional representation. Recently, the role of the presidents of the regions' conference has strengthened, although it is subordinate to the state–regions conference. Horizontal cooperation mechanisms are still weak.

Conclusions

It is too soon to make strong predictions about the introduction of asymmetry in a nascent federal system such as Italy. The main contribution of this chapter is its recommendation of a network approach to asymmetry in which the emphasis is on peer or horizontal collaborative relationships among regions. This approach can address the asymmetry demands more effectively than the traditional model, which is based exclusively on bilateral relations.

This network model requires some small-scale reforms aimed at enforcing existing instruments as well as the introduction of new ones aimed at governing the impact of asymmetric federalism on the other (ordinary) regions. Further research is required to determine under which conditions the aims and expected benefits for the regions that demand additional functions will occur. Moreover, research is also needed to ascertain whether or not the central government is able to monitor their existence and persistence.

From a practical point of view, several issues with asymmetric federalism remain unresolved. First, it is unclear if it will be possible to implement asymmetric federalism without a fully developed federal system, including fiscal federalism, in place. If difference is considered to be an asset and asymmetric autonomy is adopted as a permanent approach and not a gradual gap-reducing strategy, effective network

---

* See Law Decree S.2941: Dispositions concerning the reduction of the number of Parliament members, the creation of a Federal Senate of the Republic and the form of Government.

governance models must ensure adequate oversight and strong steering capacities from the central government. In addition, the capacities of the regions with reference to financial management, strategic effectiveness, horizontal and vertical coordination, monitoring, and evaluation need to be enforced. Finally, capacity-building policies for the weaker regions are required, introducing frameworks for learning and the diffusion of innovation.

These conclusions highlight relevant implications for further research. The literature on network governance can greatly contribute to the debate on asymmetry. In particular, different forms of institutional design and steering mechanisms need to be tested against their capacity to address the key issues identified in this chapter.

Acknowledgment

I would like to thank Riccardo Mussari (University of Siena and consultant to the parliamentary commission on the implementation of federalism), Paola Pellegrino (expert on federalism), and Alessio Limonet (Valle D'Aosta Region at the time of this research). Any errors or misunderstandings are my own.

References

Agranoff, R. 2005. Federal asymmetry and intergovernmental relations in Spain. In *Asymmetry Series*, IIGR, No. 5. Kingston, ON: School of Policy Studies, Queen's University.

Bifulco, R. 2005. *The Italian system of Conferences*. Paper presented at the conference Il mondo delle Seconde Camere, Torino, 31 March–1 April.

Bifulco, R., and N. Lupo. 2010. The institutional achievements of Italian regions: one decade after the introduction of direct elections. *Italianieuropei*, Special autonomies and asymmetric federalism (Dossier) 1 (1): 178–219. Available from http://www.italianieuropei. it/en/la-rivista/archivio-della-rivista/itemlist/category/98-italianieuropei_1_2010.html.

Bifulco R., Cecchetti M., Giuffrè F., Gianfrancesco E., Demuro G., Rivosecchi G., Costa Lobo M., Menniti Ippolito A., Marino I.R., Cavaliere V., 2010. Special autonomies and asymmetric federalism (Dossier). *Italianieuropei* 1 (1): 178–219. Roma: Solaris.

Blanco Vald.s, R.L. 2004. Where are the differences? Differential facts, equity and asymmetry. In *Asymmetric federalism: the Italian and Spanish cases*, edited by D. Dominici, G. Falzea, G. Moschella. Milano: Giuffr. pp. 197–224

Bordignon, M. 2011. Italian federalism in 2011. In *Vivaio, Local and global: New institutional architectures*. Available from http://www.generativita.it/focus/vivaio/locale-e-globale-nuove-architetture-istituzionali-premium/2011/05/09/il-federalismoitaliano-nel-2011/.

Brown, D. 2005. Who's afraid of asymmetrical federalism? In *Asymmetry Series*, IIGR, No. 5. Kingston, ON: School of Policy Studies, Queen's University.

Cecchetti, M. 2010. Regional differentiation and specialty in the unity and indivisibility of the Republic. Italianieuropei, Special autonomies and asymmetric federalism (Dossier) 1 (1): 178–219. Available http://www.italianieuropei.it/en/la-rivista/archiviodella-rivista/itemlist/category/98-italianieuropei_1_2010.html.

Cepiku, D. 2011. Asymmetric autonomy in Spain. In *Special autonomies and asymmetric federalism*. edited by D. Cepiku, A. D'Adamo, G. Fiorani. Milan: McGraw-Hill, pp.51–79.

Cestari, A. 2011. Towards asymmetric federalism: The impact on regional budgets. CNA Emilia Romagna–Assemblea regionale.

Charbit, C., and M. Michalun. 2009. Mind the gaps: Managing mutual dependence in relations among levels of government. *OECD Working Papers on Public Governance*, No. 14. Paris: OECD.

Congleton, R.D. 2006. Asymmetric federalism and the political economy of decentralization. In *Handbook of Fiscal Federalism*, edited by E. Ahmad and G. Brosio. Cheltenham, UK: Edward Elgar, pp. 131-153.

Croisat, M. 1999. Le fédéralisme asymétrique: l'expérience Canadienne. In *Revue Française de droit constitutionnel* 37: 29–48.

D'Atena, A. 2006. The second Parliamentary Camera and regionalism in the Italian constitutional debate. Available from www.issirfa.cnr.it, 28 June.

Gianfrancesco, E. 2010. The implementation of Art. 116, 3 paragraph and the riequilibrium of the Italian regionalism. In Special autonomies and asymmetric federalism (Dossier), 1 (1): 178–219. Available from http://www.italianieuropei.it/en/la-rivista/archiviodella-rivista/itemlist/category/98-italianieuropei_1_2010.html.

Gibson, G. 2005. Some asymmetries are more legitimate than others—and subsidiarity solves most things anyway. In *Asymmetry Series*, IIGR, No. 5. Kingston, ON: School of Policy Studies, Queen's University.

Graefe, P. 2005. The scope and limits of asymmetry in recent social policy agreements. In *Asymmetry Series*, IIGR, No. 5. Kingston, ON: School of Policy Studies, Queen's University.

International Monetary Fund (IMF). 2011. *Italy: 2011 Article IV Consultation*. IMF Country Report No. 11/173 (July). Washington, DC: IMF.

Kay, J. 2003. *The Truth about Markets*. London: Penguin Books.

Maclure, J. 2005. Beyond recognition and asymmetry. In *Asymmetry Series*, IIGR, No. 5. Kingston, ON: School of Policy Studies, Queen's University.

Meneguzzo, M. 2008. The study of public management in Italy. In *The Study of Public Management in Europe and the U.S.*, edited by W. Kickert. New York: Routledge.

Milne, D. 2005. Asymmetry in Canada: Past and present. In *Asymmetry Series*, IIGR, No. 5, pp. 167–188. Kingston, ON: School of Policy Studies, Queen's University.

Pelletier, B. 2005. Asymmetrical federalism: A win-win formula! In *Asymmetry Series*, IIGR, No. 5. Kingston, ON: School of Policy Studies, Queen's University.

Petroski, K. 2007. The rhetoric of symmetry. *Valparaiso University Law Review* 41 (3): 1165–1234.

Quintavalle, D. 2012. Asymmetric federalism for the justice system. *LaVoce.Info*, January 31.

Riker, W. H. 1964. *Federalism: Origin, Operation, Significance*. Boston: Little, Brown.

Smith, J. 2005. The case for asymmetry in Canadian federalism. In *Asymmetry Series*, IIGR, No. 5. Kingston, ON: School of Policy Studies, Queen's University.

Tarlton, C.D. 1965. Symmetry and asymmetry as elements of federalism. *Journal of Politics* 27 (September): 861–874.

Watts, R.L. 2005. A comparative perspective on asymmetry in federations. In *Asymmetry Series*, IIGR, No. 5. Kingston, ON: School of Policy Studies, Queen's University.

Chapter 2

Emerging Issues in Italian Fiscal Federalism: The Case of Municipalities

Riccardo Mussari and Filippo Giordano

Contents

Introduction

Since 1990, the Italian public sector has undergone a massive process of reform and modernization (Mussari 2005). This process includes fundamental changes in two key fields: a broad introduction of new public management (NPM) concepts and practices; and the gradual shifting of powers, competencies, and responsibilities from the central to the lowest levels of government. The main purpose of these reforms has been to enhance efficiency, accountability, and manageability in the multi-tiered public sector, moving Italy from a centralized, unitary system to a decentralized model in which greater autonomy and a significant role are accorded to local governments. The impact and results of these reforms have been controversial. In particular, these reforms have led to duplication and confusion in areas of shared competency among different tiers of government, scarce financial autonomy of local governments, and a financial system based on historical expenditures, which has triggered an increase in Italian public spending and a decrease in intergovernmental accountability.

Despite the difficulties encountered in the reform process, the introduction of fiscal federalism in Italy, with a particular emphasis on decentralized revenue-generating responsibilities, is still recognized as an effective means of creating real autonomy for local governments and therefore enhancing responsibility for public spending decisions and accountability in the intergovernmental system. Law No. 42 of 5 May 2009 (delegation to the government on matters of fiscal federalism, in accordance with Article 119 of the Constitution) establishes the principles of Italian fiscal federalism that should guarantee a higher level of revenue autonomy for regions and local authorities, maintaining the progressivity of the tax system.

Fiscal federalism refers to the structure of intergovernmental fiscal relations in a multilevel system, in which each order of government has different expenditure responsibilities and taxing powers. Despite theoretical normative descriptions, every country defines and implements its own form of fiscal federalism. Thus an archetype of fiscal federalism does not exist, and the way in which the system works depends on the institutional and sociopolitical factors of each country.

This chapter analyzes the characteristics of Italy's fiscal federalism scheme, with a particular focus on its implications for municipalities. Even if Italian fiscal federalism is in its infancy and will need years to be implemented fully, it seems not to have been influenced by experiences in other countries. Hence some critical issues in the Italian system have already emerged, in particular within institutional environments.

Italian Public Sector Reform: The Myth of Local Autonomy

The public sector reforms of the last two decades are commonly referred to as *new public management* (NPM), which represents a paradigm shift from the traditional model of public administration to a post-bureaucratic one (Hood 1991; O'Flynn 2007). Such public sector reforms have been carried out worldwide, though often in different forms and with different foci (Pollitt and Bouckaert 2004). In particular there has been a growing tendency in countries around the world to reassign expenditure decisions and implementation capabilities to lower orders of government (Ahmad 1997).

In the Italian public system, the reform process linked to the NPM paradigm seeks to address the following issues (Rebora 1999):

- The reshaping of the public sector's macrostructure through the redefinition of responsibilities within a multi-tier system, based on the principle of horizontal subsidiarity; that is, more competencies delegated to lower levels
- The introduction of private-sector management practices and tools through the redefinition of public administration operational rules
- The downsizing of public administration through both privatization and the contracting out of services
- The improvement of accountability between citizens and public administrations (which has faced a crisis caused by corruption and scandals), as evidenced by the reform that introduced direct elections for the position of mayor (Mussari 1997)

These reforms generally involve every level of the Italian public sector (central administrations, regions, provinces, local governments, agencies, hospitals, universities) with varying degrees of intensity. In the specific case of local government, the reforms imply an increase in autonomy in three key areas (Anessi Pessina 2002):

- Organizational (managerial) autonomy through the Local Government Reform Act in 1990, civil service reform in 1993, and local government accounting reform in 1995.
- Financial autonomy through the introduction of local taxes and the progressive reduction of intergovernmental grants. In particular, in 1993 ICI (municipal property tax) was introduced, and in 1999 personal income tax surcharges were introduced by local governments.
- Decision-making autonomy, with the devolution of administrative functions and competencies from the central to local tiers of government and the simplification of administrative procedures (Laws 59/1997 and 127/97, also known as the "Bassanini Laws").

Through these reforms, Italy has evolved from a unitary state, with a strong centralized authority, to a multilevel one with greater autonomy afforded to lower levels of government. The reform process was substantially completed in 2001, vis-à-vis the reform of the second part of the Italian Constitution and the introduction of horizontal subsidiarity as a guiding principle for the assignment of responsibilities among different tiers of government. In fact, at a constitutional level, the reforms redistributed not only legislative powers between central and regional governments (Article 117), but also administrative functions between central and local governments (Article 118), and they granted greater financial autonomy to lower levels of government (Article 119) (Bordignon et al. 2007).

Although the main purpose of these reforms was to enhance efficiency, accountability, manageability, and autonomy in a multi-tiered government, their results and impact have been controversial. In particular, an overall increase in Italian public sector spending has been seen in the last 15 years. First, the shifting of powers from central to local governments failed to produce the expected expenditure reductions of central entities, while on the other side of the spectrum, local governments generally increased their expenditures to manage their new functions. In the Italian political scene, this outcome is known as the *cost of devolution*. Second, inefficient intergovernmental financial relations (characterized by grants calculated on historical expenditures, central bailout expectations, and the lack of sanction mechanisms for local government fiscal indiscipline) have tended to stimulate overspending within local governments and produce unsustainable deficits. This result reveals that decentralization may be dangerous if it allows subnational governments to expand their expenditures while pushing the costs on to others (Von Hagen et al. 2000; Rodden 2002; Rodden, Eskeland, and Litvack 2003). Third, the devolution of services, when accompanied by negative factors like sunk costs, has often generated inefficiencies and much higher public spending. Moreover, the devolution of services has often involved the establishment of private organizations owned by local governments which, being affected by politics, often prove to be inefficient and badly managed.

Another legacy of these reforms has been duplication and confusion in many areas of shared rule among orders of government. The reshaping of the public sector's macrostructure through the redefinition of responsibilities has generated a hybrid and complex form of multilevel governance. After a period of constant increases in local government autonomy since the middle of the 1980s, the central government has, since 1999, progressively reduced the financial autonomy of local governments.

The constraints imposed on public finances by the European Stability and Growth Pact have forced Economic and Monetary Union (EMU) countries to establish various rules for financial coordination, known as Domestic Stability Pacts (DSPs). DSPs seek to control budget balances and the stock of debt with reference to the general government and to guarantee that all bodies involved with and contributing to public finances do not engage in opportunistic conduct (Giuriato and Gastaldi 2009).

In Italy intergovernmental financial relations are traditionally characterized by a low level of commitment on the part of both central and local governments. As mentioned above, the presence of large fiscal imbalances, both vertical and horizontal, among different orders of government and territories, along with central bailout expectations have historically encouraged fiscal indiscipline. In order to eliminate moral hazard and to prevent local entities from shifting the costs of their fiscal irresponsibility onto the collectivity, the Italian central government—the only body directly responsible at the European level for the state of public finances—has adopted very stringent subnational rules (i.e., rules on budget balances, expenditure caps, ceilings on own local revenues). The Italian Domestic Stability Pact has had

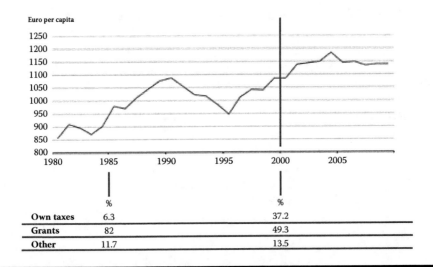

	%	%
Own taxes	6.3	37.2
Grants	82	49.3
Other	11.7	13.5

Figure 2.1 Trends in municipal expenses per capita and financial autonomy, 1980–2010. (From IFEL [Institute for Local Economy and Finance Statistics] Fondazione ANCI. 2011. Economia e Finanza Locale. Rapporto 2010. Ed. IFEL Ricerche; Organisation for Economic Co-operation and Development. 2011. *Revenue Statistics 2011*. Paris: OECD. With permission.)

modest success in aligning the fiscal behavior of subnational government units with national commitments. At the same time, it has significantly reduced local government financial and decision-making autonomy.

Figure 2.1 illustrates the trends of per capita local government spending since 1980 and following the introduction of the DSP in 2000. The ongoing increase in per capita spending after the year 2000 indicates that the DSP has not been able to fully meet its objectives to reduce overspending or indiscipline among local governments. Moreover it is clear that the local revenue mix has changed since 1980. First, between 1985 and 2000 Italy increased the share of own taxes while decreasing the share of grants for local governments, resulting from the 1990s reforms. Second, after 2000 there was a substitution effect between local tax revenue and local tariffs, mainly due to constraints on the revenue side imposed by the central government. With increased restrictions on property tax and reductions in intergovernmental transfers to local governments, municipalities sought other sources of revenue.

In order to address these concerns, the Italian government introduced fiscal federalism in 2009. Law No. 42 (5 May 2009) (delegation to the government on matters of fiscal federalism, in accordance with Article 119 of the Constitution) establishes the principles of Italian fiscal federalism that should guarantee a higher level of revenue autonomy for regions and local authorities, while maintaining the progressivity of the tax system. First, it provides for the assignment of autonomous resources to municipalities, provinces, metropolitan cities, and regions, in relation to their respective competencies and according to the principle of territoriality.

Second, the law guarantees that regions and local authorities can "shift" taxes, albeit within the constraints set by state law. Third, it states that public functions will be fully financed through equalization. Full financing will not be related to the costs actually incurred but will be based on "standard needs," which are the expenditures corresponding to an average good management cost. As a consequence, regional and local administrations are forced to be efficient in order to avoid resorting once again to fiscal leverages to obtain financing.

In order to apply these principles, Law No. 42/2009 required the government to adopt, within 24 months (delayed an additional six months), eight legislative decrees that set the rules and mechanisms under which fiscal federalism would work. Current debate questions whether or not the new form of fiscal federalism will afford real autonomy to local governments while at the same time increasing their responsibility for and accountability in public spending.

Is Fiscal Federalism a Good Deal for Italy?

Fiscal federalism refers to the structure of intergovernmental fiscal relations in a multilevel system in which each order of government has different expenditure responsibilities and taxing powers. There is a general agreement among decentralization experts that the increased accountability associated with decentralization can be assured only when subnational governments have an adequate level of autonomy and discretion in raising their own revenues. There are advantages and disadvantages to decentralizing the various functions of government from higher (and larger) to lower (and smaller) orders (Boadway and Shah 2009). The Organisation for Economic Co-operation and Development (OECD), in its recent recommendations for Italy based on the Economic Survey published in 2009, summarizes the advantages of a decentralized tax system as follows:

- Citizens' perceptions about differences in tax rates tend to make governments more responsive to their tastes and preferences, thus improving resource allocation.
- Tax decentralization tends to improve budget management efficiency as citizens become directly aware of the costs of publicly funded activities. Some authors have found a smaller size of Sub Central Governments (SCG) under tax competition conditions.
- Tax decentralization also promotes democratic accountability, because those who benefit from public services decide on taxation levels and pay the bill.
- Tax decentralization provides subcentral governments with incentives for growth-oriented economic and fiscal policies, because they may fully reap the financial benefits.
- It could reduce disparities when smaller jurisdictions benefit from capturing tax bases from neighbors' bigger jurisdictions (OECD 2009).

The literature on fiscal federalism is devoted in large part to analyzing the consequences of varying degrees and forms of decentralization and to proposing appropriate levels of decentralization for different contexts (Boadway and Shah 2009). The "proper" distribution of tax authority and expenditure responsibility is an extremely complex issue. Economists generally focus on issues of efficiency and equity, while public administration and political science scholars tend to focus on the distribution of powers, responsiveness and accountability, tax competition, and coordination (Kee 2004). However, the notion of an ideal assignment of functions is elusive because it depends upon institutional considerations, value judgements, and empirical consequences that are hard to verify (Boadway and Shah 2009). In the literature published over the last few years there has been general agreement that good and bad models of fiscal federalism do not exist. There are forms of fiscal federalism that work—that is, that enhance accountability and effectiveness in public spending—and there are other forms that do not. Recent studies in the field of fiscal federalism focus on the features that affect how normative prescriptions work in a certain country and the performance of different forms of federalism in an institutional environment.* This already huge body of literature is known as the Second Generation of Fiscal Federalism (SGFF).

While the First Generation of Fiscal Federalism was largely normative and assumed that public decision makers were benevolent maximizers of social welfare (Musgrave 1959; Oates 1972; Rubinfeld 1987, quoted in Weingast 2006), SGFF considers that in decision making, government officials tend to maximize benefits for their own constituents and political return in terms of consensus, especially as elections approach (Brennan and Buchanan 1980; Oates 2005). In this sense, institutional and political features are relevant both for understanding the capacity of fiscal federalism to improve fiscal responsibility of governments in a specific context, and for identifying which normative prescriptions can better fit within a given institutional and political environment.

If institutional features are particularly useful for understanding how a federal system performs or could perform, political considerations are important for understanding the nature and characteristics of fiscal federalism in a particular historical phase of a country. As in the case of other public policies, fiscal federalism is shaped by political bargaining among central and local governments, proponents, and opponents. Consequently, despite existing theoretical normative descriptions, fiscal federalism in any country reflects its institutional and sociopolitical context. Thus, in order to fully understand the phenomenon of fiscal federalism in a given country, it is necessary to take a holistic approach that includes economic, institutional, and sociopolitical considerations. This is particularly true in Italy, where, after the approval of the Law of Fiscal Federalism in 2009 (which established the guidelines and general principles of the system), central governments—supported by

---

* As Litvak, Ahmad, and Bird (1998) observe, "decentralization is neither good nor bad for efficiency, equity, or macroeconomic stability; but rather that its effects depend on institution-specific design" (Weingast 2006).

advisors and technical commissions—began defining operational rules and therefore how Italian fiscal federalism would actually work. During this experimental phase of the technical implementation of fiscal federalism in Italy, with central government decision making strongly conditioned by supranational institutions and international financial instability, it would be imprudent to express an opinion about the potential effectiveness of fiscal federalism. Nevertheless, it is possible to provide an overview of the Italian case, which encompasses the normative, institutional, and political features that have characterized and shaped fiscal federalism and seem to be critical to its future functioning. In particular, this chapter will focus on the financial relations between the central government and municipalities.

The Impact of Italian Fiscal Federalism on Municipalities: A Normative Perspective

The issues associated with shaping fiscal federalism in a multi-tiered system are many and encompass many theoretical aspects. In Italy, fiscal federalism has been proposed not only as the cure for fiscal imbalances, both vertical and horizontal, which have defined the country, but also as a means of improving the financial autonomy of local governments in order to enhance efficiency and accountability. Arguments for its success have stressed the necessity of giving governments an adequate level of autonomy and discretion in raising revenues, and of improving the system of equalization grants.

Insofar as autonomy and revenue generation are concerned, the literature suggests three fundamental methods of tax assignment: own taxes (independent legislation and administration), tax surcharges, and tax sharing. Each method is characterized by a different degree of fiscal autonomy or taxing power (Ambrosanio and Bordignon 2006). The Legislative Decree (LD) 292/2011* that established the rules of municipal federalism outlines the new patterns of municipal revenues that will come into force in 2014, following a transitional period from 2011 to 2013. The new municipal taxes, as of 2014, will be as follows:

- 30% of share of property transfer tax
- Municipal tax on property (primary IMU, *Imposta Municipale*)
- Municipal tax on occupation of public land (secondary IMU)

---

* Legislative decree 292/2011 is one of eight scheduled by the fiscal federalism Law 42/2009. The titles and topics of each decree are as follows: (1) state-owned land federalism, about the transfer of state properties from central to local government in order to make effective use of them; (2) Roma Capitale, which establishes a special jurisdiction for the city of Rome, with special powers and special autonomy; (3) standard needs of local government; (4) municipal federalism; (5) fiscal autonomy for regions and provinces; (6) equalization and removal of infrastructure divide imbalance; (7) sanctions and rewards for regions, provinces, and local governments; and (8) harmonization of accounting systems.

Table 2.1   Trends in Local Government Revenues

	2007	*2008*	*2009*	*2010*	*2011*	*2012*	*2013*
Own taxes	20.443	17.309	17.503	30.598	30.236	30.929	
Direct	3.695	4.001	3.916	3.906	11.619	11.619	11.885
Indirect	16.748	13.955	13.393	13.597	18.617	18.617	19.044
Grants	25.787	30.529	33.795	34.072	20.195	20.545	20.813
Ordinary	17.312	22.786	25.812	26.328	12.828	13.152	13.383
For investment	8.475	7.743	7.983	7.744	7.356	7.393	7.430
Others	16.455	17.287	17.276	17.721	18.138	18.608	19.090
Total Revenues	62.685	65.772	68.380	69.296	68.931	69.389	70.832
	%	%	%	%	%	%	%
Own taxes	32.7	27.3	25.3	25.2	44.4	43.6	43.7
Grants	41.1	46.4	49.4	49.2	29.3	29.7	29.4
Others	26.2	26.3	25.3	25.6	26.3	26.7	26.9

Source: Figures based on ISTAT data from Italian National Institute of Statistics (IFEL 2010).

- Personal income tax surcharge (optional)
- Staying tax (in particular for touristic cities)
- Earmarked taxes

Table 2.1 illustrates the impact of this new pattern on local government revenues. The decrease in intergovernmental transfers is offset by the increase in municipal own taxes, due to devolution of all property taxes (ownership, rent, transfer).

The new pattern of municipal revenues is consistent with the traditional normative approach (see, for example, Tiebout 1956; Musgrave 1959; Oates 1972) according to which local governments should eschew taxes (at least non-benefit taxes) on highly mobile tax bases and then accord a central role to property taxes and benefit taxes[*] (Krane, Ebdon, and Bartle 2004).

---

[*] The public choice literature (Tiebout 1956) states that in a system characterized by decentralized fiscal powers, politicians have incentives to set up a tax system that is perceived as desirable by citizens, when compared to the benefits they receive in terms of public goods and services provided. In the end, in a decentralized fiscal system, citizens can better evaluate and judge political decision making, which should in turn enhance efficiency and accountability in public spending and tax burdens.

However, two critical issues emerge from this form of "grant fiscalization." First, the increase of "own" taxes does not mean an increase in financial autonomy. In the Italian case, the central government has left very little taxing power in the hands of municipalities. The central government has defined tax bases for local taxes and placed strict limitations on tax surcharge and tax sharing rates. Consequently, the rates of local own taxes are defined primarily at the national level, owing to the necessity to achieve stringent national objectives recently imposed by the EU in terms of budget balances and stock of debt at the state level. Indeed, the distribution of tax powers across jurisdictions reflects the outcome of political bargaining in a particular historical situation rather than the consistent application of any normative principles (Bird 1999).

Second, the creation of a decentralized tax system may increase administrative costs and threaten transparency. For example, if a national collection system had to cope with a plethora of shared taxes between jurisdictions, this would increase administrative costs. In addition, a complex tax system, in which various jurisdictions share the same tax base and in which subcentral governments have important fiscal powers, may inhibit fiscal transparency. Voters may find it difficult to fully understand the operations of the different levels of government (Tanzi 2001), which in turn leads to less accountability. Yet, in an Italian context characterized by one of the highest rates of tax evasion among developed countries, the decentralization of tax collection systems could provide an opportunity to address this issue. In fact, the central government has already defined incentives for local governments to deal with tax evasion.

Reform of the Intergovernmental Transfer System

The rationale for transfer payments in any multi-tiered state is based primarily on the degree of both vertical and horizontal imbalances among different orders of government. Vertical imbalances occur between central and subnational governments, which each have different capacities to raise revenues to match spending. In contrast, horizontal imbalances exist among subnational governments with differing fiscal capacities and costs for public service provision. In practice, equalization is almost always motivated by equity concerns, with the basic objective being to ensure equality of access to public services, regardless of where a citizen lives. Horizontal imbalances have been a deep-rooted historical issue in Italy since the founding of its Constitution in 1861. Labeled the *north–south gap*, this imbalance exists between the wealthiest and highly developed and industrialized areas of Italy (the northern ones) and the poorest or less-developed regions (the southern ones).

In Italy, intergovernmental equalization transfer mechanisms have traditionally been based on historical expenditures. The rationale for reforming the intergovernmental transfer mechanism is based on the fact that the traditional formula failed to improve the economic disparities between north and south, while fueling

Table 2.2   Types of Expenditures and Funding Sources

Expenditure Type[a]	Coverage Method
Expenditures for fundamental functions and essential levels of service	Totally financed on a standard expenditure base through local taxes (property tax, surcharge, and tax sharing) and the equalization fund
Expenditures for other functions	Yields from own revenues, with mixed-tax revenues and with the equalization fund based on the fiscal capacity per inhabitant

[a] Law No. 42/2009 also mentions expenditures financed by special grants, through European Union financing and national co-financing as per Article 16.

inefficiency in public spending, reducing accountability, and fostering inequity in resource allocation. The literature on fiscal federalism and international practice confirms that actual expenditures are not an appropriate measure of need, because their use would provide incentives for overspending or may freeze inequitable historical patterns of expenditure (Boex and Martinez-Vazquez 2007).

Given its central role in Italy's new fiscal system, equalization is a major topic of interest among scholars and public servants in Italy (Gastaldi, Longobardi, and Zanardi 2009; Mussari and Parlato 2009; Pisauro 2009; Arachi, Ferrario, and Zanardi 2010; Petretto 2011; Rizzo and Zanardi 2011). Naturally intergovernmental transfers exist in any country, be it unitary or federal (Shah 2007), but what makes the Italian case particularly interesting is the substantial change in how these grants are determined under the current system by their methods of quantification and allocation. Article 13 of Law No. 42/2009 (LD) regulates the proper implementation (that is, after the transitional period) of equalization transfers and defines principles for quantifying transfers and determining their allocation methods. In particular, the LD establishes a correlation between types of expenditures and their coverage methods, as summarized in Table 2.2.

Municipalities are responsible for general administration, local police, public education, roads and public transportation, land/property and environmental management, and social services. These fundamental functions coincide with those used to classify municipal expenditures in both the budget and budget statements. Hence each function encompasses the expenditure needs* to fund several related local public services. For instance, local police functions subdivide expenditures into the following service categories: road police services, police administration services, judicial police services, commercial and environmental controls, etc.

Whereas most services associated with administrative, management, and control functions include internal support activities (institutional bodies, personnel

---

* Expenditure needs generally refer to the local government outlays that would be necessary to provide a particular standard of service (Boex and Martinez-Vazquez 2007).

services, financial management, etc.), expenditures for all other fundamental functions involve direct local public services with a major social impact. The importance of these services to the well-being and welfare of local communities is precisely why it is vital to understand how their expenditure needs will be determined. In contrast, the duty to guarantee full funding to these services (also provided for in the Constitution) prompts the need to define equalization fund rules in the LD—that is, quantification criteria, allocation rules, and budget allotment.

For fundamental functions, the LD has established that the amount of equalization for each order of government must be calculated using an expenditure requirement indicator based on the fiscal gap*—that is, the difference between standard expenditure needs (current and capital expenditures) for the same functions and the total, standardized, unconditional own revenues (property tax, shared, and surcharge taxes), excluding earmarked taxes, transit, and staying taxes. Given the principle that new or greater financial burdens (other than what are allowable under current legislation) cannot further encumber the state budget, it is certain that the total fund amount will be determined by the central government for single levels of government, also bearing in mind the overall constraints of public finance. Should the financial resources originating from tax revenues not be sufficient to cover standard expenditure needs, each municipality may apply for a share of the specific equalization fund in question.

With respect to equalization funds, the LD provides for the establishment of two funds within the regional budget: one for municipalities and the other for the provinces and metropolitan cities.† These funds, in turn, are sustained by a central government equalization fund.

Regardless of the formula used, the outcomes and ultimate success of the horizontal allocation approach will depend critically on how expenditure needs and fiscal capacities are measured.‡ The provisions for determining the standard cost of services and expenditure needs of municipalities were defined in Legislative Decree

---

* In international practice, there are countries that use formulas to equalize both fiscal capacity and expenditure needs (including many developed and transitional countries), countries that use mechanisms that equalize only fiscal capacity, and countries that equalize only expenditure needs differences across subnational governments. Typically, to achieve an adequate level of equalization, it is necessary to equalize both fiscal capacity and expenditure needs (Boex and Martinez-Vazquez 2007).

† Metropolitan cities are municipal jurisdictions with both municipal and provincial competencies. They encompass a large municipality and its surrounding hinterland cities. These new entities were introduced through constitutional reforms in 2001. Forecast for 2013, metropolitan city start-up seems rather far out of reach, because the Italian Parliament is still defining the working rules of these institutions.

‡ Note that while calculating expenditure needs is a necessary starting point, it is insufficient for quantifying equalization funds because it is also necessary to calculate standardized revenues. This is not a secondary issue and therefore is worth highlighting, because most efforts and attention seem to focus exclusively on standard expenditure needs, whereas the quantification of standard municipal tax revenues seems to arouse less interest (Petretto 2011).

No. 216, 26 November 2010, one of eight decrees of the fiscal federalism law. The historical spending criteria will have been abandoned as of 2012, marking a transitional phase in the implementation of fiscal federalism. Through a five-year gradual process, the application of standard expenditure needs for the six fundamental municipal functions will enter into effect. The "new system" is expected to be fully in place by 2017.

The determination of expenditure needs has been entrusted to a joint-stock company of the Ministry of the Economy and Finance (88 percent) and the Bank of Italy (12 percent), which relies on the scientific research support of the Institute for Local Economy and Finance (IFEL, *Istituto per la Finanza e per l'Economia Locale*), a foundation of the National Association of Italian Municipalities (ANCI, *Associazione Nazionale dei Comuni Italiani*). A variety of approaches have been used in different countries to quantify local expenditure needs, involving, to different extents, empirical or practical elements and a priori conceptual thinking, which range from rudimentary to quite sophisticated designs. The approach chosen by the Italian legislature is to calculate an index of relative expenditure needs for each basket of services (functions), which is able to capture factors that determine cost differences in delivering a standard package of local government services.

To estimate the expenditure needs of fundamental municipal functions, government researchers will utilize statistical and econometric models, whose data will essentially be gathered from three sources:

■ Municipal budget statements
■ Questionnaires related to each fundamental function, which every municipality is required to complete
■ Additional information obtained from official statistical sources (ISTAT)

Hence, when calculating the expenditure needs of fundamental municipal functions (Mussari and Parlato 2009), both detailed economic and non-economic data are precious and essential sources of information. Here, the Italian situation presents some critical challenges because of both the unreliability and general lack of information to quantify local expenditure needs adequately. For instance, despite the existing link between the fundamental functions as baskets of services and the functions as aggregate expenditures in municipal budgets, certified financial statements do not always provide a sufficiently reliable source of information to calculate standard expenditures for each single function for two reasons: first, accounting practices vary significantly from one local government to another, although each municipality has the same standard budget scheme;* and second, local accounting may be undisciplined, specifically to avoid central government budget constraints

---

* Essentially, some expenditures that ought to be attributed to a particular function are instead accounted for in other functions. This often occurs for the following types of spending: human resources, service usages, postal services, cleaning, maintenance, etc.

traditionally based on expenditure caps (total or current expenditure or specific expenditure items). To address these gaps, the questionnaire on fundamental municipal functions is being used to gather both non-economic information (which is often hard to obtain from official statistical sources*) and pertinent economic variables and factors that will help to determine real cost differences in delivering services. At the analytical level, these more reliable sources of economic information should provide a clear picture of the expenditures for each function.†

However, additional problems of quantitative and qualitative reliability reveal an even more complex process of expenditure needs calculation. For example, the expenditure needs assessment is based on a massive amount of service information from 8,100 municipalities, which are facing great difficulties in providing the large amount of information required by the questionnaire. Moreover, should the financial statements indeed indicate true service costs, it is still difficult to control for the non-economic information associated with those costs. In addition, governments have yet to define which basket of services precisely corresponds to each fundamental function and which standard of service each local government has to guarantee to its community.

The reliability of data is not the only issue that needs to be addressed in reforming intergovernmental transfers. The process of defining expenditure needs will be long, and the results of this effort are still uncertain. In particular it is uncertain how allocation criteria will develop—that is, how expenditure needs will be applied in order to define the real transfer needs of each municipality. At the end of the expenditure needs evaluation process, the central government will define the real criteria for quantifying intergovernmental transfers.

These issues could hamper the development of an efficient, equitable, and transparent transfer mechanism. The definition of a new equalization system in Italy seems to be linked to political arguments more so than to technical ones.

Institutional Perspective on Italian Fiscal Federalism

The study of fiscal federalism is concerned with "understanding which functions and instruments are best centralized and which are best placed in the sphere of decentralized levels of government" (Oates 1999, 1120). In economic theory this issue is known as the assignment problem. Both public finance theory (the

---

* For instance, with regard to local police functions, municipalities were asked to indicate the expansion of pedestrian areas, the annual number of street market days, the surface area of local police offices, the number of service desks open to the public, etc.

† The need to build an ex-post analytical database of function expenditures illustrates the importance of public accounting reforms in Italy. This need did not go unnoticed by the legislators, who defined the principles of bookkeeping reforms in the LD. The issues were further addressed in more recent legislation (Legislative Decree No. 118, 23 June 2011), and a much more detailed decree is due for approval in the near future.

traditional theory of fiscal federalism) and public choice literature (focusing on competitive federalism) have investigated this issue. Public finance theory (Musgrave 1959; Oates 1972) assumes that decentralizing decision making should have positive, even if unintentional, consequences for efficiency, accountability, and governance (Rodden 2006).

As mentioned earlier, recent studies in the field of fiscal federalism have paid attention to the features that affect both how normative prescriptions work and the performance of different forms of federalism in an institutional environment. For example, the beneficial effects of fiscal federalism can be altered by institutional features. Institutions create incentives that, in turn, shape future institutional developments. These institutional structures matter because they may facilitate or hinder the behavior of actors operating within the institutional structure (Krane, Ebdon, and Bartle 2004).

Analyzing the characteristics of the institutional environment—that is, how it has been defined and how it works—is crucial to understanding the critical issues of fiscal federalism in each context.* This is particularly true in Italy, where the public system as a whole has been involved in a broad process of institutional transformation toward multilevel governance. Since the 1990s, the public administration reform process has brought the Italian state from a unitary system, in which primary authority was in the hands of the central government, to a decentralized system, in which greater autonomy in decision making has been given to local governments. At the moment there are four tiers of government in Italy: central, regional, provincial, and municipal. Central and regional governments have legislative powers, while provinces and municipalities manage specific functions and have administrative and local regulatory powers. Toonen (2010) proposes an interesting framework for the analysis of intergovernmental systems, which encompasses three perspectives: intergovernmental constitution, intergovernmental relations, and intergovernmental management.

At the constitutional level, the newly reformed Italian intergovernmental system incorporates two models of federalism: first, a dual or vertical federalism model for reassigning legislative powers between central and regional governments; and second, a cooperative or horizontal model of federalism for addressing relations between municipalities and upper tiers of government. In dual federalism different policy areas are assigned to different governments. The reform in 2001, pertaining to the second part of the Italian Constitution, has redefined the policy areas in which both central and regional governments have exclusive legislative power. Article 117 of the Italian Constitution establishes 17 policy areas in which the central government has exclusive legislative power (e.g., foreign affairs, military and national security, justice, social security, economy, citizenship) and 22 policy areas wherein legislative power is shared by the state and regional governments. Regions

---

* Local governments exist within the context of an "ecology" of institutional arrangements, an ecology with political, legal–constitutional, and economic aspects (Weingast 2006).

have legislative power over these 22 policy areas, but regional legislation has to conform to the general principles established by the central government, which reinforces the unitary model of the Italian state. Finally, the regions have exclusive legislative powers over other unmentioned policy areas.

In contrast, a form of cooperative federalism defines roles and sets the rules between central/regional governments and the subregional entities responsible for its implementation. In cooperative or horizontal federalism, the division of power is defined in terms of the functions of legislation, execution, and financing (Toonen 2010). In the specific case of Italian municipalities, the reshaping of Italian public sector macrostructures has been characterized by the devolution of specific functions and administrative powers from the upper tiers of government within the unitary state, particularly in the area of services and provision of public goods to citizens. Municipal competencies and functions are established by national law, and decision-making autonomy is given to manage them.

Critical issues within the Italian intergovernmental system emerge when the characteristics of intergovernmental relations and forms of intergovernmental management, the two most important dimensions of analysis, are studied. How the intergovernmental system works relies on these two dimensions. Intergovernmental relations refer to how relationships and linkages are established between different orders of government and their degree of interconnection; intergovernmental management refers to the mechanisms of interaction among decision makers (Toonen 2010). In unitary states, in which authority and responsibility are mainly in the hands of the central government, the relationship between central and local administrations is built on the principal–agent model, in which lower governments have little autonomy to implement policies and the degree of central–local interconnection is high—that is, higher interference of central government in local decision making.

In contrast, a model of multilevel governance in which different orders of government have decision-making autonomy to implement policies requires that central–local government relations be based on a partnership model rather than on a hierarchical one. In this case the mechanisms of coordination, both horizontal and vertical, are important in order to secure a good degree of territorial integration of national services in local government, to guarantee a standard level of services for all citizens, and to involve local governments in pursuing national objectives.

Though decentralization is expected to produce a more responsive and accountable government at each level, in the Italian context the main effect has been to generate a complex intergovernmental system with more internal contradictions. The unclear boundaries of regional legislative power have generated high institutional conflicts between central and regional governments. In particular the long list of shared policy areas and the constitutional residual principle, according to which what is not specifically mentioned in the Constitution is of exclusive regional competence, have sparked thousands of "attribution conflicts" that are now being brought before the Constitutional Court. Moreover, the weakness of horizontal and vertical coordination seems to be more critical. In Italy there is no constitutional body in which the regions can actively participate in the national legislative process and in the definition of national policies and subnational resource allocation. In Italy the mechanisms of coordination are set by national law. The central regional coordinating body is called the *State–Regions Conference* and is mainly an advisory body that supports national decision making in regional affairs, although its competencies have recently been expanded.

The lack of agreement between state–regions has not prevented the central government from moving ahead in decision making. The power of the central government to impose decisions is reinforced by the weakness of horizontal coordination among territories, with most of them defending their own political and territorial interests. In order to decrease political conflicts, the central government often prefers to reach agreements with subnational governments based upon general principles in policy decision making and to manage territorial and political interests in the implementation phase through a one-to-one central–local bargain. However, these bargaining outcomes can conflict with the general principles. This dynamic has been problematic for intergovernmental commitment; has amplified differences among territories in terms of economic development, efficiency, and effectiveness in service provision; and has hampered efforts to increase interregional equity.

In addition, the institutional relations between the central government and municipalities have been affected by the fragmented process of decentralization. Moreover, the devolution of functions from central and regional governments to the municipalities was not accompanied by a parallel devolution of adequate resources to manage these new responsibilities. The concept of local government autonomy is established at the constitutional level but is often limited in practice by operational and administrative rules defined by the central administration. The degree of interdependency between central and local governments remains high and often leads to administrative duplication and overlap. Parikh and Weingast (1997) point out that the distribution of authority reflects the distribution of power. In other words, central bureaucracies tend to retain certain forms of administrative power in their own hands rather than cede total autonomy to local governments.

Given the lack of coordination mechanisms and the necessity to pursue national policies and objectives, the central government seems to have maintained a top-down approach in decision making and used prescriptive administrative regulation to manage central–local relations, in particular in the field of financial relations. This excess of norms, weakness of control, and lack of sanctioning and rewarding mechanisms have often stimulated territorial indiscipline and a low level of intergovernmental commitment. Recent studies by political scientists posit a direct link between federal political institutions and fiscal indiscipline (Treisman 2000; Wibbels 2000; Rodden 2002).

The impact analysis of the last two decades of decentralization reforms on Italian intergovernmental systems reveals:

- A conflicting multilevel system, with many overlaps in central and regional legislative powers
- A lack of horizontal and vertical coordination mechanisms
- A top-down approach to decision making by the central government
- A high degree of interconnection in central–local relations, which limits the autonomy of local governments in decision making
- A low level of intergovernmental commitment, with diffuse territorial indiscipline as a reaction to the autonomy limitations imposed by the central government
- A diffuse perception of intergovernmental inequity due to vertical and horizontal imbalances

Consequently, even if the rationale for its introduction was to improve the Italian intergovernmental system, the implementation of fiscal federalism seems to be strongly affected by a conflict-ridden and uncertain institutional environment. Yet these institutional issues are critical for the effective implementation of fiscal federalism. Strictly intertwined, they stem from the uncertainty of the legislative process and the unclear objectives of fiscal federalism, the centralization of the decision-making process, and the weakness of a coordination mechanism between central and local governments in decision making.

The initial impact of fiscal federalism and how it will truly work in the future remain uncertain. The fiscal federalism law (No. 42/2009) and subsequent decrees have only established principles and guidelines. Several applicative acts (approximately 70, 18 alone for municipal federalism) still have to be passed in order to put these principles into practice. As a result, the real timing for implementing fiscal federalism remains unknown. Moreover, the effectiveness of fiscal federalism will also rely on the rules to be set in the applicative laws, which could also be changed and adapted as new circumstances arise in the political and institutional debates over the next few years. In fact some crucial issues within the law 42/2009 were deliberately not defined in unequivocal terms in order to offer legislators a variety of options for enacting more than one form of fiscal federalism. This is particularly true in the field of equalization and local financial autonomy.

The equalization goals of the intergovernmental transfer systems are different in international practice: they enable a similar level of service affordability, similar levels of fiscal resource availability, similar levels of service at similar levels of taxation, and equal distribution on a per capita basis (Boex and Martinez-Vazquez 2007). In Italy if there is general agreement on improving vertical imbalances between central and local governments, how to improve the horizontal imbalances between developed areas and the poorest ones without encouraging overspending and inefficiency* remains the most debatable political issue more than 150 years after Italian unification. In a context characterized by the reduction of the overall amount of transfers, the tendency to maintain the status quo in order to reduce political and institutional conflict between parties and governments prevails.

The central government's determination not to compromise—through decentralization—its capacity to pursue national objectives triumphs over the necessity to improve financial autonomy at lower levels of government. The central government continues to impose many financial constraints on local governments in order to achieve the stringent national objectives imposed by the EU at the national level, mostly in terms of budget balances. These challenges are consistent with the centralization of the legislative process and the weak coordination mechanism in decision making. As Shah suggests, there are four alternatives for determining the structure of fiscal relations among orders of government: the central government alone can decide the structure; a technical commission can design and reform the system, as in Australia; federal–state committees can negotiate the terms of the system, as in Canada; and, a joint intragovernmental commission can act as an intralegislative commission, such as the upper house of the German parliament (Shah 1998).

According to Italian law there are three bodies involved in the fiscal federalism decision-making process:

1. *Parithetical Technical Commission for Fiscal Federalism Implementation*, an advisory and technical body composed of delegates of all central government bodies and each tier of government.
2. *State–Cities Conference*, a body with advisory and decision-making functions, which fosters cooperation between the state and municipalities.
3. *Parliamentary Commission for fiscal federalism implementation*, a political body composed of members of the two chambers of parliament. It supports government in fiscal federalism decision making and sets the applicative rules.

Despite the presence of a technical commission and a body for central–local coordination, fiscal federalism relies on a political body and central government decisions. This goes against the principles of federalism but is consistent with the Italian institutional environment, traditionally characterized by the lack of a coordination mechanism and a more politicized decision-making process.

Conclusions

Recent studies in the field of fiscal federalism have focused on the features that affect how normative prescriptions work in a given country and the performance of

---

* "Intergovernmental grants create the appearance that local public spending is funded by nonresidents" (Rodden 2002).

different forms of federalism in an institutional environment. What emerges is that an archetype of fiscal federalism does not exist, and the way in which the system works depends on both institutional and sociopolitical factors. Institutional and political features are relevant both for understanding the capacity of fiscal federalism to actually improve the fiscal responsibility of governments in a specific context and for determining which normative prescriptions can better fit within a given institutional and political environment.

The institutional literature identifies four key elements for fiscal federalism, as perfectly summarized by Sorens (2011). First, local governments must have decision-making autonomy and considerable power to tailor the provision of public goods and services to local circumstances. Second, local governments face hard budget constraints and must have fiscal autonomy. In other words, subnational governments must be able to face the financial consequences of their policy decisions, so that they cannot spend beyond their means (Shah 1997; Weingast 2006). This will ensure intergovernmental fiscal discipline. Third, there is a common market so that subnational governments may not enact barriers to the free flow of goods, capital, and labor across their borders (Sorens 2011). Fourth, the allocation of political authority must be institutionalized. This condition requires that decentralization not be under the discretionary or unilateral control of the national government (Weingast 2006). Even if Sorens admits that no political system perfectly fulfils these four criteria for fiscal federalism, the Italian case highlights several critical issues that support the hypothesis that the Italian intergovernmental system diverges dramatically from an ideal type.

Since the approval of the Law of Fiscal Federalism in 2009, Italy has undergone a long experimental phase, wherein central governments, supported by advisors and technical commissions, have begun to define operational rules and therefore how Italian fiscal federalism will actually work. Although the principles established in the laws are consistent with the normative prescriptions and aims of fiscal federalism, the implementation of fiscal federalism seems to be strongly conditioned both by supranational institutions and international financial instability, and by the tyranny of the status quo (McLure 2001). The conflict-ridden and uncertain institutional environment seems to negate the potential benefits of fiscal federalism. In particular, the Italian intergovernmental system is characterized by a lack of central–local coordination mechanisms, a top-down approach to decision making by the central government, and a high degree of interconnection in central–local relations. It contrasts with the necessity to preserve both the programmatic and fiscal autonomy of local governments underlined by the literature. Moreover, although the reform of the Italian Constitution has introduced the concept of local autonomy, the elements required for a programmatic and efficient fiscal autonomy have not been institutionalized and remain at the discretion of the central government.

In order to improve the accountability of the Italian intergovernmental system, Italy's brand of fiscal federalism must address three key challenges:

1. The degree of fiscal autonomy must be able to guarantee both the central government's control over public finance and the capacity of local governments to match spending.
2. The design of an intergovernmental transfer system must preserve equity without compromising efficiency in public spending.
3. Institutional constraints must be imposed to improve intergovernmental commitment and reduce political conflict.

References

Ahmad, E., ed. 1997. *Financing Decentralized Expenditures: An International Comparison of Grants.* Cheltenham, UK: Edward Elgar.

Ambrosanio, M.F., and M. Bordignon. 2006. Normative versus positive theories of revenue assignment. In *Handbook of Fiscal Federalism*, edited by Ehtisham Ahmad and Giorgio Brosio. Cheltenham, UK: Edward Elgar, pp. 306–338.

Anessi Pessina, E. 2002. *Principles of Public Management.* Milan: EGEA.

Arachi, A., Ferrario, C.A., and A. Zanardi. 2010. Regional redistribution and risk sharing in Italy: The role of different ties of government. *Regional Studies* 44: 55–69.

Bird, R.M. 1999. *Rethinking Sub-national Taxes: A New Look at Tax Assignment,* International Monetary Fund, WP/99/165.

Boadway, R., and A. Shah. 2009. *Fiscal Federalism: Principles and Practices of Multiorder Governance.* Cambridge: Cambridge University Press.

Boex, J., and J. Martinez-Vazquez. 2007. Designing intergovernmental equalization transfers with imperfect data: Concepts, practices, and lessons. In *Fiscal Equalization. Challenges in the Design of Fiscal Equalization and Intergovernmental Transfers*, pp. 291–344, edited by Jorge Martinez-Vazquez and Robert Searle. New York: Springer.

Bordignon, M., F.M. Ambrosanio, A. Zanardi, and A. Staderini. 2007. *Fiscal federalism in Italy: Facts and issues.* Speeches given during the seminar New Perspectives for Financial Intermediation in Economic Context Evolution. Castello dell'Oscano–Perugia, 22-23-24 marzo 2007.

Brennan, J., and J. Buchanan. 1980. *The Power to Tax: Analytical Foundations of a Fiscal Constitution.* Cambridge: Cambridge University Press.

Gastaldi, G., E. Longobardi, and A. Zanardi. 2009. Sharing of the personal income tax among levels of government: Some open issues from the Italian experience. *Rivista Italian degli Economisti* 14 (1): 157–190.

Giuriato, L., and F. Gastaldi. 2009. The domestic stability pact in Italy: A rule for discipline? MPRA, Munich Personal RePEc Archive, Paper No. 15183, posted 12 May.

Hood, C. 1991. A public management for all seasons? *Public Administration* 69 (1): 3–19.

IFEL Fondazione ANCI. 2011. Economia e Finanza Locale. Rapporto 2010. Ed. IFEL Ricerche.

Kee, J.E. 2004. Fiscal decentralization: Theory as reform. In *Financial Management Theory in the Public Sector*, pp. 165–186, edited by Aman Khan and W. Bartley Hildreth. Westport, CT: Praegers.

Krane, D., C. Ebdon, and J. Bartle. 2004. Devolution, fiscal federalism, and changing patterns of municipal revenues: The mismatch between theory and reality. *Journal of Public Administration Research and Theory* 14 (4): 513–533.

Litvack, J., J. Ahmad, and R. Bird. 1998. Rethinking decentralization in developing countries. *The World Bank Sector Studies Series*. Washington, DC: World Bank.

McLure, Charles E. 2001. The tax assignment problem: Ruminations on how theory and practice depend on history. *National Tax Journal* 54: 339–363.

Musgrave, R. 1959. *Public Finance*. New York: McGraw-Hill.

Mussari, R. 1997. Autonomy, responsibility, and new public management in Italy. In *International Perspectives on the New Public Management*, edited by Lawrence R. Jones, Kuno Schedler, and Stephen W. Wade. London: JAI Press, pp. 185–201.

Mussari, R. 2005. Public sector financial reform in Italy. In *International Public Financial Management Reform: Progress, Contradictions and Challenges*, edited by James Guthrie, Christopher Humphrey, Olav Olson, and L.R. Jones. Charlotte, NC: Information Age Press, pp. 139–168.

Mussari, R., and S. Parlato. 2009. Local equalization and standard need. Comments on articles 13 and 21. In *Fiscal Federalism*, edited by V. Nicotra, F. Pizzetti, S. Scozzese. Roma: Donzelli, pp. 193–211.

Oates, W. 1972. *Fiscal Federalism*. New York: Harcourt Brace Jovanovich.

Oates, W. 1999. An essay on fiscal federalism. *Journal of Economic Literature* 37: 1120–1149.

Oates, W. 2005. Toward a second-generation theory of fiscal federalism. *International Tax and Public Finance* 12: 349–373.

O'Flynn, J. 2007. From new public management to public value: Paradigmatic change and managerial implications. *Australian Journal of Public Administration* 66 (3): 353–366.

Organisation for Economic Co-operation and Development (OECD). 2009. Economic Survey of Italy 2009. Paris: OECD.

Organisation for Economic Co-operation and Development (OECD). 2011. *Revenue Statistics 2011*. Paris: OECD.

Parikh, S., and B.R. Weingast. 1997. A comparative theory of federalism: India. *Virginia Law Review* 83: 7.

Petretto, A. 2011. Costs and standard need in municipalities: Great institutional innovation or utopia? *IRPET, Regional Observatory on Fiscal Federalism*, November.

Pisauro, G. 2009. Financial relations between State and Regions. In *Fiscal Federalism*, edited by V. Nicotra, F. Pizzetti, and S. Scozzese. Rome: Donzelli, pp. 71–82.

Pollitt, C., and G. Bouckaert. 2004. *Public Management Reform: A Comparative Analysis*. Oxford: Oxford University Press.

Rebora, G. 1999. *A decade of reform*. Milano: Guerini e Associati.

Rizzo, L., and A. Zanardi. 2011. Filling fiscal gaps in Italy: A challenging task for the federal reform. In *IEB's World Report on Fiscal Federalism '10*. Barcelona: IEB-Institut d'Economia de Barcelona, pp. 74–78.

Rodden, J. 2002. The dilemma of fiscal federalism: Grants and fiscal performance around the world. *American Journal of Political Science* 46 (3): 670–687.

Rodden, J. 2006. *Hamilton's Paradox: The Promise and Peril of Fiscal Federalism*. New York: Cambridge University Press.

Rodden, J., G. Eskeland, and J. Litvack, eds. 2003. *Fiscal Decentralization and the Challenge of Hard Budget Constraints*. Cambridge, MA: MIT Press.

Shah, A. 1997. Fiscal federalism and economic governance: For better or worse? Paper presented at the Technical Consultation on Decentralization, Rome, Italy, 16–18 December.

Shah, A. 1998. Fostering fiscally responsive and accountable governance: Lessons from decentralization. In *Evaluation and Development: The Institutional Dimension*. World Bank Series on Evaluation and Development Transaction.

Shah, A. 2007. Institutional arrangements for intergovernmental fiscal transfers and a framework for evaluation. In *Intergovernmental Fiscal Transfers*, edited by Anwar Shah. Washington, DC: World Bank, pp. 293–318.

Sorens, J. 2011. The institutions of fiscal federalism. *Publius* 41 (2): 207–231.

Tanzi, V. 2001. Pitfalls on the road to fiscal decentralization. Economic Reform Project. Working paper. Washington, DC: Carnegie Endowment for International Peace.

Tiebout, C.M. 1956. A pure theory of local expenditures. *Journal of Political Economy* 64 (October): 416–424.

Toonen, T. 2010. Multi-level governance and intergovernmental relations: Integrating theoretical perspectives. In *Governance and Intergovernmental Relations in the European Union and the United States: Theoretical Perspectives*, edited by Edoardo Ongaro, Andrew Massey, Marc Holzer, and Ellen Wayenberg. Cheltenham, UK: Edward Elgar, pp. 29–50.

Treisman, D. 2000. Decentralization and inflation: Commitment, collective action, or continuity? *American Political Science Review* 94 (4): 837–857.

Von Hagen, J., M. Bordignon, M. Dahlberg, B. Grewal, P. Petterson, and H. Seitz. 2000. Subnational government bailouts in OECD countries: Four case studies. Inter-American Development Bank working paper R-399.

Weingast, B.R. 2006. Second generation fiscal federalism: Implications for decentralized democratic governance and economic development. Available from http://ssrn.com/abstract=1153440 or http://dx.doi.org/10.2139/ssrn.1153440.

Wibbels, E. 2000. Federalism and the politics of macroeconomic policy and performance. *American Journal of Political Science* 44: 687–702.

Chapter 3

Integrating User Voices into the European Financial Services Policy Process

Heather McKeen-Edwards

Contents

Introduction

The recent global financial crisis has re-energized the discussion of how to achieve legitimacy in policy making and public management for the financial sector. As many governmental bodies increasingly turn to regulatory reform, it is essential to ensure that financial regulation is both effective and representative of broad societal interests. The recent reforms in the European Union (EU) are no exception to this trend. The European Commission's post-crisis roadmap to improve financial regulation explicitly highlights consumer protection and user interests as key elements of effective and legitimate financial governance, concluding that "the interests of European investors, consumers and SMEs [small and medium sized enterprises] must be at the centre of the reform" (European Commission 2009, 4). Given the importance of building a sound financial system that is beneficial to society as well as the economy, the legitimacy of financial governance is crucial.

Legitimacy is a multifaceted and contested concept, yet few would argue that policy, and public management more generally, can be effective without it. Scharpf (1999) has maintained that EU governance should be more concerned with output legitimacy (government *for* the people, focused on the problem-solving quality of legislation) than input legitimacy (government *by* the people, focused on the participatory quality of legislation) because the preconditions of the latter—a collective identity and demos—do not exist at the European level. However, the use of democratic accountability, consultation, and participation to enhance legitimacy in the process of policy making has become a common focus of EU institutions. For some, input legitimacy can include all strategies that the European bodies employ to democratize the procedures for creating policies, including non-state actor consultation and participation in policy making. The potential for consultation to increase input legitimacy in the EU has been assessed in a number of different arenas (Héritier 1999; Lord 2001; Lord and Beetham 2001; Skogstad 2003). For Schmidt (2004, 2010) this process of consultation is still an important source of legitimacy. However, she argues that it is not really "governance *by* the people," as it does not involve political participation in the EU, but rather "governance *with* the people," or throughput legitimacy, which is achieved through consultation with organized interests. This form of legitimacy depends on establishing a coordinative discourse among various EU policy actors as opposed to promoting political participation and citizen representation. Whether it is conceptualized as input or throughput legitimacy, however, the integration of societal interests through consultation and participation has been increasingly recognized as an important part of legitimating transnational policies.

This chapter examines efforts to incorporate the voice of users, such as consumers and investors, and other societal stakeholders into EU financial governance. Some scholarly works have looked at different aspects of consumer and other user representation (Bradley 2007; Emmenegger 2010; Iglesias-Rodriguez 2011) and the relationship between input and output legitimacy (McKeen-Edwards and Roberge

2007; Mugge 2011) in this sector. However, this chapter provides a more systematic examination of the different methods used by European institutions to engage these interests directly. It identifies two mechanisms used in addition to open consultation, and assesses whether or not they contribute to an increase in consumer voice in three stages of the policy process: agenda setting and framing, policy formulation, and decision making.

Overview of the European Union Financial Services Policy-Making Process

Since the First Banking Directive was created in 1977, financial services policy at the European level has evolved to encompass a wide range of activities and instruments. Between the 1970s and 1990s, various directives expanded the reach of European-level governance in banking, securities, and insurance. However, progress toward a truly unified financial marketplace in Europe was inconsistent and slow. With the introduction of the Euro currency, renewed emphasis was placed on creating a more consistent European regulatory framework, culminating in the Financial Services Action Plan (FSAP) in 1999. This plan attempted to integrate the continent's securities markets over a five-year period through 42 directives (European Commission 1999). In order to accomplish this ambitious agenda, the policy process in the sector was also changed. Based on recommendations in the 2001 report of the Committee of Wise Men, chaired by Baron Lamfalussy, the new process incorporated a four-level comitology-based structure (Committee of Wise Men 2001). This approach was intended to speed up the policy-making process by separating the process of creating directives and regulations. The setting of broad regulatory principles in directives still falls within the co-decision process of Level I. However, once these broad principles are approved, the more detailed aspects are elaborated in regulations by a sector-specific committee of the European Commission, based on input from a committee of relevant national financial supervisors (Level II). Levels III and IV focus on ensuring consistent and national implementation, respectively, of directives and regulations through targeted policies.

The successful implementation of FSAP and the Lamfalussy framework marked significant developments in the role that the EU played in the governance of finance, and established a more comprehensive regulative process at the transnational level (Freixas, Hartmann, and Mayer 2004; Grossman and Leblond 2011). In 2005, the FSAP was followed by another white paper on financial services policy that introduced a set of new initiatives to integrate the still largely fragmented retail financial services sector (Bradley 2007; Ayadi 2011). At the same time, the reach of the Lamfalussy process was also expanded beyond securities into the banking and insurance sectors. More recent changes have largely left the comitology approach untouched at Levels I and II, but have increased the supervisory power of the European sphere (Level III) with the introduction of new European supervisory agencies, such as the European Banking Authority (EBA), the European Securities and Market Authority (ESMA), and the European Insurance and Occupational Pensions Authority (EIOPA). These new bodies have replaced the non-binding coordinating committees of regulators, which previously existed at this level, thus strengthening the importance of the European level in financial regulation. Given the increased importance and complexity of the European financial policy environment, ensuring the effective incorporation of user voices is important for the legitimacy of the governance that emerges.

Mapping Efforts to Enhance Users' Voices in the European Union Financial Policy Process

The introduction of the comitology process occurred at the same time as the shift to incorporate forms of broad and open consultation; this method was explicit within the FSAP and the Lamfalussy process. It was reiterated more precisely in the EU's Consumer Policy Strategy 2002–2005 that states, "The Commission will reinforce a regulatory approach in the field of financial services based on early, broad and systematic consultation of all interested parties, including consumers and end-users" (European Commission 2002). However, achieving input legitimacy in financial regulation through open consultation is difficult in practice given that non-business constituencies are generally underrepresented and lack resources relative to industry actors.

The inequality between industry and social interests is apparent in the response rates to calls for consultation. McKeen-Edwards and Roberge (2007) revealed that there were often low levels of civic participation in the consultation processes of the Committee of European Securities Regulators (CESR) between 2002 and 2005, as 77 percent of responses came from industry bodies or corporations. This relative inequality has not diminished with time. In 2010 and 2011, the European Commission undertook four consultations on aspects of retail financial services: tying and other potentially unfair commercial practices (April 2010); access to a basic payment account (November 2010); legislative steps for the Packaged Retail Investment Products (January 2011); and a study on interest rate restrictions (March 2011).[*] Even in these consultations, the percentage of responses from

---

[*] The choice to examine these consultations does not imply that user groups were not active in responding to consultations in other areas of financial services. Rather they were chosen to show that the low response percentage persists even in policy discussions that are directly applicable to retail users.

consumers/users never exceeded 25 percent.* This percentage to the retail financial services consultations is particularly instructive because one would assume a higher response rate from users given the immediate relevance of the subject matter.

The inequality in these results stems from two trends. First, the financial industry has developed a well-resourced lobby that has the ability to respond to consultations, and has built a solid relationship with national and European regulators. Second, many interest groups for users are not necessarily well placed to address this imbalance on their own. Bradley, for example, finds that consumer groups in particular are more likely to be "excluded from effective participation in supranational standard-setting due to the combined effects of opaque processes, framing, and lack of resources" (2008, p. 74). Additional constraints can also occur because of the short time frame for response in most consultations and the technical language used (FIN-USE 2006). Even the Commission recognized these challenges when it noted that "it has been difficult to put into practice the kind of wide ranging and continuous dialogue that is required, as user groups often do not have the necessary resources or expertise, especially at the EU level, to cover all the issues" (European Union 2003, p. 1).

Because legitimacy through consultation requires widespread and diverse participation, these inequalities in the involvement of societal actors create a public management problem that needs to be addressed. To counteract this tendency, the EU has made use of two additional mechanisms: the creation of expert groups to represent user interests, and the inclusion of representatives from these groups in the stakeholder committees of the various European supervisory authorities.

Creating an Expert Group to Represent User Interests

The establishment of expert committees with a mandate from the European Commission to present and promote the interests of users in EU policy making is one means of increasing their input into financial services policies. The Commission's use of expert committees is not unique to this sector of policy making. In fact, such committees have become increasingly important across a wide range of policy areas at this level, with 802 currently identified in the Register of Commission Expert Groups. These expert groups vary in size, as well as in the combinations of public and private members, the formality of their structures, and their permanence. What unites them is the task of providing advice to the relevant

---

* April 2010 consultation—55 responses (11% consumers); November 2010 consultation—76 responses (25% users/consumers); January 2011 consultation—140 responses (14% users/consumers); March 2011 consultation—47 responses (15% consumers/users). See European Commission. n.d. "Consultations" (http://ec.europa.eu/internal_market/consultations/index_en.htm).

Commission departments. In essence, each expert body is "a forum for discussions, providing high-level input from a wide range of sources and stakeholders in the form of opinions, recommendations and reports" (European Commission n.d.).

In 2003, the Commission proposed the creation of an expert committee to represent consumers and SMEs in the financial services policy process. This move was intended to create a form of "structured dialogue" around the interests of these users by providing a clear connection to the policy process through the Commission. The FIN-USE Expert Forum of Financial Services Users (FIN-USE) came into existence in 2004 and completed two three-year mandates before being disbanded in June 2010. At the time of its creation, then Internal Market Commissioner Frits Bolkestein stated:

> Setting up this forum is part of our drive to make sure all interested parties, including retail and small business users, have the chance to contribute to policy-making on financial services... The Forum will give those users a stronger voice and help them to play a more active role in defining the policies of which they will be major beneficiaries. (European Union 2003, p.1)

FIN-USE was a permanent formal expert group; that is, it was set up by a Commission decision and with a mandate that did not end upon the completion of a single task or policy. It was composed of experts,* appointed through an open call for applications, with work experience in financial services and professional experience with user-related issues. The composition of the committee also ensured a mixture of specializations and geographical diversity (Ramboll Management 2006).

FIN-USE had two primary tasks. First, it was expected to respond to requests for opinions and recommendations from the European Commission on specific initiatives. Second, it was to proactively identify key issues that affect users. During its two mandates a significant amount of its work focused on preparing responses to and opinions on proposed legislative actions. However, the forum also issued some proactive opinions and reports. In addition, FIN-USE members met with Commission and other government officials and participated in a variety of external financial events each year to explain and promote the importance of consumer and user interests.

At the end of FIN-USE's second mandate in 2010, the European Commission decided to merge its functions with another Commission-supported committee, the Financial Services Consumer Group (FSCG),† thus creating a new expert

---

* In 2004 the initial 12 experts were appointed, with the size of the committee increasing to its final composition of 15 members before it was disbanded.

† Financial Services Consumer Group (FSCG) was a subgroup of the European Consumer Consultative Group (ECCG) created in 2006. Unlike FIN-USE its members were representatives of national and EU consumer organizations rather than individually appointed experts (European Commission 2006; Vander Stichele 2008). Moreover, it specifically focused on discussing and articulating the interests of consumers only, and there was no expectation that it would produce the kind of policy input that FIN-USE generated (Ramboll Management 2006).

committee known as the Financial Services User Group (FSUG). When creating this new committee in a 20 July 2010 decision, the European Commission (2010) also modified its membership by incorporating representation for retail investors, consumers, and small business.* This change was in response to the call to increase the voice of these investors made in the 2009 roadmap, *Driving the European Recovery*. Matching the change in representation, FSUG also expanded to 20 appointed members, 11 representing consumers and retail investors.

There are many structural similarities between FSUG and FIN-USE. Organizationally, both are appointed committees whose members have expert knowledge of financial services and are directly connected to user perspectives and interests. In fact, there are seven members who served on FIN-USE immediately prior to the change, including the first FSUG-elected chairman and vice-chairman. Moreover, FSUG has a similar mandate to its predecessor. Of its four explicit tasks, the first two involve advising the Commission in its preparation of policies and providing insight and opinions on practical implementation, and the third is to proactively identify areas that affect users. These generally map to the tasks of FIN-USE. The final explicit role calls for FSUG to "liaise with and provide information to financial services user representatives and representative bodies at the European Union and national level, as well as to other consultative groups administered by the Commission" (European Commission 2010).

Inclusion in the Stakeholder Committees of the Various European Supervisory Authorities

The second distinctive mechanism for capturing user interests in the policy process beyond open consultation was the creation of heterogeneous stakeholder committees within the European supervisory authorities (ESMA, EBA, and EIOPA) in 2011. Committees to represent the interests of stakeholders are not a completely new development post-crisis. Early versions, known as Market Participants Consultative Panels, were established within the previous Level III committees of supervisors at the suggestion of the European Parliament. However, in the new EU supervisory authorities (ESMA, EBA, EIOPA), these groups have become significantly more institutionalized. Earlier versions were established at the pleasure of the committee of regulators, but the new supervisory authorities are mandated by EU statute to create and consult with a stakeholder committee. Therefore, these current stakeholder committees represent the first "formal institutionalization of stakeholder participation" in EU financial policy making (Iglesias-Rodriguez 2011, p. 3).

---

* The small business component is limited to micro-enterprises—that is, firms with 10 or fewer employees and a balance sheet or turnover (gross sales) of less than $2 billion euro (European Commission 2005).

The statute for each supervisory authority* details the composition of the stakeholder committee, as well as its roles and powers within the authority. The 30-member committees must incorporate representatives from a variety of different interests with at least five independent academics and ten industry representatives joining another 15 members who represent consumers, users, SMEs, employees' representatives, and, in the case of the insurance committees, relevant professionals. Clearly, this stakeholder body includes many people who represent user interests. This marks a shift from the composition of earlier committees, which had the discretion to determine whether or not to incorporate user representatives. For example, in 2008, CESR's Market Participants Consultative Panel had 16 members, all executives "from the highest corporate level of financial sector companies across Europe" (CESR 2008, p. 84).

In terms of policy input, each stakeholder committee plays an active advisory role within its respective authority and with the Commission and must be consulted on the design and implementation of regulatory technical standards. Each committee is also to be consulted on proposed guidelines for the competent authorities or financial institutions. The committee may submit opinions or advice to the authority on any issue related to its tasks and responsibilities. Moreover, it has the right to request that the authority investigate an alleged breach or non-application of EU law.

Can Expert and Stakeholder Groups Increase User Voice in European Union Financial Services Policy?

Assessing the ability of these mechanisms to enhance the voice of users in EU financial service directives and regulation is a difficult task because final policies reflect a blend of several different interests. However, institutional features and practices in previous policy initiatives can be used to assess whether these two mechanisms have improved user voice. When one looks at these elements, it is clear that these mechanisms have contributed to increasing user voice from what it would have been if only the opportunity to respond to open consultations had been provided. Both of these mechanisms have institutionalized aspects of user interests and input in the policy process because of their formal connections with the European Commission and the different European supervisory authorities.

However, it is also apparent that these two mechanisms cannot ensure the full integration of consumer voice at all stages of the policy process. There are multiple places where user interests are still not as effectively incorporated as they may appear to be when looking only at the institutional landscape. By examining in greater detail the role of these mechanisms at three different stages of policy

---

* European Union regulations 1093/2010, 1094/2010, and 1095/2010.

design—agenda setting and framing, policy formulation, and decision making—this complex and nuanced relationship is revealed.

The agenda setting and framing stages of the policy process are important for emerging regulatory initiatives because they lay the foundation on which subsequent policy actions are built. The former involves the process of issue identification and policy initiation, while the latter captures the efforts of state and non-state actors to define or redefine a particular issue or problem. Examining the policy process at this point is essential because the impact of users on policy formulation discussions can be affected in situations where framing has been controlled by other groups (Bradley 2008).

To date, the stakeholder committees have not been particularly active in the early stages of framing and agenda setting because of their connection to Level III supervisors. This may change as their role develops over time, but as currently structured these committees are better placed to address the policy formulation stage. Institutionally, however, FIN-USE and its successor FSUG have the potential to take on roles in agenda setting because they are mandated to proactively identify key issues that affect users. In this capacity FIN-USE issued several reports on a variety of issues throughout its mandate, including the importance of consumer voice (2006, 2009), the effects of the financial crisis on consumers (2008b, 2010), and financial education (2008a). Through these reports, FIN-USE actively sought to frame issues and promote particular regulatory innovations. In its short existence, FSUG has also worked to frame regulation through a letter to the Commissioner of the Internal Market and the supervisory agency heads calling for increased focus on consumer protection and not simply market stability in their agendas. However, this role has been limited because the Commission is not mandated to follow up, which means that FSUG does not necessarily set the regulatory agenda.

The above points indicate that the expert fora currently in place do have the potential to influence framing and agenda setting, although this is mitigated by their identity as consultative bodies. Yet at the highest level of framing and agenda setting, there still appears to be a lack of proper representation and input from users. One can look at the High-Level Group on Supervision (also known as the De Larosière Group), which developed the recommendations at the foundation of the new EU regulatory and supervisory agenda post crisis. The De Larosière Group was able to produce a comprehensive report in a very short time frame. However, the formulation phases included little direct input from consumers as there were no consultations with FIN-USE or any other European consumer or investor associations. This can be contrasted with the group's invitation to provide oral evidence to 12 high-level public officials active in European or international governance bodies, 14 European and international financial associations, and representatives of the four large insurance companies (De Larosière Group 2009). Their absence from the high-level discussions that framed the post-crisis response indicates that the role of these expert groups in agenda setting is somewhat circumscribed.

Shifting focus to the second stage, policy formulation, the integration of user voice is still present, but the role of each mechanism is altered slightly. In the policy formulation phase, the main objectives are the development of a set of policy instruments and policy choices to address the problems. In this case, it is clear that the creation of both a dedicated expert forum and an inclusive stakeholder group have influenced this process. In absolute terms, there has been an obvious increase in the opportunities for input in policy design with the addition of these two mechanisms. First, through its clear connections to the policy process within the Commission, FIN-USE and its successor, FSUG, have the potential to create "structured dialogue" between the interests of users and these processes.* Like its predecessor, FSUG provides advice, insights, and opinions to the Commission, and various Commission bureaucrats will present issues at the forum's meetings. Moreover, the expert committees have been active in responding to calls for consultation. FIN-USE provided a wide range of responses to, and opinions and positions on, proposed EU directives and work areas. The rate of response also increased throughout the forum's life span, from 12 opinions and reports in its first 2.5 years to 20 documents in the 2009–2010 year. FSUG continued this role, issuing 16 responses to European or international initiatives in its first year (FSUG 2011a). The importance of expressing these views is more obvious when one considers that the responses received to open consultation on each of these policies is heavily skewed in favor of financial industry actors and other business interests.

As in agenda setting, the impact of these discussions and submissions is mitigated by the consultative nature of the opinions, which means that the expert fora have limited power to actually adjust legislation beyond issuing responses and calls for changes. FIN-USE actively acknowledged that consumer interests had not been as effectively integrated into the policy process as they could have been, and that despite the best efforts of forum members and Commission staff, it had "comparatively weak influence on policy making at the highest levels compared to the influence of the powerful financial services industry lobbies" (2009, p. 4).

The stakeholder committees play their most prominent role in the policy design and formulation stage as each European supervisory authority is required by statute to consult with these groups. In terms of participation, the inclusion of user voice is most institutionalized in these stakeholder committees of the supervisory agencies. The mandated inclusion of users, consumers, SMEs, and employee associations has meant that various well-respected consumer advocates, including a number of FSUG members, have been selected to serve on each committee (FSUG 2011b). The limitation of relying on this mechanism alone for input is that committees are heterogeneous, which means that recommendations and responses will

---

* An independent external evaluation at the end of its first mandate described FIN-USE as "a relevant, effective and efficient forum for bringing the perspectives of consumers and SMEs into the policy-making process in the financial services field" (Ramboll Management 2006, p. 1).

not necessarily match the interests of users completely. This weakness has been identified by users themselves, who have expressed concern about the composition of different stakeholder committees and its effects on the inclusion of user interests. In particular, user groups have highlighted the low numbers of consumer and non-industry actors on the stakeholder committees of the EBA and EIOPA. For example, the EBA stakeholder committee's membership is mandated to represent

> in balanced proportions credit and investment institutions operating in the Union, their employees' representatives as well as consumers, users of banking services and representatives of SMEs. At least five of its members shall be independent top-ranking academics. Ten of its members shall represent financial institutions, three of whom shall represent cooperative and savings banks. (European Union 2010, p. 17)

The ambiguous definition of "users" in these statutes has been interpreted by the EBA to include representatives from industries that provide services to the banking industry. Therefore the five members classified as users on this stakeholder committee represent KPMG LLP, PricewaterhouseCoopers, Federation of European Accountants, Standard & Poor's Ratings Services, and Deloitte. The selection of these actors illustrates a very different definition of "user" than is seen in other EU documents including the composition of the Financial Services User Group. Because of these concerns, FSUG sent letters of complaint to the Chairmen of the EBA and EIOPA, while three other user groups (BEUC, The European Consumers' Organization, and Euroshareholders) have filed complaints with the European Ombudsman[*] arguing that these groups did not meet the mandated division of members. Clearly, the continued evolution of the committees presents a range of possibilities and challenges to consumers and user interest representation through these mechanisms.

Finally, looking at the decision-making or adoption stage of the policy process, these mechanisms have had little effect on increasing user voice because their input is consultative in nature. Ensuring user voice is present at this stage of the process requires a return to the more traditional techniques to influence decision makers at the European level. This lobbying also supplements any national mechanisms that may be in place to ensure that user voice is included in policy making. However, the influence of user voices at the national level should not be overstated. A recent study for BEUC shows that while some member states have active user representative bodies and institutionalized mechanisms for their input, others have very little development in these areas (Reifner and Clerc-Renaud 2011).

---

[*] At the time of writing, the current cases related to the composition of the stakeholder committee are 1966/2011/EIS, 1876/2011/EIS, and 1875/2011/EIS for the EBA and 1874/2011/EIS and 1877/2011/EIS for EIOPA. No decision has been made in any case.

Best Practice and Future Considerations

This case offers several insights into institutionalizing and enhancing user voice at the transnational level. The mechanisms implemented highlight the importance of encouraging engagement from underrepresented groups on multiple fronts in a sector that has traditionally been dominated by industry. In this case, each mechanism has increased the presence of user voice beyond what would have been achieved through open consultation alone. As expert groups, FIN-USE and FSUG have been given the ability to influence both agenda setting and policy formulation. The stakeholder committees of the supervisory authorities also create an additional space for user input into the policy process. These bodies can have more direct influence on the policy formulation process through their institutionalized position, yet that same position can shift their focus away from agenda setting. Given the structural imbalance between industry and public interest responses to regulation, an explicitly appointed, properly funded committee of experts or equal inclusion on a stakeholder body can make an important contribution to increasing the voice of users.

However, it is important to realize that these bodies cannot fully replace broad, open, and accessible consultation with a wide range of user stakeholders. Although they clearly draw attention to user interests, both of the mechanisms also underscore a tension between expertise and representation. As government appointed groups, their claims to be representative can be more tenuous, especially in the case of an expert committee. Therefore, these mechanisms should be seen as important supplements to, rather than replacements for, interest representation, redressing the imbalance that occurs across the financial services sector at the national, regional, and international levels.

A second key finding is that the act of creating institutional structures or spaces does not in itself guarantee increased voice at all stages of the policy process. In the first two stages, each mechanism adds access points for users to the policy design process, but these are limited. The role and impact of FIN-USE or FSUG are constrained by their consultative status, while the stakeholder committees are not composed solely of users, meaning that their recommendations will reflect a range of interests. Furthermore, the absence of these bodies, and any user voice more generally, from the discussions of the De Larosière Group also highlights that presence in one area does not mean access to other parts of the policy process. Therefore, the simple existence of these mechanisms cannot ensure that user interests will necessarily be integrated into policy making effectively. In essence, these policy tools are useful and necessary conditions for ensuring user input but are not sufficient.

Instead, these expert fora and inclusion on stakeholder committees are useful methods to provide, in the words of Emmenegger (2010), the "procedural consumer protection instrument" of voice. The task now is to ensure the consistent translation of that voice into consideration by regulators and policy makers. Some ways to formalize this translation involve the inclusion of provisions that require the Commission or other relevant EU body to respond formally and directly to issues raised by the proposals.

Finally, even taking into account these concerns, these two mechanisms would be useful supplements to improve the legitimacy of other regulatory bodies in financial services, particularly the international standard-setting bodies like the Basel Committee for Banking Standards, the International Organization of Securities Commission, and the International Association of Insurance Supervisors which have been actively redesigning global best practices for financial governance over the last few years. The use of expert bodies explicitly representing the interests of small end-users or explicitly diverse stakeholder committees to provide essential input from users in these standard development processes could provide a potentially fruitful mechanism to increase the voice of these underrepresented groups in these transnational bodies. The clear structural imbalance between industry and users at the European level is even more prominent when looking at international regulations. Studies by Tsingou (2009) and others have highlighted the power of financial industry actors and associations in the construction of international standards. The potential benefits of these mechanisms in overcoming the logistical difficulty of organizing the interests of diverse and fragmented end-users (like small business, consumers, and retail investors) on a global level would improve, although not wholly address, this structural imbalance.

References

Ayadi, Rym. 2011. *Integrating Retail Financial Markets in Europe: Between Uncertainties and Challenges*. Brussels: Centre for European Policy Studies.

Bradley, Caroline. 2007. Consumers of financial services and the multi-level regulation in the European Union. *Fordham International Law Journal* 31 (5): 1212–1234.

Bradley, Caroline. 2008. Financial trade associations and multilevel regulation. In *Multilevel Regulation and the EU: The Interplay between Global, European, and National Normative Processes*, edited by Andreas Follesdal, Ramses A. Wessel, and Jan Wouters. Leinden: Brill Academic, pp. 73–100.

Committee of European Securities Regulators (CESR). 2009. CESR Annual Report 2008. Paris.

Committee of Wise Men. 2001. The final report of the Committee of Wise Men on the regulation of European securities markets. Brussels, 15 February.

de Larosière Group. 2009. The High-Level Group on financial supervision in the EU. Brussels, 25 February.

Emmenegger, Susan. 2010. Procedural consumer protection and financial market supervision. EUI working papers, Law No. 2010/05. 15 February.

European Commission. 1999. Financial services: Implementing the framework for financial markets: Action plan. COM(1999)232. Brussels, 11 May.

European Commission. 2002. Communication from the Commission to the European Parliament, the Council, the Economic and Social Committee and the Committee of the Regions—Consumer policy strategy 2002–2006. Official Journal C137, 8 June, 0002–0023.

European Commission. 2005. White paper on financial services policy (2005-2010). COM(2005)629 final. Brussels, 5 December.

European Commission. 2006. Financial services: Commission hosts first meeting of Financial Services Consumer Group. IP/06/806, Brussels, 20 June.

European Commission. 2009. Driving European recovery: Volume 2: Annexes, communication for the spring European Council. COM(2009)114 final. Brussels, 4 March.

European Commission. 2010. Commission decision of 20 July 2010 setting up a Financial Services User Group, Official Journal C 199, 21 July: 0012-0014.

European Commission. n.d.(a) Register of Commission expert groups and other similar entities: Expert groups explained. Accessed 21 June 2011. Available from http://ec.europa.eu/transparency/regexpert/faq.cfm?aide=2.

European Commission. n.d.(b) The EU Single Market: Consultations. Accessed 17 February 2012. Available from http://ec.europa.eu/internal_market/consultations/index_en.htm.

European Union. 2003. Press release: Financial services: Commission to set up expert forum to look at policies from users' point of view (FIN-USE). IP/03/1119, Brussels, 25 July.

European Union. 2010. Regulation (EU) No. 1093/2010 of the European Parliament and of the Council of 24 November 2010 establishing a European Supervisory Authority (European Banking Authority). Official Journal L 331, 15/12/2010: 0012-0047.

FIN-USE. 2006. The consumers' voice in the European financial services sector, 16 January. Brussels: FIN-USE, European Commission. Accessed 23 December 2011. Available from http://ec.europa.eu/internal_market/fin-use_forum/docs/cons_voice-en.pdf.

FIN-USE. 2008a. Financial education: Changing to second gear, envisioning the way ahead, January. Brussels: FIN-USE, European Commission. Accessed 23 December 2011. Available from http://ec.europa.eu/internal_market/fin-use_forum/docs/fin_education-2008_01_en.pdf.

FIN-USE. 2008b. Reforming mortgage and credit markets—An opinion, December. Brussels: FIN-USE, European Commission. Accessed 23 December 2011. Available from http://ec.europa.eu/internal_market/fin-use_forum/docs/reform_mortgage-credit_markets-2008_12_en.pdf.

FIN-USE. 2009. Position paper on consumer voice in financial services, May. Brussels: FIN-USE, European Commission. Accessed 23 December 2011. Available from http://ec.europa.eu/internal_market/fin-use_forum/docs/consumer_voice_en.pdf.

FIN-USE. 2010. Summary report on reforming EU financial markets: Putting financial users at the heart of financial market reform. Brussels: FIN-USE, European Commission, June. Accessed 23 December 2011. Available from http://ec.europa.eu/internal_market/fin-use_forum/docs/reforming_eu_fin_markets_en.pdf.

Financial Services User Group (FSUG). 2011a. Minutes: FSUG meeting of 27 January 2011. Accessed 1 January 2012. Available from http://ec.europa.eu/internal_market/finservices-retail/docs/fsug/minutes/2011_01_27_en.pdf.

Financial Services User Group (FSUG). 2011b. FSUG annual report. Accessed 1 January 2011. Available from http://ec.europa.eu/internal_market/finservices-retail/docs/fsug/annual_report_2011_en.pdf.

Freixas, Xavier, Philipp Hartmann, and Colin Mayer. 2004. The assessment: European financial integration. *Oxford Review of Economic Policy*, 20 (4): 475–489.

Grossman, Emiliano, and Patrick Leblond. 2011. European financial integration: Finally the great leap forward? *JCMS: Journal of Common Market Studies* 49 (2): 413–435.

Héritier, Adrienne. 1999. Elements of democratic legitimation in Europe: An alternative perspective. *Journal of European Public Policy* 6 (2): 269–282.

Iglesias-Rodriguez, Pablo. 2011. The role of interest groups in EU financial regulation after the European Supervision Authorities in the financial field: The case of the stakeholder groups. European Society of International Law Conference Paper Series, no. 10/2011, Tallinn Research Forum, 26–28 May.

Lord, Christopher. 2001. Assessing democracy in a contested polity. *Journal of Common Market Studies* 39 (4): 641–661.

Lord, Christopher, and David Beetham. 2001. Legitimizing the EU: Is there a "postparliamentary basis" for its legitimation? *Journal of Common Market Studies* 39 (3): 443–462.

McKeen-Edwards, Heather, and Ian Roberge. 2007. Striving for legitimacy: Financial services sector policymaking in the EU after Lamfalussy. *Current Politics and Economics of Europe Special Issue* 18 (2): 223–243.

Mugge, Daniel. 2011. Limits of legitimacy and the primacy of politics in financial governance. *Review of International Political Economy* 18 (1): 52–74.

Ramboll Management. 2006. Evaluation of FIN-USE, independent report for the European Commission, DG Internal Market and Services, July. Accessed 2 December 2011. Available from http://ec.europa.eu/dgs/internal_market/docs/evaluation/finuse.pdf.

Reifner, Udo, and Sebastien Clerc-Renaud. 2011. Financial supervision in the EU: A consumer perspective. A report submitted to BEUC—The European Consumers' Association. Hamburg. February. Accessed 18 February 2012. Available from http://docshare.beuc.org/docs/1/JCGJPFJAAINEFCNDEBDNBENMPDWY9DB67N9DW3571KM/BEUC/docs/DLS/2011-00396-01-E.pdf.

Scharpf, Fritz. 1999. *Governing in Europe, Effective and Democratic?* Oxford: Oxford University Press.

Schmidt, Vivien A. 2004. The European Union: Democratic legitimacy in a regional state? *Journal of Common Market Studies* 42 (5): 975–997.

Schmidt, Vivien A. 2010. Democracy and legitimacy in the European Union revisited: Output, input and throughput. KFG Working Paper Series, No. 21, November.

Skogstad, Grace. 2003. Legitimacy and/or policy effectiveness? Network governance and GMO regulation in the European Union. *Journal of European Public Policy* 10 (3): 321–338.

Tsingou, Eleni. 2009. Regulatory reactions to the global credit crisis: Analyzing a policy community under stress. In *Global Finance in Crisis: The Politics of International Regulatory Change*, edited by Eric Helleiner, Stefan Pagliari, and Hans Zimmermann. London/New York: Routledge: 21–36.

Vander Stichele, Myriam. 2008. Financial regulation in the European Union: Mapping EU decision making structures on financial regulation and supervision, a report commissioned by European Network on Debt and Development, WEED, Bretton Woods Project and Campagna per la Reforma della Banca Mondiale, December.

Chapter 4

Structuring the Game and Surmounting Obstacles: Case Studies from Europe in Multilevel Public Management

Elisa Scotti

Contents

Foreword: Multilevel Governance and Administrative Law

In the European Union (EU), the decision-making process is complex, taking place with increasing frequency in multilevel contexts that arise from the convergence of many different dynamics: decentralization and federalism, on the one hand, and European integration, on the other, as well as pluralism and the differentiation of interests. Increasingly, the process involves many orders of government, including municipalities, provinces, regions, and the European Union, neighboring countries (within the EU and beyond) and numerous authorities protecting different interests, such as the environment, the landscape, privacy, competition, and ethnic minorities. It also involves the public, citizens, and special interest groups. With so many actors, how can decisions be made?

The traditional approach to decision making was hierarchical—that is, a system in which authorities have a fixed, top-down order and in which civil society is excluded from the process. This hierarchical model has now been replaced by a more modern approach. Multilevel governance (MLG) is the formula that currently encapsulates the new vision (Piattoni 2010).

In particular, over the past few decades, the decision-making process has involved both public and private entities at several territorial levels and in different policy sectors; the relationships created among them are not hierarchically ordered but are instead flexible and based on a different approach. Public authorities seem to have abandoned the traditional task of commanding and controlling. Instead, they now facilitate and coordinate decision-making processes within a network of multifaceted relationships based on principles of openness, participation, responsibility, effectiveness, and consistency, as well as on the fundamental search for consensus.

The MLG method embodies the most modern principles of public administration (democracy, autonomy, participation) and is one of the cornerstones of recent public administration reforms. In early 2000, the European Commission identified the reform of European governance as one of its strategic objectives. The 2001 White Paper on governance reform and the 2002 communication entitled *Towards a Reinforced Culture of Consultation and Dialogue—General Principles and Minimum Standards for Consultation of Interested Parties* placed the emphasis on territorial cooperation networks representing the various entities of the institutional, economic, and social partnership (European Commission 2001b, 2002). EU policies for the distribution of structural and cohesion funds[*] provide a paradigm of this new model. In both the design and implementation phases, these cohesion policies are based on principles of participation, agreement, and partnership (Marks 1993; Hooghe 1996).

---

[*] Structural and cohesion funds are financial instruments created by the EU in order to promote economic and social cohesion in the European Union.

At the state level, the Italian constitutional reform of 2001 gave more power to the regions and local bodies. The Constitution now provides that "The Republic is composed of the Municipalities, the Provinces, the Metropolitan Cities, the Regions and the State. Municipalities, provinces, metropolitan cities and regions are autonomous entities having their own statutes, powers and functions in accordance with the principles laid down in the Constitution." (Art. 115); the Republic is no longer "divided in Regions, Provinces and Municipalities" (Art. 115, previous version) (Cerulli Irelli 2004). With this new provision the Constitutional Court has clarified that the relationships among the state, regions, and local bodies are based on the principle of mutual understanding and fair cooperation in the exercise of competing powers (Constitutional Court, Decision 303/2003 [Bifulco 2006]). In practice, this means that when competences overlap, the decision-making process must be based on consensus. In this context, Italian law on administrative procedure (Law n. 241/1990) regulates decisions involving public entities in different jurisdictions (such as the State Environmental Department, the Cultural Department, regions, municipalities) by requiring negotiation among all parties (the *Services Conference*; Articles 14 et. seq., Law 241/90 [Sandulli 2011]).

In the environmental sphere, the Aarhus Convention (AC 1998)* provides all citizens and environmental associations, in particular, with specific rights to access information and participate in related public policy-making and decision-making processes. The principles of the Aarhus Convention are acknowledged in both the EU and national regulations governing environmental procedure, such as the Environmental Impact Assessment (EIA) and the Strategic Environmental Assessment (SEA).† These regulations stipulate that the public must be informed and consulted and that decisions must take into account the results of these consultations.

These important innovations to the institutional framework, stressing coordination and consensus, definitely help to improve multilevel governance's chances of success. However, as this chapter will demonstrate, multilevel governance doesn't always work. In some cases, multilevel governance represents a successful solution, while in others, especially because of the need for unanimous agreement, it can become a trap (the joint decision trap [Scharpf 1988]) or a tragedy (the tragedy of the anticommons or the tragedy of the impotent decision maker [Heller 1998]).

---

* Concluded at Aarhus, Denmark, on 25 June 1998. It was promoted by the United Nations Economic Commission for Europe (UNECE) and ratified by Italy through Law n. 108 in 2002, and approved in 2005 by the EU through Council Decision 2005/370/EC.

† Environmental assessment ensures that the environmental implications of decisions are taken into account before decisions are made. Environmental assessment can be undertaken for individual projects, on the basis of Directive 85/337/EEC, as amended (known as "Environmental Impact Assessment"—EIA Directive) or for public plans or programs, on the basis of Directive 2001/42/EC (known as "Strategic Environmental Assessment"—SEA Directive). The common principle underlying both directives is that plans, programs, and projects that are likely to have a significant impact on the environment must be subject to environmental review prior to their approval or authorization (http://ec.europa.eu/environment/eia/home.htm).

In fact, despite every good intention, it is impossible to guarantee the adoption of decisions, even though they may be vital and broadly shared, because the network of relationships as a whole is beyond the jurisdiction of each of the parties involved. Also, it is not possible to guarantee that any given agreement is truly the result of consensus and not merely a consequence of larger entities overpowering the weaker parties (Rawls 1999).

This chapter will highlight this ambivalence by exploring some success stories and problematic experiences in order to understand whether or not multilevel public management is capable of replacing the traditional hierarchical approach to governance.

Success Story I: Partnerships for Sustainable Territorial Development

Integrated Territorial Plans

Within territorial governance, there are many examples of the successful application of models of multilevel governance based on negotiation and a strategic approach. Territorial policies must necessarily overcome the vertical and horizontal separation of tasks and functions that characterize the current public system. Because territorial issues also have an immediate impact on citizens, they require the involvement of the public in decision making (Amorosino 2003).

European law has provided significant impetus to multilevel governance. The EU has promoted the direct participation of regions and local bodies through partnerships as part of numerous initiatives aimed at the sustainable development of the territories (such as the leader, urban, and equal programs). As part of the Community Regional Support Network 2000–2006, these partnerships have taken many forms: territorial pacts, integrated territorial projects, local development plans, and local action groups, all of which share the following common characteristics:

1. *Integration*, which implies consideration of the entire local system, including all of its component parts, its socio-institutional relationships and the interdependence between sectors and values. Integration is then translated into a strategic approach for a specific area (such as a tourist district or industrial zone), which overcomes the different spheres of competence by creating a multi-issue public management network.
2. *A bottom-up approach*, which is intended to optimize the territory and the roles of various players within it, and to prioritize the contribution of municipalities, local bodies, economic operators, social entities, and interested citizens.
3. *Partnership*, which involves defining the program in consultation with all interested public and private entities, regardless of level of responsibilities or jurisdiction (national, regional, and local).

The outcome of this European policy has been positive. From 2000 to 2006, many different Integrated Territorial Plans were approved, establishing an innovative approach to the relationship between the regions and the territorial entities. This approach continues today in the implementation of regional policies for 2007–13. In these instances, the partnerships have taken root in part because the political, economic, social, and civil parties are active in both proposing projects and implementing them (Amorosino 2001).

The Integrated Plans for Sustainable Urban Development (PIUSS), developed by the Italian region of Tuscany to implement policies for economic and social growth in urban areas, are a striking example of the success of a multilevel approach to governance. Each PIUSS, which deals with many authorities (economic, social, urban, and environmental), coordinates public and private actors in the policy-making and implementation phases by applying the consensus method.

Cross-Border Cooperation

Still within the European context, the partnership method is also fundamental to the implementation of policies for cross-border cooperation (CBC), which are designed to encourage regions and cities in different member states and other countries to work together and to learn from reciprocal experiences in the context of common programs, projects, and networks. Partnership thus becomes a tool for promoting, outside the jurisdiction of the EU, administrative, social, and economic reforms inspired by European governance models.

Various initiatives are envisaged in this area for the 2007–13 period, all of which are based on partnerships among regions, among cities,* in border areas, or between European regions and candidate or potential candidate countries (Instrument for Pre-Accession Assistance [IPA]).†

Success Story II: IPA Adriatic CBC Programme

The case study below considers the Instrument for Pre-Accession Assistance (IPA) and, in particular, the IPA Adriatic CBC Programme.

IPA is a financial instrument for countries applying for entry into the European Union. These are known as "candidate countries" and "potential candidate countries." The first group comprises the former Yugoslav Republic of Macedonia,

---

* See, respectively, the INTERREG IVC and the URBACT programs, and the European Neighbourhood and Partnership Instrument (ENPI).
† See Council Regulation (EC) no. 1085/2006, 17 July 2006, establishing an Instrument for Pre-Accession Assistance (IPA). See http://europa.eu/legislation_summaries/agriculture/enlargement/e50020_en.htm and the IPA Adriatic Cross-Border Cooperation Programme (2011), available from http://www.abruzzosviluppo.it/filedoc/1269253632-Implementing_Manual_final.PDF.

Croatia, and Turkey. Potential candidate countries are Albania, Bosnia and Herzegovina, Iceland, Montenegro, and Serbia, including Kosovo.* For these countries, IPA provides a dual level of solidarity and cohesion: the first, in economic terms, is associated with the provision of European funds; the second is an institutional one, associated with the exchange of knowledge and methods for public action (in terms of both policy making and decision making). It also promotes the fundamental principles of the EU—namely, the rule of law; human rights, including the fundamental freedoms; minority rights; gender equality and nondiscrimination; cross-border cooperation; and administrative, economic, and social reforms.

More specifically, the IPA consists of the following five components, each covering priorities defined according to the needs of the recipient countries:

I. *Support for transition and institution building* provides financing for capacity building and institution building. It supports measures to drive stabilization and the transition to a democratic society and market economy.
II. *Cross-border cooperation* supports cooperation between candidate and potential candidate countries, and with EU member states and regions.
III. *Regional development* supports investments and associated technical assistance in areas such as transport, environment, and economic cohesion.
IV. *Human resources development* concerns preparation for participation in cohesion policy.
V. *Rural development* contributes to sustainable rural development and involves the framing of common agricultural policy and related policies.

Components I and II are open to all candidate and potential candidate countries, while components III through V are open to candidate countries only (European Council 2006).

Against this backdrop, the IPA Adriatic CBC Programme was created, springing from joint programming undertaken by the collaborating countries. It involves all of the regions bordering the Adriatic Sea, be they members, candidate, or potential candidate countries to the EU, and therefore including the entire eastern coast of Italy, the former Yugoslav republics (Bosnia and Herzegovina, Montenegro, Serbia, Croatia, and Slovenia), as well as Greece and Albania. Its objective is to strengthen cooperation and sustainable development in the Adriatic region by implementing initiatives based on four priority areas: economic, social, and institutional cooperation; natural and cultural resources and prevention of risks; accessibility and networks; and technical assistance (European Commission 2007).

Numerous projects have been approved under the IPA Adriatic CBC Programme. Among them, a paradigmatic example of multilevel governance is the Alterenergy project, "Energy Sustainability for Adriatic Small Communities."

---

* See Annex I–II to the Regulation [EC] No. 1085/2006.

Alterenergy Project

The overall aim of this project is to define an Adriatic community for sustainable energy development through a common, shared strategy for addressing climate change based on equilibrium between environmental protection, competitiveness, and the security of the Adriatic region's energy supply. The project focuses on developing replicable models for the sustainable and integrated management of energy sources (energy–environmental plans, pilot infrastructure projects, and communication campaigns designed to foster an awareness of sustainable energy). It encompasses small communities (fewer than 10,000 inhabitants) that populate the Adriatic area and aims to improve their ability to plan and manage energy-saving initiatives and renewable energy generation.

Recently approved as part of the IPA Adriatic Programme and accepted for European funding (2011), the Alterenergy project illustrates multilevel governance in action, with EU institutions, states, regions, and other public bodies all cooperating and interacting successfully. Based on a broad partnership, the project embraces all eligible Adriatic countries under the leadership of the Apulia region, with technical and scientific support from the Apulian Regional Agency for Technology and Innovation (Agenzia ARTI Puglia).

The following partners—a wide variety of institutions at different territorial levels—are involved in the project: the regions of Abruzzo, Emilia Romagna, Friuli Venezia Giulia, Marche, and Molise; Veneto Agricoltura (a regional agency for agriculture, forestry, and agro-industry); ENEL SPA (associate partner); GOLEA Goriška local energy agency; Ministry of the Economy–Energy Directorate (associate partner); Istria County; Primorsko Goranska County; Split and Dalmatia County; Dubrovnik and Neretva County; Ministry of Foreign Trade and Economic Relations–Department for Secondary Energy and Projects; Serbian Energy Efficiency Agency; the Municipality of Kotor; Ministry of Economy, Trade, and Energy; the Region of Epirus; and finally the Greek CRES (National Centre of Renewable Energy Sources and Saving).

Planning for the project began in 2006 and was completed in September 2011. The region of Apulia and the Albanian government, which have been collaborating since 1994 through the previous cross-border cooperation program (the Interreg IIIA Italy-Albania), were the driving forces behind the initiative. The project developed through meetings, fora, and negotiations among all parties and in particular between the proponents and the EU Commission.

The first step was to formalize inclusion in the IPA Adriatic area. To this end, a meeting took place in March 2006 with regard to a potential Italy–Albania Strategic Project. A letter of intent was drawn up in order to safeguard the cooperation between Albania and Italy and the associated funds. The letter was signed that same month by both the prime minister of Albania and the head of the region of Apulia; it was subsequently sent to the president of the commission in Brussels. The

European Commission and the Italian Ministry of Foreign Affairs then discussed the new cross-border cooperation program.

In 2007, the Italian city of Bari hosted a conference on "Investments and Legality in Albania" during which the future cooperation between the two countries was discussed. Next, following a series of specialist fora and meetings, all members of the IPA Adriatic CBC Programme acknowledged the value of past collaboration between the two countries, and they agreed to the explicit mention of the Italy–Albania Strategic Project in the program. The IPA Adriatic Operational Programme refers to implementing a strategic project specifically for Italy and Albania:

> The Programme partnership recognises the value of the Italy-Albania cooperation which has been supported by the two countries and the EU over recent years. As a result, the Programme partnership invites Albania and Italy to develop a strategic project which will be of benefit for the whole Adriatic Programme area. The involved Albanian and Italian partners must aim to expand the partnership for this strategic project to other interested partners from the Programme area. The Albanian and Italian partners are invited to submit to the Joint Monitoring Committee—in one of its first meetings—the strategic project, including a financial and activities plan. (European Commission 2007, p.65)

The next step in the process involved the approval of the Alterenergy project, also through multilevel negotiation. The project was presented to all representatives of partner countries and to the public, via conferences, events, and meetings held between 2008 and 2010. On 5 December 2008, for example, the project was outlined at the Innovation Festival in the Italian city of Bari. In 2009, it was examined by both the IPA Adriatic Programme Supervisory Committee and the Italian National Committee Meeting for the IPA Adriatic Programme. The following year, the planning team for the Alterenergy project met with key national partners in order to present details of the initiative and the resources dedicated to each participating state/region (Polignano 2010). In July 2011, Alterenergy was officially presented to the Joint Monitoring Committee;* it was approved by all partners in September 2011.

As mentioned above, Alterenergy focuses on developing energy–environmental plans and pilot projects in the small communities that populate the Adriatic region, promoting energy development, sustainability, and efficiency. It is divided into six work packages (WPs): project management; communication, information, and awareness-raising campaigns; integrated energy management models; integrated

---

* "The JMC is composed of representatives from the central and regional/local governments of the participating Countries. A representative of the European Commission shall attend the JMC meetings. Environmental and economic and social partnership representatives may also participate, whenever appropriate, as observers" (IPA Adriatic Cross-Border Cooperation Programme, 2011, 7).

plans for sustainable energy; support for business and investment; and pilot project implementation.

The third step in the initiative, currently underway, is planning the project's implementation and execution. This step also requires cooperation and negotiation among all parties. To this end, meetings are being held to bring together all relevant institutional bodies from the energy sector (regions, ministries, and energy advertising agencies) and from all partner countries. The meetings discuss financial–administrative procedures and ways of embarking on the project. For example, discussions were held recently regarding the WP "Integrated Energy Management Models." The aim was to develop an understanding of the sector and a common method for defining sustainable energy plans for the target community.

Alterenergy is scheduled to run for four years with a budget of around €12.5 million. It is expected to achieve a range of goals, including identifying common integrated energy management models; improving local communities' ability to plan, implement, and manage energy-saving schemes and renewable energy generation; raising awareness, both among the public and local economic entities (SMEs, professionals), of the opportunities for and benefits of energy efficiency and the environmentalization of the energy mix; strengthening cooperation and increasing the availability of viability studies and replicable pilot projects; and increasing investment opportunities both for the public sector and for private businesses operating in the green economy sector.

Problematic Experiences: The Introduction of Public Works

Public works is a sector in which multilevel governance seems to be somewhat less straightforward. What procedure should be used for decision making in this field? Is it possible to use a method based on effective coordination and consensus among all implicated orders of government and policy sectors? Is it useful to include the public affected by the decision?

These questions are complicated. First, infrastructure planning generally leads to widespread benefits and localized disadvantages for local communities, and it gives rise to the NIMBY (not in my backyard) syndrome. Substate levels of government (regions and local authorities), together with citizens, therefore tend to oppose public works projects; for this reason, their inclusion in the decision-making process can seem to be ill advised. Involving them could, in fact, create conflict, thereby giving rise to the "tragedies" of the anticommons and the impotent decision maker (or joint decision trap).

Second, these traditional opponents tend to be excluded from the decision-making process by the law, which frequently provides specific regulations for decisions of this kind. In the institutional framework, especially for the most important infrastructure planning, authority is generally vested in the highest territorial levels (state and EU). Moreover, the approval procedures are usually accelerated and do not guarantee the effective involvement of all orders of government or all of the policy sectors implicated. The regulations do not include local communities or interested members of the public in the decision-making process. The state can always overcome disagreement unilaterally.

In Italy, this problem is particularly acute because the law does not provide for the involvement of citizens in decision-making processes concerning infrastructure and, in particular, the location of infrastructure. However, recent proposals have tried to introduce some form of public consultation into these procedures, such as the public inquiry or the public debate, following the French and British models (Casini 2007; Revel et al. 2007; Macchiati and Napolitano 2009). Nonetheless, even these models are subject to considerable criticism, given their limited ability to incorporate all necessary viewpoints and their restricted power to resolve issues in a manner that preserves the democratic nature or the acceptance of choices of this type (Cassese 2007; Bétaille 2010).

Despite these concerns, the involvement of local bodies and the public in decision making (and therefore in policy making) remains a key challenge. In fact, as recent experiences demonstrate, if the opponents of the decisions are excluded, the "tragedy" is not avoided but merely postponed. Local authorities and citizens who are excluded from the decision-making phases tend to impose their points of view during the implementation phase: through legal arguments, through the use of shutdowns and protests, or through requests for exorbitant compensation. Interestingly, they often succeed in imposing their points of view, even though it may be after the fact and through non-legal means.

At the EU level, one case clearly illustrates this state of affairs. It comes from the implementation of the Trans-European Networks—Transport (TEN-T), which was set out in the Maastricht Treaty of 1992 as key to guaranteeing the smooth functioning of the internal market and strengthening the economic and social cohesion of the EU (Predieri and Morisi 2003). The TEN-T priority projects constitute the fundamental axis for transportation within the EU and are shaped by the EU using a top-down process, based on agreements with member states and without the involvement of the various territorial levels affected or the general public.

First articulated in the 1991 European Commission communication entitled *Europe 2000: Outlook for the Development of the Community's Territory*, the driving force behind the development of these trans-European networks came from the *Growth, Competitiveness, and Employment* White Paper, which was drawn up by the Commission and presented in December 1993 by then-President of the European Commission, Jacques Delors* (European Commission 1991, 1993).

---

* The European Commission is composed of one commissioner per member state, up to a certain size. As of 2014, the commission will be reduced in size and will consist of several members corresponding to two-thirds of the number of member states. In the reduced-size commission, the commissioners will be selected according to a system of equal rotation among member states.

During that same month, the European Council in Brussels* set up a special group to assist in defining the projects to be implemented. The group was headed by the vice president of the commission, Henning Christophersen, and was composed of representatives of the heads of state and of government.

In December 1994, the "Christophersen Group" finished its work, presenting a conclusive report to the European Council in Essen in which they proposed 26 large-scale priority projects (Christophersen Group 1994). Fourteen of these projects were approved by the European Council. Decision 1692/96 of the European Parliament and Council ratified the responsibility of member states for implementing the network, stipulating that the commission would examine the progress of the work every five years.

Toward the end of the 1990s, however, it became clear that the TEN-T program was not progressing and that some of the biggest priority projects were being blocked. In 1998, the first report on the progress of the program revealed these difficulties and delays, which were also highlighted in the Commission's White Paper in 2001 on European transport policy (European Commission 2001a). The obstruction was attributed not only to widely known financing difficulties, but also to ineffective multilevel governance, which was unable to cope with many different competences across all levels and across borders. European-level attempts to overcome this "crisis" led to the founding of a high-level group headed by the former commissioner, Van Miert, and composed of representatives of member states. One representative was designated by the ministries of transport of each member state; one representative was designated as an observer by the 12 countries set to enter the EU in either 2004 or 2007; and one representative came from the European Bank to monitor funding issues. This group was charged with the task of supporting the European Commission as it reviewed the TEN-T guidelines.

The Van Miert report, presented to the Commission on 30 June 2003, identified a limited number of priority projects based on criteria including the project's economic viability, the relevant member state's commitment to complying with a fixed schedule when programming the works, the project's impact on the mobility of goods and people between member states, as well as its impact on cohesion and sustainable development (High Level Group 2003). This review phase was carried out using the method first followed—that is, without involving the regions, local bodies, or the general public even though the Van Miert report highlighted the governance and NIMBYism problems hindering the projects.

Following the publication of the Van Miert report, there was a participatory phase open to all affected by the projects: the commission invited all interested parties to share their own observations and concerns related to the review of the TEN-T, submitting them in writing no later than 10 September 2003. This

---

* The European Council includes the heads of state or government of the member states, together with the Council president and the president of the Commission. The EU Minister for Foreign Affairs also takes part in the Council's work.

consultation process was, however, met with several criticisms, including that it was seen as a formality because of the time frame for consultation and the way in which it was organized. Far from being preliminary and instrumental to the work of the high-level group, it was held afterwards and therefore had a limited impact on the final decision.

After the consultation and on the basis of the report, the European Commission drew up a new list of 30 priority projects that were to start before 2010. The list, presented in 2003 upon the conclusion of the work, led to a redefinition of the priority projects, divided into four sections according to priority: projects already approved at Essen, to be implemented before 2010; high-added-value projects to commence before 2010 and to be completed before 2020; high-added-value projects with a longer-term schedule; and projects important for territorial cohesion.

At the legislative level, Decision No. 884/2004/CE of the European Parliament and of the Council addressed the governance question by establishing a framework based on coordination and on the broadening of the decision-making processes. The decision stipulated that project approval must be subject to strategic environmental evaluations that would be open to the public. It also set out the possibility of appointing a European coordinator to facilitate the implementation of the most important cross-border projects.

The role of the European coordinator is fundamental. As early as 1994, its importance was highlighted in the Christophersen Group's report:

> We have accelerated preparation of the priority projects, and several are already under construction. However, it takes time to prepare and implement complex projects of exceptional scale, involving several Member States. That is why we recommend the creation of suitable project-specific "authorities" to be in charge of project promotion. This is the most efficient way of bridging over different priorities and regulatory conditions in the Member States concerned, and to involve the private sector. (Christophersen Group 1994, p.1)

According to Decision No. 884/2004/EC, of the European Parliament and of the Council (OJEU L 161, 30.04.2004, 1).

> The European Coordinator shall: (a) promote, in cooperation with the Member States concerned, joint methods for the evaluation of projects and, where appropriate, advise project promoters on the financial package for the projects;
>
> (b) draw up a report every year for the European Parliament, the Commission and the Member States concerned on progress achieved in the implementation of the project(s) for which he/she is responsible, new regulatory or other developments which could affect the

characteristics of the projects and any difficulties and obstacles which may result in a significant delay in relation to the dates indicated in Annex III;

(c) consult, together with the Member States concerned, regional and local authorities, operators, transport users, and representatives of civil society with a view to gaining fuller knowledge of the demand for transport services, the possibilities of investment funding and the type of services that must be provided in order to facilitate access to such funding.

Therefore, the European coordinator is charged with overcoming project implementation crises by, on the one hand, looking for financing, and on the other, attempting to resolve multilevel governance problems through coordination of the various entities concerned and involvement of the regions, local bodies, and citizens who have until recently remained outside the proceedings related to the TEN-T networks.

Although ultimately the principle of public consultation open to all interested parties has been formally sanctioned, this innovation appears to have come too late. The projects were long decided, and at this stage, the consultations now run the risk of being nothing more than a formality, simply serving as a forum for information gathering without any real possibility of affecting, other than marginally, decisions that are already firm. In fact, in 2010, as the European Commission observed in the *Roadmap to a Single European Transport Area,* of the 30 TEN-T priority projects related to the EU's main transport hubs, only five were completed (European Commission 2010, 2011).

Since 2009, the Commission has altered the policy-making model generally used for TEN-T, in accordance with the guidelines previously established in the 2001 White Paper on governance. With its February 2009 Green Paper on the future development of TEN-T, the Commission embarked on a revision of the TEN-T policies, based on the recognized need for public consultation (European Commission 2009). That same year, a first consultation was held, the results of which led to a second consultation on the future trans-European transport network policy in 2010 (European Commission 2010).

The Lyons–Turin–Milan–Trieste–Koper–Ljubljana–Budapest High-Speed Rail Line

One example relating to events surrounding a TEN-T priority project may help to further elucidate this problematic context—the cross-border Lyons–Turin–Milan–Trieste–Koper–Ljubljana–Budapest high-speed rail line. This project was one of the priority strategies identified by the Essen European Council in 1994; the decision was not preceded by public consultation at the EU level. For the section of the project subject to Italian interests, the proposal was put forward by the Italian government without involving the regional or local authorities, or interested citizens. In fact, all of the latter clearly expressed their opposition to the project, and NO TAV* groups were organized outside of institutional headquarters with the intention of blocking implementation of the high-speed project (Bettini 2006). These protest groups were immediately joined by local bodies who were affected by the project and excluded from the public decision-making process (Algostino 2011).

Because of the vocal opposition from the NO TAV movement, which resorted both to lawsuits and to protests of various types, the implementation of the project ground to a halt. These groups subsequently participated in the open public consultation in 2003, after publication of the Van Miert report mentioned above. Their observations did not, however, result in a review of the project or in the reopening of negotiations, an outcome that generated strong criticism. In fact, the deadlock was not resolved, and opposition among the communities concerned grew ever stronger.

In order to resolve this impasse, the Italian government and the EU Commission reopened the decision-making processes, inviting participation from all sectors and institutional levels concerned, as well as from the general public. First, the Italian government waived the use of the simplified and accelerated decision-making procedures that had made it possible to avoid an environmental impact assessment of the final project. As provided by Decision 884/2004/CE, a European coordinator responsible for the issue was appointed and a negotiating procedure was then introduced by the government, to be managed by the Technical Observatory for the Turin-Lyons rail link.

Founded in 2006, the observatory is composed of technical representatives from the Province of Turin; the Region of Piedmont; the Ministries of the Environment, Infrastructure, Home Affairs, and Health; and RFI, the Italian rail network company. The observatory is responsible, although a posteriori, for encouraging and overseeing the participation of local communities and their public and private representatives in an effective dialogue with those entities. Seventy meetings have taken place, with approximately 300 hearings involving 60 international experts and continuous negotiation with local bodies and citizens. This dialogue has resulted in a partial modification of the project, compensation measures, and an assurance of the transparency of the procedure and the provision of appropriate information to the communities (Pizzanelli 2010).

Nonetheless, the conflict has been only partially settled; many local representatives and opposition movements have refused to continue discussions. As a result, public force has been required at times to ensure the commencement of the project, and, even at this stage, doubts remain over what the final version of the project will look like and whether it will be completed.

---

* TAV stands for *Treni ad alta velocità*, or "high-speed trains" in English.

Conclusions

The case studies examined in this chapter emphasize the central role of multilevel governance based on effective coordination, participation, and consensus. The first case demonstrates the effectiveness of action founded on the involvement of all interested parties. In contrast, the second illustrates the failure of action taken without the involvement of all parties, even more so when the process sidesteps those most immediately affected by the decisions in question—that is, the regions, local bodies, and the general public.

However, the case studies also highlight the obstacles that public management has to overcome in order to coordinate all parties involved in multilevel contexts effectively. The greatest obstacle is disagreement, which is a common occurrence in multilevel contexts and which is inevitable whenever decisions are not unanimously acceptable because of negative external factors. In these cases, the decision-making process often leads to a deadlock, generating the tragedies mentioned earlier.

Managing conflict is, therefore, one of the main challenges faced by multilevel public management. One tempting solution for administrators and legislators may be to return to the unilateral, top-down models of the past. However, reducing the participatory phases and the opportunities for debate and negotiation among all interests involved, and maintaining an authoritative, top-down, and hierarchical approach will only reduce the acceptability of the choices made. Choices made under such circumstances often cannot be implemented (Habermas 1996; Bifulco 2011).

Moreover, even when it is not possible to overcome disagreement, the application of the fundamental principles of multilevel governance, in terms of participation and mediation, can significantly reduce the degree of institutional and social conflict (Waldron 1999).

Herein lies one of the current challenges for regulation: defining methods for managing disagreement that incorporate the principles of multilevel governance based on coordination and on the search for consensus without returning to outdated authoritarian and centralized models. In this perspective, multilevel governance must be understood as a procedural mechanism, which can be instrumental in achieving "fair" decisions but which, per se, is not able to guarantee the fairness of the final decision (Romano 1987; Rawls 1999).

Because the consensus on "opposed" choices can be achieved only partially using a procedural mechanism, the substantial parameters that the public decision maker is required to observe thus become very important. These are the principles of equality, reasonableness, and the sustainability of the choice, which must form the basis of any public decision, irrespective of the decision-making process applied. And which, even in negotiated procedures, constitute an essential guarantee for interests that are powerless and unorganized (Romano 1999). These interests are, by and large, the losers in the multilevel public arena, which is dominated by stronger public and private powers despite the formal involvement of all interested parties (Cassese 2001).

References

Algostino, Alessandra. 2011. *Democrazia, rappresentanza, partecipazione. Il caso del movimento no TAV* [Democracy, representation, participation. The case for the NO TAV movement]. Naples: Jovene.

Amorosino, Sandro. 2001. Gli indirizzi dell'Unione Europea per l'organizzazione del territorio comune e le funzioni statali e regionali-locali. [European Union guidelines for common territorial organisation and state and regional/local functions]. *Diritto dell'Unione Europea* 383–392.

Amorosino, Sandro. 2003. Il governo del territorio, tra stato, regioni ed enti locali. [Territorial government, between state, regions and local bodies]. *Rivista giuridica dell'edilizia* 77–90.

Bétaille, Julien. 2010. La contribution du droit aux effets de la participation du public: de la prise en considération des résultats de la participation. [The contribution of law to the effects of participation by the public: Consideration of the outcome of participation]. *Revue juridique de l'environnement* 197–219.

Bettini, Virgilio. 2006. *TAV: i perché del NO [TAV: Why we say "no"]*. Turin: UTET Libreria.

Bifulco, Raffaele. 2006. Leale collaborazione (principio di). [Frank and fair cooperation (principle of)]. In *Dizionario di diritto pubblico [Dictionary of Public Law]*, edited by Sabino Cassese, Vol. IV, 3356–3364. Milan: Giuffrè.

Bifulco, Raffaele. 2011. Democrazia deliberativa. [Deliberative democracy]. In *Enciclopedia del diritto [Encyclopaedia of Law]*. Annali IV, 271–294.

Casini, Lorenzo. 2007. L'inchiesta pubblica, analisi comparata. [The public inquiry, comparative analysis]. *Rivista trimestrale di diritto pubblico* 43–92.

Cassese, Sabino. 2001. L'arena pubblica. Nuovi paradigmi per lo Stato. [The public area. New paradigms for the state]. *Rivista trimestrale di diritto pubblico* 601–650.

Cassese, Sabino. 2007. La partecipazione dei privati alle decisioni pubbliche. Saggio di diritto comparato. [Private participation in public decision making]. *Rivista trimestrale di diritto pubblico* 13–41.

Cerulli Irelli, Vincenzo. 2004. Sussidiarietà (diritto amministrativo). [Subsidiarity (administrative law)]. In *Enciclopedia Giuridica Treccani.* Updating XII. Rome: Istituto della Enciclopedia Italiana, 327–378.

Christophersen Group. 1994. Report to the Essen European Council. IP/94/1102.

European Commission. 1991. Communication: Europe 2000: Outlook for the development of the community's territory. 91/C 339/18.

European Commission. 1993. White Paper: Growth, competitiveness and employment. COM (93) 700.

European Commission. 2001a. White Paper: European transport policy up to 2010: The time for choices. COM (2001) 370.

European Commission. 2001b. White Paper: European governance. COM (2001) 428 def/2.

European Commission. 2002. Communication: Towards a reinforced culture of consultation and dialogue—General principles and minimum standards for consultation of interested parties. COM (2002) 278 def.

European Commission. 2007. IPA Adriatic Cross-Border Cooperation Programme. 2007CB16IPO 001.

European Commission. 2009. Green Paper: TEN-T: A policy review. Towards a better integrated trans-European transport network at the service of the common transport policy. COM (2009) 44 final.

European Commission. 2010. Working document: Consultation on the future trans-European transport network policy. COM (2010) 212 final.

European Commission. 2011. Roadmap to a single European transport area—Towards a competitive and resource efficient transport system. COM (2011) 144 final.

European Council. 2006. Regulation (EC) No. 1085/2006.

Habermas, Jürgen. 1996. *Between Facts and Norms*. Cambridge, MA: MIT Press. German ed.: Faktizität und Geltung. Beiträge zur Diskurstheorie des Rechts und des demokratischen Rechstaats [1992].

Heller, Michael. 1998. The tragedy of the anticommons: Property in transition from Marx to Markets. *Harvard Law Review* 111: 621–688.

High-Level Group on the Trans-European Transport Network. 2003. Report. TREN-2003-00960-02-00-EN-REV-00.

Hooghe, Liesbet. 1996. *Cohesion Policy and European Integration: Building Multi-Level Governance*. New York: Oxford University Press.

IPA Adriatic Cross-Border Cooperation Programme. 2011. *IPA Implementation Manual*, final version. Available from http://www.abruzzosviluppo.it/filedoc/1269253632-Implementing_Manual_final.PDF (accessed Jan. 10, 2013).

Macchiati, Alfredo, and Giulio Napolitano, eds. 2009. *È possibile realizzare le infrastrutture in Italia? [Is It Possible to Create Infrastructures in Italy?]*. Bologna: Il Mulino.

Marks, Gary. 1993. Structural policy and multi-level governance in the EC. In *The State of the European Community: The Maastricht Debate and Beyond*, edited by Alan W. Cafruny, Glenda Goldstone Rosenthal, 391–411. Boulder, CO: Lynne Rienner.

Piattoni, Simona. 2010. *The Theory of Multi-Level Governance. Conceptual, Empirical and Normative Challenges*. New York: Oxford University Press.

Pizzanelli, Giovanna. 2010. *La partecipazione dei privati alle decisioni pubbliche. Politiche ambientali e realizzazione delle grandi opere infrastrutturali. [Private Participation in Public Decisions: Environmental and Implementation Policies for Large-Scale Infrastructure Projects]*. Milan: Giuffrè.

Polignano, Claudio. 2010. La governance dei programmi di cooperazione territoriale europea. [The governance of European Territorial Cooperation Programmes]. Available from http://www.fondieuropei2007-2013.it/upload\TransMediterraneo\Seminario_BO_28092010\PDF_SLIDE\Polignano_IPA_ALTERENERGY.pdf (accessed Jan. 10, 2013).

Predieri, Alberto, and Massimo Morisi, eds. 2003. *L'europa delle reti. [The Europe of Networks]*. Turin: Giappichelli.

Rawls, John. 1999. *A Theory of Justice*, rev. ed. Oxford: Oxford University Press. [First ed. 1971.]

Revel, Martine, Cécile Blatrix, Loïc Blondiaux, Jean-Michel Fourniau, Bertrand Hériard-Dubreuil, and Rémi Lefebvre, eds. 2007. *Le débat public: une expérience française de démocratie participative [The Public Debate: A French Experiment in Participatory Democracy]*. Paris: La Découverte.

Romano, Alberto. 1987. Il cittadino e la pubblica amministrazione [The citizen and the public authorities]. In *Il diritto amministrativo degli anni '80. Proceedings of the XXXth Conference on Scientific Studies of Administration*, edited by G.M. Rigamonti, 155–220. Milan: Giuffrè.

Romano, Alberto. 1999. Amministrazione, principio di legalità e ordinamenti giuridici. [Administration, the principle of legality and legal systems]. *Diritto amministrativo* 111–142.

Sandulli, Maria Alessandra, ed. 2011. *Codice dell'azione amministrativa.* [*Code of Administrative Action*]. Milano: Giuffrè.

Scharpf, Fritz W. 1988. The joint decision trap: Lessons from German federalism and European integration. *Public Administration* 66: 239–278.

Waldron, Jeremy. 1999. *Law and Disagreement.* Oxford: Clarendon Press.

Chapter 5

Policy Governance in Complex Multilevel Systems: Innovation Management in Canada

Charles Conteh

Contents

Introduction

Transitions in public management research and practice toward service delivery or policy implementation processes that reflect the complexities of the operating environment of public policy governance have been witnessed in recent years. These trends indicate a shift in emphasis from narrow, intra-organizational and managerial issues to interorganizational relationships and multi-actor governance processes within the pluralist environment of public service delivery (Osborne 2010).

The analytical shift in public management is not simply the fancy of academics but rather a reflection of major transitions taking place in the real world of public management. The twenty-first century is proving to be an increasingly complex, unpredictable environment for public management in particular, and public policy governance in general, as the traditional relationship between the state and citizens continues to change. Citizens are increasingly becoming value creators in every public policy issue, seeking to be co-producers of public services. This means that what constitutes the public policy space is larger than before, and the boundaries of the public sector are being redrawn, presenting an expanded range of opportunities for as well as challenges to the roles, relationships, and tools that public agencies have at their disposal. In such environments, public agencies (and even governments) are differentiated by their response to this new complexity: some will "muddle-through" while others will harness that complexity to create competitive advantage. These new approaches to thinking about and practicing public management require creative public sector leadership, the reinvention of "citizen" or "service user" relationships, and the building of operational dexterity.

The growing complexity of public management subsystems transcends national boundaries. Scholars have identified two major transnational trends over the past three decades—namely, globalization and shifts in political culture. Globalization refers to social, economic, and even political interdependence that makes it possible to imagine supra-territorial connections among policy actors once separated by geography and culture (Pal 2006). Shifts in political culture are somewhat related to the phenomenon of globalization, as societies and subgroups search for meaning and reconstruct identities that may reinforce or undermine conventional narratives of nationhood. Moreover, highly educated and technologically connected societies are transmitting information and knowledge through social network media outside the influence of the state, resulting in the dispersion of symbolic power and the decline of deference for political leaders.

This shift in political culture has been seeping into the processes of public management as new social movements become increasingly motivated by "rights-driven" and interest-driven politics manifested in phenomena such as popular participation, grassroots mobilization, issue networks, assertive ethnicity, and regionalism. The resulting social fragmentation is responsible for the complexity and dynamism of modern public management. These phenomena are often at odds with technocratic approaches to public management. Although governments used to provide services directly to citizens, questions are now being raised about co-production arrangements with citizen groups, subnational identities, and transnational interests. The instruments of public management are thus expected to adapt to the imperatives of change.

Another dimension of the changing environmental context of public management is the current economic climate. Again this phenomenon relates to the forces of globalization. The recent global financial meltdown dating back to 2007 and the dramatic industrial, financial, and regulatory changes that prompted seismic shifts in global trade and manufacturing reflect the deeper structural features of globally integrated economies. The challenge before all governments is to mitigate the threats of global economic integration while leveraging the opportunities that it provides.

While pressure is mounting on governments to engage their economies and societies proactively, recent years have also brought with them challenges for advanced democracies (mostly Organisation for Economic Co-operation and Development [OECD] countries) facing large budget deficits that necessitate drastic spending cuts. Sustainable cost reductions transcend a mere resizing to include reshaping public service provision and delivery models. Like never before, the currents of these recent changes mean that governments around the world and at all levels are thinking about new ways to engage their front lines and share responsibilities with other actors in society, often by working across organizational boundaries and formally incorporating citizen inputs and participation. Thus the compounding and contradictory pressures of more proactive public sector engagement on the one hand and structural deficits on the other are forcing governments toward greater innovation in cost efficiency, inclusion, and participation. As a Chinese proverb maintains, every crisis can be an opportunity for positive transformation and change.

Among the core competencies identified for public sector leadership under the environmental conditions described above, one of the most frequently cited has been collaborative management. This competency is central to proactive initiatives geared toward building leadership capacity within public agencies to meet current and future challenges and opportunities of public management in complex and dynamic environments. Collaborative management has become a ubiquitous concept transcending disciplines and research traditions. It suggests that in the face of the centrifugal forces of national and global socioeconomic transformation, public agencies from all levels are required to cooperatively generate creative and integrated solutions to ensure coherence and effectiveness in the delivery of public services as required by the citizens within a tight fiscal environment.

Governments around the world are embracing these apparent contradictions and their challenges in light of the value propositions that such collaborative public management entails. Thus, the important questions to explore in public management relate less to the issues within particular public sector agencies and more to understanding new models of public service delivery involving interjurisdictional and intersectoral co-production. This chapter is premised on the assertion that public policy governance is increasingly characterized by the imperatives of collaborative or multi-organizational arrangements for solving socioeconomic problems.

Innovation Policy Governance in Multilevel Systems

The governance of innovation policy is an interesting case that illustrates the emergent policy and environmental context of public management. Innovation refers to an economic process rather than merely science and engineering activities. It suggests new or better ways of doing things, which create or add value (Council of Canadian Academies 2009). It extends beyond products to include improved processes and novel forms of business organization and public service delivery. Innovation is considered to be the bedrock of economic development in the knowledge-based economy or "new economy."

This shift toward the new economy is underpinned by structural and institutional changes brought about by globalization. Several emergent changes have driven home the urgency of innovation policy. Among them are the following: (1) the intensification of global competition, especially with the rapid rise of what are now referred to as the BRIC countries (Brazil, Russia, India, and China), creating both challenges and opportunities; (2) the shift toward less resource-intensive and more ecologically sound production methods, which allows for the continuation of economic growth and development; (3) the demographic time bomb of industrialized countries' aging populations, which threatens productivity as the proportion of the working population plateaus and begins to decline; and (4) the unfolding and outstanding developments in the transformative technologies of information and communications, life sciences, and advanced materials, which provide new and immeasurable opportunities.

Innovation has been considered the key driver of labor productivity growth (increased output per hour worked) and thus the main source of a nation's economic success and socioeconomic prosperity (Howitt 2007; Industry Canada 2009). Productivity growth is strongly related to the international competitiveness and commercial dynamism on which high employment and good jobs ultimately depend. Factors influencing the choice of innovation as a business strategy transcend the firm, sectoral (meso), and national (macro) levels. Key factors include the following: structural characteristics of private firms; competitive intensity of the various economic sectors (particularly in those where technology or customer tastes change rapidly); climate for new ventures (referring to a range of early-stage venture financing, presence of research institutions, and an ecosystem of supplier firms to help nurture an innovation from concept to commercialization); public policies that encourage or inhibit innovation (such as taxation, regulations, targeted assistance programs, or public procurement favorable to innovation); and business ambition, such as entrepreneurial aggressiveness and growth orientation (often reflected in the dedication of businesses to market expansion and taking sectoral control). Business ambition may also be referred to as the *entrepreneurial ethos*.

For example, new ventures refer to the *green shoots* of the innovation system. They are essential to the nurturing and commercialization of new ideas and the creation of new competition. The most significant enabling conditions can be grouped into three broad categories:

1. Venture financing
2. Acquisition of commercial skills
3. Technology transfer

Venture financing and acquisition of commercial skills refer to the sources and availability of risk capital and mentorship supporting the development of new firms from concept to sustainable business. Technology transfer represents the institutional and public policy mechanisms for the dissemination, application, and commercial realization of research and intellectual property developed within universities and government laboratories (Industry Canada 2009; OECD 2009).

In this context, the challenge for public management is to mitigate the threats of global economic integration while leveraging the opportunities for regions and sectors of a country's economy to adapt to the imperatives of exogenous and endogenous forces of change successfully. As the capacity of states to actively intervene and regulate their economy decreases, the state is viewed less as a regulator of markets, and more as a facilitator of market processes led by private corporations (Mackenzie, Sheldrick, and Silver 2005). Thus, while the state's role is changing, it is, nevertheless, actively involved in the promotion and development of the new economy (Roy 2007).

Management of the new economy is characterized by the building of a complex and intricate fabric of national and regional innovation systems. Some of the major institutional players in this governance infrastructure are private and public research-intensive firms, research universities, and government laboratories. This trend has given rise to the growing importance of sophisticated network governance systems involving government, business, university, community, and civic actors (OECD 1997; Holbrook and Wolfe 2003). Innovation governance systems presuppose dense linkages and dynamic interactions among key actors (Cooke and Morgan 1998; Holbrook and Wolfe 2003). This co-production of actors constitutes the essence of interdependence among the public, private, and civic sectors.

The governance of innovation systems requires an architecture that transcends and integrates the various levels of government and institutionalizes a network governance framework. In this regard, public management is about multisector and multi-actor engagement energized by global forces. Both tensions and harmony in the relationship between global phenomena and national governance arrangements can be leveraged by public managers to stimulate creativity, innovation, and adaptation (Roy 2007). Innovation policy governance illustrates the fact that public management increasingly relates less to the issues within particular public sector agencies and more to the understanding of new models of public service delivery that consist of co-production among the public, private, and civic sectors as well as across levels of government. Innovation policy management also provides an example of the limitations of some of the central assumptions of public management scholarship and practice. In particular, managing innovation systems calls into question the assumption of technocratic rationality in organizational behavior in an increasingly complex society and economy. The discussion in the following section provides several specific examples from Canada to further illustrate the imperatives of interorganizational and interjurisdictional co-production in innovation policy. It should be emphasized that while the cases are drawn from Canada, the examples are illustrative of similar phenomena in advanced industrialized countries (OECD 2009).

Examples from Canada

As noted earlier, a significant characteristic of innovation systems or clusters is that they tend to be geographically concentrated and locally driven ecosystems or networks that support and sustain the creation and dissemination of new ideas and ventures aimed at economic reinvention. In the province of New Brunswick, for instance, structural changes in the economy resulting from increasing globalization have reinforced the growing importance of exploring emerging sectors such as the biotechnology industry to address the seismic dislocations of traditional industries (Government of New Brunswick 2006). These emerging sectors in turn require geographically concentrated and locally driven ecosystems of innovation that tend to thrive in the demographic clusters of cities where social capital and knowledge networks are more likely to be found (Holbrook and Wolfe 2003). Innovation thrives in systems where high levels of interaction and collaboration take place among economic and community stakeholders.

Fostering networks of geographically concentrated innovation clusters thus requires equipping cities with a certain coordinating authority and the legitimacy to provide more active and strategic leadership. In New Brunswick, this means that the Greater Moncton region (the commercial capital of the province) is emerging as a strong and assertive jurisdiction in its own right, with governance systems involving networks of government, business, community, and civic actors (Bourjeois and Trepanier 2010). In December 2006, for instance, the Moncton Technology Planning Group (MTPG), commissioned by the city's Economic Development Office, released an economic development action plan aimed at accelerating a knowledge-based economy in the Moncton area (City of Moncton, Department of Economic Development 2007). The central emphasis in the strategy is on the growth of Moncton's existing information and communications technologies (ICT) sector strengths and the existing and emergent research capacity in area institutions. What these developments point to is the gradual, de facto decentralization of authority to cities to carry out functions entailing greater responsibility and policy discretion in promoting local economic development.

The New Brunswick government, in turn, has recognized to a certain extent the strategic significance of cities in the emerging economy, as evident in its 2002 *Prosperity Plan* (a long-term plan to pursue emerging sectors in the bio-economy, modular fabrications, and component construction, among others, through an aggressive innovation policy) (Government of New Brunswick 2002). Although municipalities are still creatures of the provinces in Canada, the New Brunswick government's *Prosperity Plan* identifies them not merely as residual institutions for performing rudimentary tasks like road maintenance and garbage collection, as was the case in previous decades, but rather as indispensable partners in the search for local innovation and adaptation.

Local government actors in the province are now considered essential participants in the governance arrangements of a knowledge economy that prioritizes nurturing innovation clusters in every sector in the province. In particular, the provincial government seeks to engage municipalities in a comprehensive framework to invest in institutional infrastructure that will more closely integrate rural, northern, and urban regions in pursuit of economic development (Canadian Institute for Research on Regional Development 2000). This partnership, as shown in the provincial government's "International Trade Strategy," is also considered germane to New Brunswick's ambition to become Atlantic Canada's energy hub, a leader in energy efficiency, and a world-class producer of goods and services for the global energy sector (Government of New Brunswick, Department of Intergovernmental Affairs 2009).

In addition, in 2006, a new development plan for New Brunswick, entitled "Achieving Self-Sufficiency," was unveiled under a new government (Government of New Brunswick 2006). The purpose of this plan was to give greater attention to local and rural regions in the institutional infrastructure of innovation governance in the province. The thrust of the document is the transformation of the economy (with a focus on fostering innovation), the building of the workforce for a knowledge-based economy (mostly through education and training), and the reformation of the institutions of government for greater efficiency and effectiveness in service delivery, and the adoption of single-window delivery models.

More importantly, the plan emphasizes the priority of the provincial government to work more closely with critical partners. In particular, the document targets the nurturing of relationships with strategic partners in the private and nonprofit sectors, as well as with the federal and municipal governments. The emphasis on partnership is consistent with the 2006 plan's focus on supporting technology clusters and priority core technologies through the development of strategic alliances in education, training, and recruitment of highly qualified personnel, and attraction of investment by outside sources.

The government's recognition of the strategic significance of collaborative, intergovernmental relations is further evident in the 2006 plan's emphasis on strategic partnerships among certain provincial departments and the federal government's economic development agency in the region—the Atlantic Canada Opportunities Agency (ACOA). The stated aim of this collaboration is to provide streamlined access to business support programs at all levels. The provincial government maintains that this partnership will develop standards and implement provincial planning policies to provide planning certainty for investors, and put in place innovative incentives to encourage sustainable management of economic development resources.

The federal government is navigating a similar trajectory. A significant characteristic of the federal government's strategy for innovation policy intervention is its supportive (rather than competitive) role behind provincial leadership in economic development. An example of this is the Atlantic Innovation Fund (AIF). In 2001, in recognition of the prevalence of innovation policy within New Brunswick and the rest of Atlantic Canada, the federal government through ACOA launched the AIF, which is designed to work jointly with the provincial and municipal governments as well as the private sector in New Brunswick (and other provinces in Atlantic Canada) for the development of new ideas, technologies, products, and markets for a global, knowledge-based economy (Canada: ACOA's Departmental Performance Report 2001). The AIF aims to support research and development (R&D), leading to the launch of new products, processes, and services. It also seeks to improve the province's capacity to commercialize R&D. Through the AIF, ACOA has made strategic investments aimed at deepening partnerships with the government and non-state actors in New Brunswick, particularly the chambers of commerce and universities, to increase the innovation capacity of the province. The government of New Brunswick's launch of its New Brunswick Innovation Foundation (NBIF) two years after the AIF is a testament to the success of ACOA's pursuit of collaborative governance. The AIF and NBIF complement each other not only in the substance of their policies but also as intergovernmental funding mechanisms.

Similar examples of multilevel governance in innovation policy can be found in the province of Manitoba. A key element of innovation policy governance in Manitoba is the increasingly strategic importance of Winnipeg as the critical locus of industrial and trade policy coordination in the province (Economic Development Winnipeg 2011). Although municipalities tend to be "creatures" of the provinces in Canada, they have been assuming greater policy responsibility and attendant policy autonomy and discretion, especially in the governance of local economic reinvention. With a population of just over 700,000, Winnipeg claims approximately 60 percent of the province's residents. The unique demographic concentration of Manitoba's population within three hours' drive of the city adds to the strategic significance of the municipality in the new governance environment (Western Economic Diversification Canada 2009).

Over the past decade, Winnipeg's knowledge-based industries have matured into significant forces in the provincial economy (Economic Development Winnipeg Inc. 2011). For example, the city is home to 40 life sciences companies and 30 research and development groups with expertise in areas such as health, environmental, and agricultural biotechnology (Government of Manitoba 2011). Winnipeg's notable biotech and research organizations include Innovative Magnetic Resonance Imaging Systems (IMRIS), Monteris, Manitoba Institute of Cell Biology, Medicure, the International Centre for Infectious Diseases, the

Canadian Science Centre for Human and Animal Health, and the National Microbiology Laboratory.

An interesting dimension to these developments in Manitoba is that the provincial government seems to reinforce the institutional implications of these trends in Winnipeg and other smaller cities in the province (Western Centre for Economic Research 2004). In 2005, for example, the provincial government established the Building Manitoba Fund, which expanded the personal income and corporation income tax revenue-sharing arrangements with municipalities, and provided municipalities with added sources of growth revenue. Therefore, Manitoba and New Brunswick both reflect a broader systemic transformation in which cities act like "city-states" complete with institutional capacities for effective policy engagement in economic development (Western Economic Diversification Canada, Economic Research and Market Studies 2009, 2010).

Moreover, the federal government, through its regional economic development agency, Western Economic Diversification Canada (WD), now also has "national agreements" consisting of several national programs the agency delivers in the western provinces including Manitoba (Western Economic Diversification Canada, 2009–2010). The point worth noting is that through these agreements, the federal government now collaborates not only bilaterally with the provincial government but also with industry, municipal, and community partners in investments that support a range of activities, including support for knowledge clusters in the province. WD's emergent focus on multidimensional and multilateral partnerships now constitutes a fundamental characteristic of the agency's delivery strategy, not only in Manitoba but across Western Canada. The federal agency actively reaches out to multiple partners, thereby blurring the once sacrosanct boundaries of the public sector in what constituted intergovernmental agreements (Western Economic Diversification Canada 2009–2010).

Another indication of WD's adaptation to the complexity of its operating environment is the fact that the agency began to interpret its contractual relationship with Manitoba as "supportive of local joint action under provincial leadership."[*] The federal government increasingly sees itself as a strategic partner (in supportive roles) with the provincial government and the municipalities in the province (WD's Departmental Strategy 2009). Interorganizational collaboration in Manitoba had to make more room for local actors in joint action with the various orders of government. While the federal government remains keen on maintaining some level of visibility, its support of provincial policy leadership allows for critical spaces of adaptation in maneuvering around interjurisdictional complexity. These examples demonstrate how innovation policy governance in Canada is now more focused on programs involving joint, longer-term strategic investment and collaborative, intergovernmental decisions alongside the private and non-profit sectors.

---

[*] Interview between the author and a senior official at Western Economic Diversification Canada in Winnipeg, Manitoba, July 2011.

Similar examples can be found in the province of Ontario. For instance, the Federal Economic Development Initiative for Northern Ontario (FedNor) is an agency that has been increasingly pursuing close engagement with major cities in the region over the past decade. In particular, FedNor has engaged with the City of Greater Sudbury in a project to assess underserviced industrial land related to future development in innovation policy in the forestry and mining sectors (Government of Canada 2009). In the past, part of FedNor's approach as a federal agency was to consult with Industry Canada (a federal department) to prevent local projects from conflicting with federal departmental policies. But the agency seems to be departing from this framework since, rather than setting preconditions or dictating the terms of projects, it is now engaged in enabling municipal authorities to make projections and plans about the industrial future of their cities. Concern about political legitimacy in the region, it seems, means the risks of failing to respond to municipalities' demands for closer partnership can no longer be ignored. It is worth noting that compared with the relative success of ACOA in New Brunswick and WD in Manitoba, FedNor is still dealing with the challenge of reconciling Industry Canada's national frame of reference in innovation policy development with the particular nature of municipalities' approaches to local economic development.

In Southern Ontario, the newly created (2009) federal agency for economic development (FedDev) also has a mandate that reflects the changing physiology of government, with an emphasis on co-production network arrangements among orders of government, and between the public sector and non-state actors in innovation policy. For example, the agency aims to provide tools to facilitate the building of partnerships with a range of actors for the creation of the Golden Horseshoe Region's global competitive edge in innovation (FedDev 2011).

FedDev, in particular, seeks to work closely with provincial ministries such as the Ontario Ministry of Research and Innovation (MRI), also a relatively new organization (2005) with a mandate to make innovation a driving force of Ontario's economy and to project this new Ontario onto the national and international stage (Ontario, Ministry of Research and Innovation 2011).* MRI's own program activities are directed at facilitating Ontario's transition to an idea- and innovation-based economy especially supportive of new knowledge-intensive industries. One of the ministry's key programs is the Ontario Network of Excellence, which works directly with entrepreneurs, academia, and businesses to build globally focused, investor-ready companies. This involves supporting researchers, entrepreneurs, and businesses as innovators in all stages to help bring unique products and services to market. The ministry's partners are drawn from a range of actors including research hospitals, universities, entrepreneurs, venture capitalists, businesses, and government agencies. Key programs such as the Research Excellence Program, Ontario

---

* For further details on the Ontario MRI, see the following Web site: http://www.mri.gov.on.ca/english/programs/default.asp.

Research Fund, and the Innovation Demonstration Fund all fund and promote transformative, internationally significant research of strategic value to the province. The Innovation Demonstration Fund, for instance, provides financial support of up to 50 percent of eligible costs to help Ontario companies with the commercialization and initial demonstration of their innovative technologies.*

The aforementioned examples of ideational and structural changes in the Canadian economy mean that innovation policy governance is becoming more diverse and complex. Such transformations have implications for state restructuring (Timonen 2003; Doornbos 2006). Management of innovation policy is characterized by the building of complex and intricate collaborative institutional frameworks (or regional innovation systems) that transcend several jurisdictions and mobilized interests, including the private sector and research institutions. This means a deepening of the complexities of federalism in countries like Canada, the United States, and Australia, as well as the multilevel governance systems of most European countries (Krasnick 1986; Bosch and Durán 2008; Anderson 2010).

The imperatives of the new economy, therefore, require a rethinking of the institutional infrastructure of economic development policy implementation or public management. The governance of innovation systems requires an architecture that transcends and integrates the various orders of government, as well as institutionalizes a network governance framework incorporating and legitimizing the nexus between proximity, innovation, and economic growth and development. The organic clusters among market actors, knowledge producers, and civic interests, which emanate from identification with their immediate surrounding communities, can be leveraged into formal mechanisms of engagement and collaborative forms of governance (Cooke and Schwartz 2007).

In a country like Canada where federal agencies are mandated to support economic adjustment in subnational regions, economic development policy governance within a multilayered institutional system reflects the new context of regional development. Structured hierarchies in multilevel systems are confronted with the need to adjust their policy delivery processes to increasingly complex environmental conditions. The complexity of the modern economic environment in particular necessitates viewing regional development policy implementation as a process of interorganizational and interjurisdictional cooperation. Mechanisms for building synergies among actors in both the public and private sectors are increasingly important. Networked regional economies require collaborative approaches to market governance where public managers make connections across organizations and share ideas, resources, and power with state and non-state actors. This means that regional development agencies' strategic choices of policy intervention are based on the specific environmental and institutional characteristics of a given region.

---

* Interview with a program officer at the Ontario MRI, Toronto.

The preceding discussion indicates that the imperatives of the new economy require a rethinking of regional economic development policy governance in Canada and other multilevel governance systems. First, it calls for policy alignment across orders of government through the development of frameworks that give central importance to "place" as both a geographical and institutional construct. Second, it requires horizontal collaborative governance among the public, private, and community sectors, where the private sector in particular regions can be seen less as an object of economic development and more as an agent of adaptation to global and local changes. Third, the emphasis of public policy governance mechanisms is on building strategic alliances to manage the many dependencies that are a natural and necessary component of service delivery or policy implementation in highly politicized environments. Finally, economic development policy governance involves finding and sustaining a good fit between the mission and strategies of public agencies and the forces in their external environment that create both opportunities and threats.

Implications for Public Management

In complex multilevel governance systems such as Canada, the United States, Australia, and the European Union, authority tends to be dispersed among orders of government (local, regional, provincial, national, and supranational) as well as across loci and sectors, which include market actors and civil society. While there is a growing appreciation for the imperatives of policy governance coordination across these multiple orders and loci, there is not enough attention given to how different political systems actually adapt their institutional and policy designs to operate effectively in the emergent complexity of multilevel governance systems design.

To take the example of Canada further, although the Constitution grants de jure responsibility for economic development policy to provincial governments, in practice this responsibility is shared between the federal centre (in Ottawa) and its constituent units in the provincial capitals (Simeon 2006). Moreover, although municipalities are "creatures" of the provinces in Canada, in reality they have enjoyed greater policy responsibility and attendant policy autonomy and discretion, including the governance of local economic development (Sancton 2009). Finally, even though public agencies are granted the official mandate and responsibility for policy domains such as economic development, these mandates are increasingly shared with non-governmental organizations and active citizen groups. Each of these nodes of governance suggests different and increasingly assertive manifestations of policy engagement outside the traditional boundaries of economic development policy intervention. Understanding the imperatives of joint policy action across these multiple orders and loci within a given political system is necessary.

From this analysis of innovation policy, public management in interjurisdictional and interorganizational policy subsystems is a process of constantly finding an appropriate fit between the task environment, strategy, and structure of an agency, thereby assuring continued organizational effectiveness. The complexity of managing interjurisdictional and interorganizational network systems is three-fold. First, it is inherently difficult to predict future events in such environments. Second, the commitments that public agencies make have secondary consequences (often the reaction of other agencies in the environment), which are extremely difficult to anticipate. Third, unanticipated consequences occur because directing and controlling network interaction cannot be engineered with any degree of precision.

Public management is increasingly about strategic partnerships and network models of service delivery innovation and reform. The emphasis is on strategic partnerships that facilitate interjurisdictional and interorganizational cooperation and allow governments to find solutions to social problems or commission innovation aimed at productivity and economic development. As such network models of policy governance are becoming ubiquitous, the critical objective of research becomes partly an appreciation for the "politics" of these partnerships and partly an understanding of the requisites of effective management of these interorganizational relationships.

Finally, traditional public administration focuses on the agency and its programs, emphasizes hierarchical structures and command-and-control management processes, strictly distinguishes between public and non-governmental agencies (private or not-for-profit), and pays close attention to management skills to cater to these elements. The new approach is more integrative, in the sense that it draws useful elements (Argyris 1957) from traditional public administration. However, it emphasizes the strategic imperative of environmental forces, promotes network approaches to public service production and delivery by blurring the boundaries of the public sector, views processes of policy implementation as characterized by negotiation and persuasion, and pays attention to enabling and relational skills for public managers.

The implications of this discussion for public management theory are three-fold. First, the present approach views concepts such as strategic planning and performance management as instruments of feedback and self-regulation. They serve strategic purposes, often geared toward the facilitation of organizational learning and adaptation in turbulent environments. Second, the discussion emphasizes the importance of building coalitions of strategic alliances in order to successfully manage the many dependencies that are a natural and necessary consequence of operating in highly politicized environments. Third, public management can be understood as consisting of finding and sustaining a good fit between an agency's mission and strategies, its internal systems and structures, and the forces in its external environment that create both opportunities and threats.

Conclusion

While this chapter has focused on Canada, the cases mirror similar processes of public policy governance in other industrialized countries. The complexity of modern political and economic environments means that public policy governance should be seen as a process of navigating institutional boundaries, rather than simply optimizing program output. At a broader level, the federal, provincial, and even municipal governments' operations reflect the changing currents of policy ideas concerning the role of the state in the economy. The example of innovation systems management illustrates how public management increasingly requires a governance architecture that transcends and integrates the various orders of government, and institutionalizes a network governance framework. Some of the major institutional players in the infrastructure of innovation policy governance are local, private, and public research-intensive firms; research universities; and government laboratories. This trend has given rise to the growing importance of sophisticated local network governance systems involving government, business, university, community, and civic actors. Innovation governance systems presuppose dense, geographically concentrated linkages, and dynamic interactions among key actors, which lead to interdependence among the key public, private, and civic sectors. In this regard, public management is about multisector and multiactor engagement energized by global forces. The tensions and complements in the relationship between global phenomena and national governance arrangements can be leveraged by public managers to stimulate creativity, innovation, and adaptation. Strategic innovation development policy intervention increasingly relates less to the issues within particular public sector agencies and more to understanding new models of public service delivery, which consist of co-production between the public and private sectors as well as across orders of government.

The practical implications for public managers operating within complex, interjurisdictional and interorganizational policy environments are as follows: (1) strategic public management entails the adoption of a proactive rather than a reactive approach to an agency's interaction with its external environment; (2) the public manager will continuously attempt to discover trends and identify opportunities as well as anticipate future problems; (3) public agencies will tend to use systematic approaches to identify issues and establish organizational priorities; (4) public agencies will build the requisite expertise in forecasting, strategy development, and constant evaluation; (5) public management will involve expanding the range of interaction between public agencies and stakeholders; and (6) operating in complex network systems requires the active involvement of top management in close interaction with frontline staff for the development and implementation of successful response strategies. Such a close interaction between top management and frontline staff allows for more accurate and precise boundary-spanning strategies by which agencies are able to monitor environmental forces and identify issues and trends systematically.

References

Anderson, G. 2010. *Fiscal Federalism: A Comparative Introduction*. Don Mills, ON: Oxford University Press.

Argyris, Chris. 1957. *Personality and Organization. The Conflict between System and the Individual*. New York: Harper.

Bosch, N., and J.M. Durán. 2008. *Fiscal Federalism and Political Decentralization: Lessons from Spain, Germany and Canada.* Cheltenham, UK: Edward Elgar.

Bourjeois, Yves, and Michel Trepanier. 2010. Same size, same social characteristics, same performance? Comparative study of Moncton and Trois-Rivières. A presentation at the Innovation Systems Research Network 12th Annual Conference, 5–7 May 2010. Toronto, Ontario.

Canada. 2009. FedNor. Available from http://fednor.gc.ca/eic/site/fednor-fednor.nsf/Intro (accessed June 2010).

Canada. Atlantic Canada Opportunities Agency. 2001. Departmental Performance Report 2000–2001. Ottawa: Public Works and Government Services Department. Available at http://www.tbs-sct.gc.ca/rma/dpr/00-01/acoa00dpr/acoa00dprtoc_e.asp (accessed July 2010).

Canadian Institute for Research on Regional Development, and Donald Savoie. 2000. Community economic development in Atlantic Canada: False hope or panacea? Available at http://www.acoa-apeca.gc.ca/eng/publications/ResearchStudies/Pages/CommunityEconomicDevelopmentinAtlanticCanadaFalseHopeorPanacea.aspx (accessed July 2010).

City of Moncton. Department of Economic Development. 2007. Accelerating technology-based economic growth and entrepreneurship in Greater Moncton. Available at http://www.moncton.ca/Assets/Business+English/Accelerating+technology-based+economic+growth+and+entrepreneurship+in+Greater+Moncton+-+Executive+Summary+and+Recommendations.pdf (accessed January 2011).

Cooke, P., and K. Morgan. 1998. *The Associational Economy: Firms, Regions and Innovation.* New York: Oxford University Press.

Cooke, P., and D. Schwartz. 2007. Creative regions: An introduction. In *Creative Regions: Technology, Culture and Knowledge Entrepreneurship*, edited by P. Cooke and D. Schwartz. London: Taylor & Francis, pp. 1–20.

Council of Canadian Academies. 2009. Innovation and business strategy: Why Canada falls short. Available at www.scienceadvice.ca.

Doornbos, Martin R. 2006. *Global Forces and State Restructuring: Dynamics of State Formation and Collapse.* Basingstoke, UK: Palgrave Macmillan.

Economic Development Winnipeg. 2011. Economic overview. Available from http://www.economicdevelopmentwinnipeg.com/winnipegs-economy/overview (accessed June 2011).

FedDev. 2011. 2011–2012 Report on plans and priorities. Available from http://www.feddevontario.gc.ca/eic/site/723.nsf/eng/h_00115.html (accessed December 2011).

Holbrook, Adam, and David Wolfe. 2003. *Knowledge, Clusters and Regional Innovation: Economic Development in Canada.* Montreal: McGill-Queen's University Press.

Howitt, Peter. 2007. *Innovation, Competition and Growth: A Schumpeterian Perspective on Canada's Economy.* Toronto: C.D. Howe Institute. Available from http://www.cdhowe.org/pdf/commentary_246.pdf (accessed March 2011).

Industry Canada. 2009. Performance Reports 2009–2010. Available from http://www.ic.gc.ca/eic/site/ic1.nsf/eng/h_00226.html (accessed June 2011).

Krasnick, M., and Royal Commission on the Economic Union and Development Prospects for Canada. 1986. *Fiscal Federalism.* Toronto: University of Toronto Press.

Mackenzie, Michael, Byron Sheldrick, and Jim Silver. 2005. *State Policies to Enhance the New Economy: A Comparative Perspective.* Available from http://www.policyalternatives.ca/sites/default/files/uploads/publications/Manitoba_Pubs/2005/State_Policies.pdf (accessed January 2010).

Manitoba. 2011. Manitoba agriculture, food and rural initiatives: Financial assistance and funding programs. Available from http://www.gov.mb.ca/agriculture/financial.html (accessed June 2010).

New Brunswick. 2002. Greater opportunity: New Brunswick's Prosperity Plan 2002–2012.

New Brunswick. 2006. Action plan to be self-sufficient in New Brunswick. New Brunswick: Office of the Premier.

New Brunswick. Department of Intergovernmental Affairs. 2009. New Brunswick's international strategy. New Brunswick: Office of the Premier.

Ontario. Ministry of Research and Innovation. 2011. Programs and funding. Available from http://www.mri.gov.on.ca/english/programs/default.asp (accessed July 2011).

Organisation for Economic Co-operation and Development (OECD). 1997. *Regional Competitiveness and Skills*. Paris: OECD.

Organisation for Economic Co-operation and Development (OECD). 2009. Investing for growth: Building innovation regions. Meeting of the Territorial Development Policy Committee. Available from http://www.oecd.org/document/27/0,3343,en_2649_33735 _33711480_1_1_1_1,00.html (accessed January 2010).

Osborne, S. 2010. Delivering public services: Time for a new theory. *Public Management Review* 12 (1): 1–10.

Pal, L.A. 2006. *Beyond Policy Analysis: Public Issue Management in Turbulent Times*. Scarborough, ON: ITP Nelson.

Roy, J. 2007. *Business and Government in Canada*. Ottawa: University of Ottawa Press.

Sancton, Andrew. 2009. Introduction. In *Foundations of Governance: Municipal Government in Canada's Provinces*, edited by Andrew Sancton and Robert Young. Toronto: University of Toronto Press, pp. 3–19.

Simeon, R. 2006. Federal-provincial diplomacy: The making of recent policy in Canada: With a new preface and postscript. In *Studies in the Structure of Power, Decision-Making in Canada*, edited by Social Research Council of Canada. Toronto: University of Toronto Press, pp. 48–66.

Timonen, Virpi. 2003. *Restructuring the Welfare State: Globalization and Social Policy Reform in Finland and Sweden*. Cheltenham: Edward Elgar.

Western Centre for Economic Research. 2004. A primer on Western Canadian entrepreneurship. Available from http://www.wd.gc.ca/eng/56.asp (accessed July 2011).

Western Economic Diversification Canada. 2009. 2009–2010 Departmental Performance Report. Ottawa: Public Works and Government Services Canada. Available from http:// www.tbs-sct.gc.ca/dpr-rmr/2009-2010/inst/wco/wco00-eng.asp (accessed July 2011).

Western Economic Diversification Canada. 2010. WD Procurement Strategy, 2009–2010. Available from http://www.wd-deo.gc.ca/images/cont/11766-eng.pdf (accessed January 2011).

Western Economic Diversification Canada. 2010. Tomorrow's gateways: Value capture strategies in key sectors and potential for foreign direct investment in Western Canada, IE Market Research Corporation. Available from http://www.wd.gc.ca/eng/12814.asp (accessed June 2011).

Western Economic Diversification Canada. Economic Research and Market Studies. 2009. Efficient cities: The interrelationship between effective rapid transit systems and the optimal utilization of land use entitlements. Available from http://www.wd.gc.ca/ eng/56.asp (accessed August 2011).

ACTORS IN MULTILEVEL PUBLIC MANAGEMENT

Chapter 6

Politics over Policy: Multilevel Public Management of the Financial Services Sector in Canada

---

Ian Roberge

Contents

Introduction

On 22 December 2011 the Supreme Court of Canada unanimously ruled as unconstitutional the federal government's proposed Canadian Securities Act. The legislation was to have created a national securities regulator in lieu of the current structure in which supervisory and regulatory authority is exercised by the provinces. The federal government had referenced its proposed legislation to the top court in an effort to circumvent the objections of some provincial governments. The Supreme Court's opinion ends for the foreseeable future the half-century debate over the creation of a national securities commission in Canada. The federal government's initiative was strongly supported by Ontario and a majority of market actors, but it was firmly opposed by Québec, Alberta, and Manitoba, among others. In its decision, the Supreme Court made clear that it was not passing judgment on whether or not the proposal was good public policy, but rather on the constitutionality of the legislation. Jurisdictional politics, in this case, came to overshadow the public policy debate. The present chapter considers the politics of securities market supervision and regulation in Canada.

Jurisdictional authority across the financial services sector in Canada is fragmented. On the one hand, the federal government is responsible for banks and parts of the insurance industry (solvency of firms). On the other hand, the provinces have jurisdiction over the securities sector, cooperative banking and trusts, and parts of the insurance industry (provinces have authority over civil and contract law). Governments across the country and market actors throughout the years have expressed serious concerns about the effectiveness, efficiency, and competitiveness of the supervisory and regulatory arrangement for securities markets. The two solutions that came to be the most debated were the creation of a national securities commission and the adoption of the passport model (to be described later in the chapter). Provinces, except Ontario, moved forward with the passport model, which they have now successfully implemented. The federal government, supported by Ontario, decided in 2009 to establish a national securities commission. As noted above, it drafted a bill that it submitted for reference to the Supreme Court. The federal government established a transition office with the expectation that the new regulator would be operational by 2012. Yet the court's opinion dealt, what appears to be at the time of writing, a definitive blow to the project for a national securities commission.

The conflict between actors who support the creation of a national securities regulator (the federal government, Ontario, and the majority of market actors) and those who oppose it (Québec, Alberta, and Manitoba) has proven to be profound and irreconcilable. How is the conflict between Canada's federal government and many of the country's provinces to be explained? How are actors' preferences and interests to be understood? In its decision, the Supreme Court argued that governments should cooperate to resolve their differences. Cooperation, as will be discussed in this chapter, has been particularly difficult in this policy area. Why has this been the case? What are the lessons to be learned for scholars and practitioners? This chapter's main argument is that jurisdictional politics and wrangling about the process dominated the public policy debate, making the politics of the case more important than the merits of policy options under consideration. Proponents and opponents were unable to convince one another or even to negotiate a compromise, which led quasi-inevitably to a debate about who had the authority to do what. Actors' policy preference, in turn, reflected their own self-interest with only passing reference to what might be good public policy. Multilevel public management, as this case illustrates, is inherently political.

Presented in this chapter is the debate surrounding the creation of a national securities regulator. Consideration is given to the political and jurisdictional imperatives, focusing on key actors. To conclude, important lessons from this case are identified. It is important to note that a theoretical explanation for jurisdictional politics is not presented in this chapter. Rather, the intent is to provide an in-depth look at the politics of multilevel public management. The research for this chapter reflects the publicly available primary and scholarly literature.

A National Securities Commission versus the Passport Model

The Canadian constitution was constructed to favor the central government's leaving largely local matters to the provinces. Financial services sector policy was thus divided between the federal government and provinces. At the time of confederation, banking and the printing of money were deemed to be national in scope, and as such, they were made a federal responsibility. Securities markets in Canada were barely beginning, small, and left to the provinces; the Toronto Stock Exchange was incorporated with the Ontario government in 1878 (TMX 2010). The evolution of the Canadian financial services sector can be seen as path-dependent with various critical junctures along the way. The federal government made, most recently, substantive banking policy changes in 1987, 1992, and 2001. In 1987, the federal government began dismantling industry pillars (banking, securities, insurance, and trusts) when it allowed banks, through subsidiaries, to partake in the activities of securities markets. Coleman (2002) has argued that there ensued a centralization of authority at the federal level since banks, as federally regulated entities, came to dominate across pillars. Despite this de facto centralization, there remained, at the turn of the millennium, much duplication and overlap in the regulation of Canadian finance.

The supervisory and regulatory structures of securities markets in Canada also find their origins in the 1867 Canadian constitution: the trading of securities falls under provincial jurisdiction. With the globalization of finance, many states came to review how they supervised and regulated their securities markets. In Canada, the discussion about the creation of a national securities commission intensified through the first decade of the new millennium. The debate focused on who had jurisdictional authority and process, and not on the best policy to ensure effectiveness, efficiency, and safe markets. The politics of multilevel governance, of jurisdiction, overtook all other conversations.

A National Securities Commission

The debate surrounding a national securities commission has persisted for decades, with reference made to it as early as the 1930s (Lortie 2011). In 1964, the Royal Commission on Banking and Finance, generally referred to as the Porter Commission, recommended the creation of a national regulator (Canada, Royal Commission on Banking and Finance 1964). The debate re-emerged at regular intervals since then, but the calls for the creation of a national securities commission became more strident over the course of the last decade when no fewer than four different attempts to create a national regulator were made. The first came when then Minister of Finance John Manley created the *Wise Persons Committee*. In 2003, shortly before the publication of the committee's report, aptly called *It's Time* (Wise Persons Committee 2003), the preliminary report on the legislation governing the Ontario Securities Commission (OSC) was submitted to the Ontario government. The first chapter of this draft report was devoted to arguing in favor of a national regulator (Crawford 2002). There seemed to be sufficient political momentum to push an initiative through. The political scene in Ottawa in 2004 became unstable, however, with the election of a minority government, and the federal government did not arduously pursue the project because doing so would offend at least one important constituency: Québec. Thus, the policy window quickly closed.

Two other unsuccessful attempts followed. The Ontario government put together an advisory panel led by Purdy Crawford, the same individual who had led the review of the OSC, to consider models for the creation of a pan-Canadian supervisory and regulatory structure (Crawford Panel 2006). The panel recommended that provinces pool their jurisdiction to create a national body. The advantage of the proposal was clear, as it recognized provincial autonomy in the field. During this period, the Investment Industry Regulation Organization of Canada, a self-regulatory body, undertook a review of regulations governing Canadian securities markets (Task Force to Modernize Securities Legislation in Canada 2006). There also emerged a discussion on the merits of a national structure. Both attempts appeared as anticlimactic following the work of the Wise Persons Committee and did not lead to concrete action.

In the midst of the global financial and economic crisis, the federal government finally decided to take the lead in 2009 and to work toward the establishment of a national securities commission. Williams (2009) even suggests that this has been Canada's main, if not sole, financial services sector policy response to the crisis. The federal government established an advisory committee to consider the option and present a draft Canadian securities act. The Hocking report (Expert Panel on Securities Regulation 2009) presented the policy rationale for a national securities regulator and a path for implementation. Based on the work of the expert panel, the federal government drafted its Canadian Securities Act. The federal government justified its action through the trade and commerce clause of the Canadian constitution, by which it can regulate transprovincial commercial activity. The Supreme Court rejected this argument, stating that market transactions had not fundamentally changed and were still based on contract law. The court did not say, however, that the federal government could not exercise some authority over securities markets, most importantly to prevent and minimize systemic risk. When the Supreme Court rendered its opinion, the Department of Finance withdrew the proposal.

The federal government, in retrospect, faced other unanticipated difficulties with its project. The proposed Canadian Securities Act largely copied, for reasons of consistency and ease, provincial regulation. The Supreme Court noted that the federal government failed to demonstrate, in that respect, why it needed to have supervisory and regulatory authority over the provinces. In addition, the federal government proposed an opt-in scheme, as recommended in the Hocking Report, which would allow willing provinces to participate, reluctant provinces to join at any time, or any province to stay out of the scheme altogether. The opt-in format seemed politically advantageous because no province would be forced to adhere to the new system. The scheme became problematic, however, when the court ruled that the federal government failed to justify a need for federal intervention, given that reticent provinces could have continued to exercise their own authority.

The federal government focused on the process and attempted to demonstrate that it had jurisdictional competence. The policy advantages of a single regulator were too often simply assumed. There have always existed multiple arguments in favor of a national securities office. It is beyond the scope of this chapter to restate them all, except to say that proponents believed the new system would be more effective and efficient. Canadian securities markets would become more competitive with the proper supervisory and regulatory structure. Currently, thirteen provincial and territorial regulatory authorities have to work together and collaborate to fulfill their mandate. The Hocking Report argued that Canadian regulation was falling behind due to this complexity, and supporters argued that the structure was expensive and rife with overlap and duplication. Yet there have been instances when matters have fallen through the cracks. For example, Canada's asset-backed commercial paper crisis in 2007—the largest financial crisis in Canadian history—happened because the federal solvency regulator for banks, the Office of the Superintendent of Financial Institutions, and the provincial securities regulators failed to see the problem brewing. Every actor argued that the growing crisis was not within its jurisdictional realm, and there was a general failure to coordinate. Harris (2010) and Chant (2009) provide compelling explanations for the crisis. One of the strongest arguments favoring a national regulator is that current arrangements have made it difficult to respond to the needs of small, individual investors. Canadian regulators have lax enforcement powers, with some major cases being tried elsewhere before a case is even mounted in Canada. The matter at hand is whether a national securities commission would have made things better or simply replicated many of the failures. Opponents noted that gains were hypothetical and never demonstrated. Proponents, in fact, never succeeded in showing that their preferred policy option would better serve ambiguous policy objectives.

The Passport Model

The passport model is the de facto alternative to the creation of a national securities commission. Drawn from the experience of the European Union, the model allows emitters to list across the country after having dealt with a single provincial regulator. Though the decentralized provincial architecture remains, the passport model offers relative simplicity to market actors who have to deal with only one provincial regulatory office. The passport model requires that regulators work with each other to harmonize their supervisory and regulatory approach. They must also have corresponding, or at least similar, regulation in place. The Provincial and Territorial Securities Initiative was launched in 2004 with the stated goal to implement the passport model. The system is now in place, and all provinces adhere to it except Ontario which, so far, has steadfastly refused to participate. The Canadian Securities Administrators, a voluntary organization that brings together all provincial regulators, has carried through with multiple initiatives to harmonize and simplify rules and practices across the country. Provinces, many of which are particularly recalcitrant to the idea of a national regulator, have thus come up with a credible alternative.

There are, again, many arguments in favor of the passport model. They are generally presented in a way that makes clear the opposition of actors defending this point of view to a single regulator scheme. The most recurring argument is that the passport model respects Canada's constitution and provincial autonomy. The focus, once more, is on jurisdictional authority rather than policy. Provincial governments argue that they have shown that they can collaborate and that the arrangements work well irrespective of repeated public attacks. Canadian markets fared fairly well, despite the asset-backed commercial paper crisis, during the most recent upheavals on global financial markets. International organizations have often praised the safety and soundness of markets in Canada. According to proponents of the passport model, Canadian markets have prospered, and the cost of operating on them is not necessarily more than doing so elsewhere in the world. In a report published by the Institute for Research in Public Policy, Lortie makes note of these key arguments (Lortie 2011).

Some Observations

From a multilevel governance perspective, there are clear implications to each model. The single regulator model represents centralization, with much greater power to be enjoyed at the federal level. Though a national regulator would have had local offices, it is unclear just how much autonomy they would have enjoyed. It is also not clear how the model would have responded to local concerns, a major preoccupation for many of the sceptics. Opponents also argued that centralization would likely stifle supervisory and regulatory innovation, with a blanket application of rules across the country. The passport model has both advantages and disadvantages. For it to work, extensive horizontal collaboration and coordination is required. There is a need to ensure that rules are harmonized or, at least, relatively equivalent. The structure is less coordinated, which also means it is quite flexible. The speed and ease of response to political and market upheavals will vary across jurisdictions, meaning that it can take time to provide a coordinated response during a crisis. The EU had difficulty responding cohesively to the 2007–2008 global financial crisis (Yamashita 2011), which led it to reconsider and further centralize its supervisory and regulatory structure. Jurisdictional politics impact public policy outcomes in many ways (McRoberts 1993); these considerations largely apply to this case.

Canada is the only major industrialized state without a national securities regulator. The joint-decision trap (Scharpf 1988) shows that the best policy option is likely to be blocked when regional actors have and exercise a policy veto. Such insight is difficult to apply to this case because each side can claim policy superiority. The failure by both sides to unequivocally show the superiority of their policy and convince one another of its merits reinforced the jurisdictional and political nature of the debate.

Jurisdictional and Political Considerations

Financial services sector policy in Canada has often been made based on political considerations—a situation that is not unique to this country. Actors' crude political calculations help to explain important policy decisions, such as the refusal of the Canadian government in the late 1990s to allow bank mergers (Harris 2004). As such, the political nature of the debate surrounding jurisdiction and process for the supervision and regulation of securities markets is not all that surprising. The objective of this section is not to present a formal model by which to understand the politics of multilevel public management. Rather, the description of actors' various interests and rationales will highlight the politics of the debate and the unwillingness and inability of actors to find a middle ground. It is important to remember that there is a policy rationale both for and against the creation of a national securities commission. From a jurisdictional perspective, the federal government was confident (along with many constitutional experts) that its trade and commerce argument would carry in front of the Supreme Court. Provinces, in turn, were equally confident that market operations still fell under contract law giving them authority over the policy field. The argument of this paper, and of this section, is not that there was no policy consideration, but rather that political, process, and jurisdictional concerns came to dominate the debate. In this section, the preferences and interests of the federal government, Ontario, and market actors all favoring a single regulator scheme are considered, as is the position of Québec and Alberta, both of which have long opposed it.

From a political standpoint, the federal government was always reluctant to create a national securities regulator for fear of upsetting the provinces, especially Québec. By 2009, the political landscape had changed, which provided the federal government with an opportunity to pursue the project. First, the Conservatives came to power proposing a somewhat new way to think of federalism, which they termed "open federalism" (Bickerton 2010). Though the concept has never been clearly defined, open federalism, if it were truly practiced, would alter the division of power through a revised interpretation of the constitution. Most importantly, the federal government, according to open federalism, would have responsibility over all matters of national economic significance, including the supervision and regulation of securities markets, and provinces would be left to manage the social sphere, including health and education. It is beyond the purview of this chapter to consider implications of such a shift, except to say that some observers have argued that open federalism smacks of neo-liberalism (Harmes 2007). The creation of a national securities commission is not, in and of itself, part of a neo-liberal agenda. Nonetheless, it is likely that a centralized model would lead to fewer regulations, which helps to explain, to a certain extent, why industry players favor the option. The project to create a national securities commission fits neatly into the concept of open federalism.

Second, the Conservative Party's electoral calculations changed as they began their second minority mandate. It is popular political wisdom in Canada that in order to win a majority government, it is necessary for a party to dominate either Ontario or Québec, and to do fairly well in the other province. It is within Ontario and Québec that the most seats are to be gained. Based on this premise, the federal government long hesitated to take the lead in creating a national securities regulator because such a project would not bring votes in Ontario and would be a vote loser in Québec where, above and beyond the particulars of the case, the appearance of federal intrusion in a traditionally provincial sphere of authority, on principle, would raise the ire of the population. The Conservative Party first formed a minority government in 2006, surprisingly winning 10 seats in Québec. Despite its best efforts, the party was not able to capitalize on these gains, and its good fortunes there quickly vanished. When the Conservatives were re-elected in 2008, they barely held onto their seats, and they no longer had any expectation of a major breakthrough in the province. There were no longer any political favors to be had in Québec. The government thus moved to implement its preferred policy option.

Finally, insofar as the position of the federal government is concerned, Minister of Finance Jim Flaherty has acted as a policy entrepreneur, or broker, on this file. Flaherty was Treasurer of Ontario when the OSC review took place and the issue of a national regulator reappeared. He became convinced that it was good public policy. The project, believed Minister Flaherty, would be good for Ontario and Canada. Without his personal involvement and efforts in this matter, it is unlikely that the federal government would have moved forward on the file.

The Ontario government also strongly supported the creation of a national securities commission. Beyond convictions, politics are again at play. The Ontario government believes that a national securities regulator, headquartered in Toronto, would serve to bolster the city as a global financial capital. Strengthening Toronto is especially important as the province's economy shifts ever further away from its industrial base toward the service sector. There are few global financial capitals around the world, and they are prestigious. Michael Bryant (2010), a former provincial cabinet member, has even suggested that Ontario should do a lot more to strengthen Toronto as a center of global finance. Toronto is already home to the TMX, the country's largest exchange by far, and most financial firms in Canada have their headquarters in the city. The Toronto Financial Services Alliance (TFSA) posits that there are 232,000 people now working in this field in the city, and that between 1999 and 2009 employment grew by 42 percent (TFSA 2012). The TFSA further notes that 30 percent of financial services sector jobs in Canada are based in Toronto. As a result, finance now accounts for 14 percent of Toronto's GDP (TFSA 2012). For opponents of a national regulator, the importance accorded to Toronto in the proposal has always been problematic, and a reason to reject the project. They argue that a single regulator, preoccupied with Toronto, will be hard-pressed to accommodate the diversity of securities markets across Canada. In contrast, proponents see it as an advantage, not a drawback. They believe that if Toronto gets stronger, financial markets across the country will likely become stronger as well. There are advantages, they argue, to being the home country of a global city. The Ontario government has reason to support its provincial capital.

The majority of financial services sector firms and actors, whether emitters or investors (large institutional investors and individuals), support the creation of a national securities commission. Many in the business community believe that it would be easier to deal with a sole regulator instead of various regulators across the country. Adding clarity to the supervisory and regulatory regime is perceived as a big advantage when it comes to the proposal for a national regulator. There may also be unspoken and rather crude political advantages for private sector actors in dealing with a single regulator. Would it be easier for firms to lobby a single regulator as opposed to many? Or, conversely, would it be easier to lobby a group of weak provincial regulators? In the United States, reference is often made, rightly or wrongly, to the Wall Street–Washington complex. Etzioni (2009) posits that U.S. regulators became subject to regulatory capture prior to the global financial crisis. Canada is certainly not immune to this possibility. Yet proponents of a national regulator generally argue that it would be stronger and better resourced than are current provincial regulators. In addition, the new national regulator would be better positioned to defend small investors who often feel they have no recourse in the

Canadian system. Whatever their underlying motivations, financial services sector firms have been keen to see the creation of a national securities commission.

The fiercest, or at least most vocal, opposition to a national regulator has come from Québec. The province's position reflects its vision of federalism and its own political calculus. Underneath the usually nationalistic rhetoric in Québec lies a particular decentralized vision of federalism. Québec politics is traditionally divided between federalists on the one hand and sovereigntists on the other. Even among the former, who wish for Québec to remain within Canada and not to become an independent state, there is a general understanding that provincial powers must be dutifully defended as a matter of principle. Benoît Pelletier (2010), the former minister of Intergovernmental Affairs under the Liberal government, the federalist alternative, has long argued that provinces require more autonomy within the federal union. Though the concept of subsidiarity is not often used in Canada, Québec's perspective is that provincial autonomy is to be preserved and federal intrusion to be tolerated only when in support of provincial goals or when fully justified and accepted by the province. Thus, the passport model, first presented by the Québec government, and in which provinces continue to fully exercise their constitutional authority, is a credible policy alternative that brings with it distinct benefits. In the matter of financial services sector regulation, the federal government has no particular reason to intervene because provinces are occupying the policy space. It is possible to take the argument even further: irrespective of whether provinces are doing a good job or not (which is open to debate), the provinces have constitutional authority and no reason to relinquish it, and the federal government has proven unable to justify its intervention, as eventually noted in the Supreme Court opinion.

The passport model affords many advantages to Québec, including what it perceives to be the needed flexibility to regulate its own market so as to sustain provincial economic growth. Québec's preference for the passport model is also rooted in cultural and linguistic considerations. Toronto has come to replace Montréal as Canada's financial capital. The Toronto Stock Exchange has bought the Montréal exchange, and there is concern in the Québec government about the status of Montréal, which has traditionally been recognized as the economic capital of the province. In a national structure, Montréal would be just another local center of finance, without special status. There is also concern about the role of French if market supervision and regulation come from outside of the province. Though large private-sector actors likely do not worry about language, small emitters and individual investors in Québec are sensitive to this issue, particularly when market activities take place in English. The passport model, in which provinces keep their own regulator, mitigates these nationalist apprehensions.

Just like at the federal level, there are basic political considerations behind Québec's position on financial services sector reform. Because the belief in provincial autonomy is shared among political parties, there is no incentive for any of them to compromise on such an issue. Doing so would be politically costly.

The Liberals, in power at the time the federal government decided to act, could have easily been accused by a sovereigntist opposition of not defending the interest of Québec adequately, and of falling prey to outside pressure had they supported the federal position. As noted earlier, the Québec government, along with its provincial allies, crafted a defensible alternate proposal. The Québec government was able to claim legitimately that it was not rejecting reform per se, but rather the proposal put forward by Ottawa and Toronto. The government of Québec argued that its approach was constructive and would improve the supervision and regulation of financial markets in Canada while still respecting the fundamentals of the Canadian constitution.

Given all of the considerations above, Québec could have been in a bind if the Supreme Court had not rejected the proposed Canadian Securities Act. Irrespective of the judicial politics involved, Québec appears to have dwindling political clout in Ottawa. The federal Conservative government is less and less concerned with vote-getting in Québec, which means that it is less inclined to listen attentively to the province. Far worse, market actors favor a national commission. Had a national securities regulator been created, these actors likely would have wanted to operate within that body's jurisdiction. While small, local players would have continued to embrace the Québec market, large emitters and investors might have ignored the province altogether. The Québec regulator would have been forced to cooperate closely with the new entity to ensure the continued growth of the provincial market. The consequences of such a situation are hard to ascertain. Luckily for the province, the discussion is now entirely hypothetical.

Jurisdictional and political concerns are also found in Alberta and Manitoba. The Alberta government, like its Québec counterpart, is keen to exercise autonomy and to keep control over its own economic development, which presumably is preserved under the passport model. Alberta is notably concerned about the development of its oil and gas sector, and it is resentful of past attempts by the federal government to intervene in this industry. The impact of a national regulator on the oil and gas sector's development is unclear, though the key consideration here is about decision-making authority. Alberta worried that the national supervision and regulation of the securities industry would not have responded to the needs of its market. Political and economic power can be said to have shifted westward in Canada. The Canadian economy has been shielded in part from the global financial and economic crisis thanks to the economic benefits derived from its natural resources. As such, Alberta's opposition to a single regulator was a quasi-insurmountable problem for the project's backers.

Finally, this section will consider the position of provincial regulators. They represent important actors in this case because they supervise and regulate securities markets in Canada. Had the federal plan gone ahead, they would have disappeared or seen their powers vastly diminished. While the OSC clearly supported the creation of a national regulator, other regulators were either against it or non-committal. The debate surrounding the creation of a national securities commission raised some important but largely unanswered questions about the effectiveness of provincial regulators. The too-often unspoken assumption behind the federal scheme was that provincial regulators were not performing to expectations. The Québec government made important regulatory changes when it created the "Autorité des marchés financiers" in 2004. Québec's provincial regulator has since been fairly active, unearthing and acting upon various financial scandals in the province. Provincial regulators elsewhere, however, have not been as alert. Of course, there are many ways to address capacity issues if there is political will to do it. There is no guarantee that a national regulator would be more effective.

The other part of the equation is whether provincial regulators took the position they did because they truly believed that it represented sound public policy or rather because it was in their self-interest to do so. It is possible to think that the two explanations are complementary. Public choice theory suggests that bureaucracies, if left unchecked, tend to continually expand. As actors pursue their own self-interest, it becomes impossible to act for the greater good. A national regulator would have had regional offices across the country. One of the objectives of the proposal was to obtain efficiencies through a leaner structure. Provincial regulators would have likely disappeared or lost their power. They were fighting for self-preservation. Though employees might have been able to transfer to the federal regulator or elsewhere within their provincial governments, some would have lost their jobs and would have had to find new employment. Provincial regulators and the people working within these offices clearly had a stake in the debate which went beyond their actual professional duties.

The argument, once again, is that public policy considerations were subordinate to jurisdictional politics and process, in which each actor sought to defend its own self-interest.

Lessons Learned

This case offers many lessons for multilevel public management. To conclude this chapter, three important lessons will be discussed.

The first lesson pertains to the politicization of a policy issue in a multilevel context. Clearly, the more politicized an issue that crosses levels of authority becomes, the harder it is for actors to find a compromise. Peters (1997) has noted that depoliticization can help to resolve a multilevel conflict. In relation to the case under consideration, jurisdictional politics became the dominant story in the debate. The Supreme Court specifically noted in its opinion that it was not commenting on whether or not the project was good public policy, but rather on its constitutionality. Government, market, and civil society actors all agreed on the policy objective—to make Canada's regulatory structure more effective, efficient, competitive, and safe—but a compromise solution that all could accept proved to be beyond reach. As such, the federal government tried to act unilaterally. It was rebutted by the Supreme Court. If the rhetoric were now toned down, it is possible that a solution could be found. The court noted that the federal government had authority over systemic risk, and that provinces remained responsible for day-to-day market activity. Consequently, it is possible to imagine a regulatory structure that would allow the federal government to act to prevent systemic risk, protecting Canadians against a major financial crisis, while at the same time permitting the provinces to continue regulating daily market activities. Such an arrangement would require extensive coordination, collaboration, and the ability of all actors, especially existing regulators at both the federal and provincial levels, to work together. Once the politics have been resolved, the real work to find a good public policy solution should begin, though whether or not it happens remains to be seen.

The second lesson relates more to public policy than multilevel public management, focusing on the logic of the arguments. In order to be convincing, policy options need to show specifically how the policy objective will be achieved. In this case, there was consensus on the policy objective: to make the securities markets' supervisory and regulatory structure effective, efficient, competitive, and safe. Proponents of a national securities commission argued that the existing fragmentation prevented the policy objective from being met. They assumed, without ever demonstrating it, that a national regulator would perform better. The Supreme Court noted that the federal government failed to show that there was a need to regulate nationally, for it to supersede allocated constitutional authority. Proponents had the burden of proof (Corcoran 2010), yet there was no guarantee in the plan put forward that a single regulator would obtain better results, especially because the Canadian Securities Act drew so heavily from provincial legislation. Provinces, in turn, argued that supervision and regulation could be made more effective and efficient through better coordination. They, thus, adopted the passport model—an indication of their willingness to work together. Proponents of a national regulator argued that the passport model, though a step in the right direction, did not overcome supervisory and regulatory fragmentation. Provinces, however, did not have to demonstrate the superiority of their own proposal because it was the de facto policy; they simply had to show the weaknesses of the single regulator model. Without accord on how best to meet the policy objective, the debate turned to jurisdictional politics and process.

The third lesson relates to matters assumed or ignored in the jurisdictional and political debate. If the supervisory and regulatory structure is not as effective, efficient, competitive, and safe as it should be, perhaps the fault lies with the provincial regulators. The important question may not be who is responsible for a policy field, but rather whether those actors who have the authority also have the capacity to fulfill their mandate. Do Canadian regulators have the needed resources, including the proper expertise, to carry out their mandate? How is the weakness of regulators, if that is indeed the case, to be explained? Does it reflect political choices at the provincial level? What are the other factors at play? How might the federal government support provinces in the exercise of their function? Might it be that what is really needed is a strategy based on evidence to strengthen regulators across the country? It is clearly time to go beyond the bickering to ensure, at the very least, the safety of Canadian markets.

Jurisdictional politics overtook the public policy debate surrounding the possible creation of a national securities commission in Canada. With no clear-cut best policy option, Canadians were left with a debate about which level of authority was to do what, rather than a conversation focused on sound policy. It is now time to shift the debate from process and responsibilities back to public policy. Practitioners, in fact, are best suited for the next step.

References

Bickerton, James. 2010. Deconstructing the new federalism. *Canadian Political Science Review* 4 (2–3): 56–72.

Bryant, M. 2010. Toronto as centre of global finance? *Global Brief.* Retrieved 29 November 2010. Available from http://globalbrief.ca/blog/2010/10/13/how-does-toronto-become-a-top-centre-for-global-finance/.

Canada. Royal Commission on Banking and Finance. 1964. *Report of the Royal Commission on Banking and Finance.* Ottawa: Queen's Printer.

Canada. Supreme Court. 2011. Reference by the Governor in Council concerning the proposed Canadian Securities Act, as set out in Order in Council P.C. 2010-667, dated May 26, 2010. Judgment dated 22 December, docket 33718. Retrieved Dec. 22, 2011. Available from http://scc.lexum.org/en/2011/2011scc66/2011scc66.html.

Chant, John. 2009. *The ABCP Crisis in Canada: The Implications for the Regulation of Financial Markets.* Expert Panel on Securities Regulation. Retrieved 19 April 2010. Available from http://www.expertpanel.ca/eng/reports/research-studies/index.html.

Coleman, William. D. 2002. Federalism and financial services. In *Canadian Federalism: Performance, Effectiveness and Legitimacy,* edited by H. Bakvis and G. Skogstad. Toronto: Oxford University Press, pp. 178–196.

Corcoran, Terrence. 2010. This power grab needs full review. *National Post.* Retrieved 27 May 2010. Available from http://fullcomment.nationalpost.com/2010/05/26/1699/.

Crawford Panel on a Single Canadian Securities Regulator. 2006. Blueprint for a Canadian Securities Commission: Final paper. Retrieved Dec. 17, 2012. Available from http://www.cba.ca/contents/files/misc/msc_crawfordreport_en.pdf.

Crawford, Purdy. 2002. Draft report. Five Year Review Committee, Reviewing the Securities Act. Ontario Securities Commission. Retrieved July 6, 2004. Available from http://www.osc.gov.on.ca/documents/fr/Securities/fyr_20030529_5yr-final-report.pdf.

Etzioni, Amitai. 2009. The capture theory of regulations—revisited. *Society* 46: 319–323.

Expert Panel on Securities Regulation. 2009. *Creating an Advantage in Global Capital Markets: Final Report and Recommendations.* Ottawa: Department of Finance. Retrieved 6 July 2009. Available from http://www.expertpanel.ca/eng/documents/Expert_Panel_Final_Report_And_Recommendations.pdf.

Harmes, Adam. 2007. The political economy of open federalism. *Canadian Journal of Political Science* 40 (2): 417–438.

Harris, Stephen. 2004. Financial services sector in Canada: Interests and the policy process. *Canadian Journal of Political Science* 37 (1): 161–184.

Harris, Stephen. 2010. The global financial meltdown and financial regulation: Shirking and learning—Canada in an international context. In *How Ottawa Spends 2010–2011,* edited by G. Bruce Doern and Christopher Stoney. Montréal/Kingston: McGill-Queen's University Press, pp. 68–86.

InterMinisterial Committee of Provincial Finance Ministers. 2004. A provincial/territorial memorandum of understanding regarding securities regulation. Retrieved 6 July 2009. Available from http://www.securitiescanada.org/2004_0930_mou_english.pdf.

Lortie, Pierre. 2011. *Securities Regulation in Canada: The Case for Effectiveness.* Montreal: Institute for Research on Public Policy. Retrieved 7 November 2011. Available from http://www.irpp.org/pubs/IRPPstudy/IRPP_Study_no19.pdf.

McRoberts, Kenneth. 1993. Federal structures and the policy process. In *Governing Canada: Institutions and Public Policy,* edited by Michael Atkinson. Toronto: HBJ, pp. 149–178.

Pelletier, Benoît. 2010. *Une certaine idée du Québec: Parcours d'un fédéraliste, de la réflexion à l'action.* Ste-Foy (QC): Presses de l'Université Laval.

Peters, Guy B. 1997. Escaping the joint-decision trap: Repetition and sectoral politics in the European Union. *West European Politics* 20 (2): 22–36.

Scharpf, Fritz. 1988. The joint-decision trap: Lessons from German federalism and European integration. *Public Administration* 66 (3): 238–273.

Task Force to Modernize Securities Legislation in Canada. 2006. Canada steps up: Final report. Retrieved 6 July 2009. Available from http://www.tfmsl.ca/index.htm.

TMX. 2010. TMX group history at a glance. Retrieved 20 January 2012. Available from http://tmx.com/en/pdf/TMXHistory.pdf.

Toronto Financial Services Alliance. 2012. Financial services in Toronto. Retrieved Dec. 17, 2012. Available from http://www.tfsa.ca/financial-services/TFSA.

Williams, Russell Allan. 2009. Exogenous shocks in subsystem adjustments and policy change: The credit crunch and Canadian banking regulation. *Journal of Public Policy* 29 (1): 29–53.

Wise Persons Committee. 2003. *It's Time.* Ottawa: Department of Finance. Retrieved 6 July 2009. Available from http://www.wise-averties.ca/main_en.html.

Yamashita, Eiji. 2011. The comparison of policy responses to the financial crisis between the EU post-2008 and Japan in the 1990s. In *The EU and Federalism: Polities and Policies Compared,* edited by Finn Laursen. Farnham, UK: Ashgate, pp. 203–220.

Chapter 7

Climate Change Adaptation and Multilevel Governance: Challenges to Policy Capacity in Canadian Finance

---

Russell Alan Williams

Contents

Introduction

In December 2010, Canada's Commissioner of the Environment and Sustainable Development Scott Vaughan released his annual report assessing government performance in response to environmental challenges. The report focused heavily on the general lack of progress by all federal agencies in integrating knowledge about climate change adaptation into their activities. In his introduction, Vaughan argued that

> [t]he concerns we have raised in this report are hardly new. About 20 years ago, the federal government acknowledged that the impacts of climate change would pose significant, long-term challenges throughout Canada, from more frequent and severe storms in Atlantic Canada to changes in the amount of rain available to farmers. And today, the federal government still lacks an overarching federal strategy that identifies clear, concrete actions supported by coordination among federal departments. (Canada, Office of the Auditor General 2010:2)

The environment commissioner's report highlighted governments' lack of planning for climate change adaptation—something that is not surprising given evidence from other jurisdictions suggesting similar problems (Preston, Westaway, and Yuen 2010)—and it identified a major cause of this problem: the lack of coordination among departments. The report actually underemphasized the problem in that it dealt only with federal agencies, ignoring the considerable role of provinces and local governments in responding to the issue. Climate change adaptation challenges the existing responsibilities of established agencies and the existing jurisdictional responsibilities of the different levels of government and requires extremely high levels of organizational cooperation, coordination, and information sharing for effective policy responses. In this sense, multilevel governance may be as much an impediment to climate change adaptation (at least in relation to governments' "policy analytical capacities") as the solution to modern governance challenges as it has so often been portrayed.

In the past, evaluation of climate change adaptation initiatives has tended to focus on agencies directly responsible for the management of natural resources. Canada's environment commissioner has highlighted Environment Canada, Natural Resources Canada, Fisheries and Oceans Canada, and Aboriginal Affairs and Northern Development as the agencies most responsible for managing adaptation. All are federal government agencies that seem to have the most direct stake in adapting to problems generated by changes in climate. However, climate change is not simply a policy concern for fish stocks or polar bear habitats—the kind of specific concerns with which these agencies have tasked themselves. Rather, it is a multidimensional policy challenge that affects many of the planning activities of modern governments. For example, likely changes in local climatic conditions have implications for long-term infrastructure planning (e.g., the undesirability of investing in transportation links for agricultural regions likely to become non-productive over the next few decades); for long-term economic development in regions dependent on certain ecologically sensitive natural resources; and for urban transportation planning and infrastructure decisions surrounding health and education spending. Climate change adaptation is a "problem" that needs to be more directly integrated into all agencies' deliberations.

Much of the political discussion of climate change in Canada tends to focus on "mitigation" (e.g., the various Kyoto Protocol–related efforts to reduce increases in carbon emissions and thereby reduce the scale of climatic change, efforts for which the current Canadian federal government has recently, and spectacularly, withdrawn its support), and policy questions relating to how governments should integrate knowledge about climate change into their long-term planning have been largely left to the federal, provincial, and municipal civil services to try to muddle through. As the environment commissioner's report suggests, for some time there has been considerable attention to adaptation concerns in government agencies. Many government agencies, particularly those responsible for natural resource management and infrastructure spending, "talk" about climate change effects in relation to their policy advising, yet these efforts are poorly coordinated, and the flow of information between agencies and various orders of government is unclear. The nature of the climate change adaptation policy problem highlights basic overlaps in Canada's federal system of government. All orders of government are involved in long-term infrastructure spending and planning, all orders of government have some level of concern about the impact of more extreme and volatile weather conditions on building and infrastructure planning, and all orders of government have a role in dealing with the economic implications of climate changes on local natural resource–based economies.

Crucially, climate change adaptation requires funding and support from federal and provincial government finance agencies, as access to investment in adaptation is one of the biggest impediments to coping with the changing environment (Preston, Westaway, and Yuen 2010). Thus, in a very real but poorly understood sense, climate change adaptation not only spills across various government jurisdictions, but it also raises a range of complex new policy questions in the finance sector. Unfortunately we know very little about the amount of knowledge that finance agencies have about climate change, their orientation toward the issue, and the extent to which government arrangements in finance are conducive to disseminating knowledge about the issue to relevant finance officials. Although environmental and natural resource agencies, like those listed above, are laden with policy researchers with natural science training, finance agencies are not, and yet they play a key role in analyzing and managing adaptation to climate change. The fact that they must also do this in complex, multilevel governance settings, where there may be few or no existing mechanisms for distributing this kind of policy-relevant knowledge, suggests that climate change adaption faces serious challenges from the perspective of governments' policy capacity.

Multilevel Governance and Policy Analytical Capacity

It is now commonplace to see multilevel governance (MLG) as "better" than more traditional, centralized forms of policy making and program delivery. As Hooghe and Marks put it, "centralized authority—command and control—has few advocates" (2003:233). Hollander (2009) has suggested that when it comes to environmental concerns, the frequent overlap of responsibilities in federal systems is probably "good" for environmental adaptation as it increases the number of channels for conveying environmental concerns to policy makers. However, much of this analysis rests on seeing the environment as a political and administrative problem, rather than an analytical challenge requiring the integration of new and complex ideas into government research and analyses. In simple terms, no matter the extent to which MLG might be a superior form of administration from a democratic or "points of entry" perspective, there are clear reasons to be suspicious about its impact on the policy capacity of public administrators in relation to their advising functions. For example, in his introduction to the widely cited special edition of the *Journal of European Public Policy* on MLG and policy capacity, Scharpf (1997) argued that conventional predictions about how globalization and MLG were likely to impact policy capacity were problematic. Scharpf maintained that future "problem solving capacities" of government were likely to vary from one policy issue to another, depending on the properties of the issue and the nature of governance arrangements in the sector. Scharpf argued that we needed to specify these factors more carefully (as causal mechanisms) if we were to understand what was happening to governments' policy capacity (1997, 531). Issues that require collaboration across agencies and levels of government in an MLG setting will likely be met with lower policy capacity unless effective coordinating mechanisms are in place to ensure that high-quality expertise about the problem gets to the officials who need it. Without these kinds of mechanisms, no matter how well equipped some government agencies and officials are to analyze major policy challenges (and it is usually the large "policy shops" working in central agencies that have this kind of expertise), that information will be poorly utilized by other levels of government.

In this chapter Scharpf's concern is developed by evaluating policy capacity in Canada, using finance agencies' engagement with climate change adaptation policy as a case study. In a sense the chapter mirrors governments' own instrumental concerns about how they might improve policy capacity (Bakvis 2000) by asking about the conditions under which policy capacity will be better or worse in MLG settings. Through a more careful specification of what constitutes effective policy capacity in relation to the advising functions of government agencies, it is suggested that one obstacle to "better" climate change adaptation policy is multilevel governance. Through an examination of existing governance arrangements, the available analytical resources, and a survey of policy professionals, it is argued that there are serious multilevel institutional challenges to policy advising on climate change adaption. Dealing with this type of policy problem in an MLG setting requires that we get our governance arrangements "right."

Assessing Policy Capacity

Unfortunately, measuring the capacity of policy makers to engage in "policy learning" (improving the advice they provide governments) has always been problematic. Much of the policy literature highlights institutional and political obstacles to learning and the flow of knowledge, generating considerable pessimism about policy analysis and advising in government. Whether based on the limitations to rational decision making (Lindblom 1979), "garbage cans" replete with different policy ideas in search of problems (Cohen, March, and Olsen 1972) or "discourse intuitionalism" and its break with any sense that policy analyses involve seeking "effective" solutions (Schmidt 2008), the academic sources have reinforced a view that governments' analytical capacities are limited, at least in terms of their ability to engage in evidence-based policy learning. Compounding this theoretical skepticism, the policy-advising function of the civil service has received little attention in the transition to the new public management, as efficiency has become the sole metric for judging what the civil service does, and the role of "expertise" and "advice" has faded (Holmes and Shand 1995; Bakvis 2000; Bernier and Howlett 2011). Thus, despite the common usage of capacity terminology in relation to learning, particularly by governments (Peters 1996; Anderson 2008; Canadian Policy Research Network [CPRN] 2009), capacity has not been clearly operationalized and evaluated. This is a problem because, from a practical perspective, if governments want good policy advice in the face of complex problems, improvements to existing capacity are essential.

Effective policy learning—whether construed as Etheridge's (1981) notion of "government learning" or Rose's (1988) "lesson drawing," which both stress governments' use of information to avoid subsequent policy failures—ultimately requires two conditions. First, effective learning requires that policy advisors have sufficient "policy analytical capacity" (Howlett and Newman 2010; Oliphant and Howlett 2010) in leading government agencies, through their accumulated knowledge, training, and skills, to engage effectively with new information or policy ideas. To put it bluntly, many government agencies are small and have few resources to devote to purposeful longer-term learning exercises. In many instances policy failures result simply from a lack of expertise needed to avoid relatively predictable problems. Think, for example, of the frequent planning failures of suburban municipalities when dealing with urban sprawl. There is a wealth of knowledge and experience about urban growth, which many municipal policy officials working for small municipalities fail to utilize in policy deliberations, perhaps due to poor training, insufficient staff resources, or time constraints in the nature of their work.

Second, and more widely recognized, effective learning requires that the structure of a particular policy subsystem—the relationship among different agencies and policy actors—be conducive to the exchange of policy-relevant advice. Both Hall (1993) and Sabatier (1987) in their work on policy learning highlight that effective learning, the kind that generates programmatic responses to real problems, requires that the policy-making environment be "open" to new actors or new policy ideas and integrated so that agencies can disseminate and share ideas. Oliphant and Howlett (2010) suggest that policy capacity requires a clearly recognized need for the information being provided by different agencies on a policy question, along with a culture of openness to exchanging knowledge. In other words, effective government learning or lesson drawing calls for integrated institutional arrangements—that is, established lines of communication among relevant agencies that have the general willingness to engage with new ideas. On some level, this problem of integration is even more important in an MLG setting. Regardless of how centralized or decentralized authority is in different policy areas under MLG, some issues are going to require the flow of information among different orders of government if analytical capacity is to be effective. For example, in this case, climate change adaptation in the Canadian MLG context will require that knowledge held by climate change scientists working in larger federal government policy shops be shared with administrators at the provincial and local levels if they are to plan effectively for the effects of climate change over the long term.

At the risk of considerable oversimplification, these two considerations are developed in Table 7.1. In policy domains where analytical capacity is limited and governance arrangements are poorly integrated and not conducive to disseminating new advice, it is likely that authorities will fail to respond in a programmatic fashion to new challenges; expertise is likely to be devoted to policy "firefighting" rather than more systematic anticipatory research.

Sectors with well-managed and integrated governance arrangements ensuring good communication among different levels of government, but limited analytical capacity will also struggle with effective learning because, no matter how well organized the channels for disseminating policy advice might be (or how much appetite there might be for those ideas), agencies simply lack the ability to produce the necessary advice. Logically, one might expect an analytical process marked by limited incrementalism, given the inability to examine previously untested ideas. Conversely, in a sector where analytical capacity is high but governance arrangements are less integrated, a number of outcomes seem possible. For example, if there are multiple institutions charged with overlapping mandates, high-quality analytical capacity may be used "badly" to support competing agencies and competing political agendas. Less instrumentally, agencies may simply recommend contradictory policies in the absence of coordination. Ineffective governance arrangements could also be conducive to "passing the buck" on complex new

Table 7.1 Typology of Policy Capacity

		Policy Analytical Capacity	
		High	*Low*
Governance arrangements	Integrated	Effective policy capacity Able to meet long-term challenges	Analytically impaired policy capacity Insufficient knowledge and expertise = focus on incremental change
	Non-integrated	Structurally impaired policy capacity Departmental policy struggles and incoherence	Ineffective policy capacity Policy failures and short-term firefighting

challenges, as ambiguity about responsibilities may create an environment in which agencies assume that someone else will deal with the issue—a particularly high risk on an issue like climate change adaptation where analytical responsibilities may lie with many agencies.

The real challenge is empirically assessing analytical capacity and the degree of integration of governance arrangements in relation to policy capacity. Both tasks are difficult in that assessing analytical capacity and governance arrangements in relation to a particular policy problem also requires some sense of what the structure or properties of the problem are, as Scharpf's work highlighted. In the real world, analytical capacity and governance arrangements are only "high" or "low" in relation to specific policy questions. For example, in the finance case, both may be high in relation to the current obsession with performance management measures emanating from the new public management, but both may be low in relation to what climate change adaptation means in the sector.

Case Study: The Canadian Finance Sector and Climate Change Policy

Climate Change Adaptation and the Finance Policy Sector

As noted above, climate change introduces new mandates for policy analyses to finance authorities, requiring that either existing analytical resources be tasked with this responsibility, integrating knowledge about climate change into their ongoing work, or that new analytical resources be added. Climate change adaptation is a complex issue in the finance sector as it generates very different analytical challenges. First, all internal government climate change policies and programs must in some way be overseen by finance departments, particularly those that require large spending commitments (Preston, Westaway, and Yuen 2010). For example, finance agencies are responsible for designing and implementing carbon taxes, providing funding for green initiatives within government, and providing funds for new energy sources and transportation projects responding to environmental changes. The scope of the analytical challenges in assessing these program options ultimately touches on all aspects of government climate policy. Furthermore, in Canada, the federal Department of Finance plays a central role in coordinating international initiatives on climate change, as its senior officials almost always guide Canada's international deliberations relating to economic policy. The sheer volume of mentions of international climate change issues on the Department of Finance's Web site suggests that this is a particular preoccupation of whatever analytical capacity exists inside the organization.

The challenges do not stop there, however. Finance authorities are also responsible for overseeing the private financial services industry and therefore are responsible for evaluating climate change issues as they touch on industry regulation. Two climate change concerns are particularly important in this light. First, as has been widely recognized by the financial services industry for almost a decade, both long-term climate changes (that may significantly challenge local economic activities) and increasing climate instability pose prudential risks to certain kinds of financial service companies and financial products.* Regulatory authorities need to integrate knowledge about likely climate impacts into assessments of financial risk, particularly in relation to the insurance industry and pension investments. Second, to the extent to which managing climate change may require the redirection of private investment to either more carbon-responsible practices or simply toward adaptive industries, finance authorities also may have a role in encouraging new priorities for the investment community.

Each of these challenges involves different agencies and often multiple orders of government. For example, while a federal agency, the Office of the Superintendent of Financial Institutions (OSFI), is responsible for ensuring that insurance companies and banks are not overexposed to predictable risks (e.g., lending and insurance in an agricultural region perhaps threatened by climate change), provincial finance officials play a major role in overseeing and managing considerable pension portfolios and may have similar concerns. Even more clearly, all orders of government in Canada are involved in funding transportation and energy infrastructure. Thus, the sharing of information among finance officials about the desirability of some

---

* See, for example, the analysis done by the United Nations Environment Program Finance Initiative.

investments over others from a long-term climate change perspective is probably a prerequisite of effective policy capacity in this area.

These challenges speak directly to the complexities of multilevel governance in relation to climate change, because for the most part, they do not fit into existing organizational arrangements in the Canadian context. They require considerable coordination—vertically, with other orders of government, and horizontally, across different policy domains. Given the novel nature of climate change adaptation, there are no existing mechanisms of collaboration and communication on the issue. In areas requiring intergovernmental cooperation or private sector collaboration, unless there are already established lines of communication and a general openness to discussing new policy ideas emanating from one area of government to another, institutional arrangements are not likely to generate effective policy capacity. To put it simply, climate change policy is difficult from a policy capacity perspective as it cuts across existing mandates. A government's policy capacity is likely to be more effective when problems "fit" existing responsibilities, but the particular properties of the climate change issue are problematic from a multilevel governance perspective as most of the issues require new communication mechanisms across governments.

Assessing Governance Arrangements and Policy Making in Finance

Given that the quality of governance arrangements is particularly important for climate change adaptation, the issue poses unique challenges for the federal division of responsibilities in the finance sector—the sector may be well integrated in relation to some policy problems but not others. For example, past studies have highlighted the role of federalism and the degree to which finance is a divided jurisdiction in mitigating effective policy design, in particular from the perspective of fiscal federalism. Other research has suggested weak federal governance in questions of industry regulation due to the disinterest of the Bank of Canada (Coleman 1996). Still others have noted both the weakness of the federal Office of the Superintendent of Financial Institutions (OSFI) in policy debates given the provinces' key role in regulating the securities industry (Harris 2010) and the weakness of the Department of Finance in guiding policy given the high level of political interference in key policy debates in the sector (Harris 2004). In essence, climate change adaptation aside, there are already concerns in the finance sector about the extent to which overlapping responsibilities, fragmented authority over small pieces of the finance puzzle, and interjurisdictional "turf wars" have undermined effective policy capacity in the past.

However, inside the federal government, the central role of the Department of Finance in overseeing and coordinating all government activities has been widely commented on for decades. Finance has extensive policy analytical capacity (perhaps more than any other agency in government) as ultimately it plays a role in all policy sectors through its management of the public purse. This suggests a large role for finance as a central coordinating agency in relation to all aspects of climate change adaptation, but the policy-making dynamics involved are not well documented.

What is better documented are finance authorities' relations with other sectoral participants—the external relations between federal authorities and other stakeholders—where the picture suggests cause for concern about the ability of these agencies to share information in a constructive and deliberative fashion. For example, since the advent of globalization and deregulation of the private financial services sector, key questions about industry regulation have become far more complex and politicized (Harris 2004; Williams 2004; Williams 2009), particularly when there is significant institutional competition between federal and provincial authorities. Constant proposals for the creation of a national securities regulator have gone nowhere despite broadly accepted analyses that this is a good idea in light of the industry complexity. The provincial and federal governments have "passed the buck" on some of the new regulatory problems raised by financial securitization (Harris 2010; Williams 2012); the governments have chosen to be politic over jurisdictions rather than address a new policy challenge. Despite the complexity of finance and the fact that it is usually a domain dominated by a high degree of technocratic consensus over major policy goals and needed reforms, normal patterns of coordination among different stakeholders have seemed broken for some time.

This is notable because governance arrangements from a policy-advising perspective are well developed within the federal government. The Department of Finance is undoubtedly the central agency in the sector. It has a coordinating role over other departments through its control of the budget, and a central coordinating role over other regulatory and policy-making institutions relating to financial regulation. Since the 2008 financial crisis, this role has been formalized through the appointment of a finance assistant deputy minister as chair of the Financial Institutions Supervisory Committee (FISC), which is the central committee tasked with coordinating the different Canadian finance authorities. FISC brings the Department of Finance together with the Bank of Canada, the Canadian Deposit Insurance Corporation, the Office of the Superintendent of Financial Institutions and, if it is ever created, a representative of the national securities regulator. FISC is intended to be a central "clearinghouse" for broad issues relating to finance. Through these kinds of mechanisms, the Department of Finance is well supported by its associate federal agencies in policy analyses—in particular the Bank of Canada and an increasingly well-staffed OSFI.

Of course the problem is that an issue like climate change adaptation does not fit neatly inside federal jurisdiction and authority, and the mechanisms of collaboration across jurisdictions are not as well developed. This is problematic, particularly from the perspective of using the typology of policy capacity. The sector is more or less integrated depending on how the issue interacts with existing organizational mandates and jurisdictions. Issues relating to policy questions internal to federal government arrangements are well integrated. At the other end of the continuum, issues that cross federal–provincial boundaries are not well integrated. Given the broad-reaching policy challenges associated with climate change adaptation and the need for collaboration and information sharing among government regardless of formal divisions of power and the degree of centralization or decentralization on any particular set of policy questions, it seems reasonable to suggest that governance arrangements are probably not as integrated as they need to be to support effective policy capacity.

Assessing Analytical Capacity: Lessons from the Survey Data?

Setting aside the formal institutional arrangements in which policy analysts and administrators work, analytical capacity has proven difficult to study in the past. There is little systematic information on the nature of policy work inside government, on existing analytical capacity (even in a sector as large and as important as finance), and we actually know surprisingly little about the scope of different agencies' research activities, analytical resources, and the competency of their policy analysts. Table 7.1 suggests a basic distinction between "high" and "low" analytical capacity, but the task of interpreting the analytical capacity in any sector is difficult, particularly in relation to specific policy problems, as again analytical capacity could be generally high but very weak in relation to new issues.

On the surface, analytical capacity on finance issues is quite high, at least at the federal level. A review of the budgets of key federal agencies suggests that the Department of Finance, OSFI, and the Bank of Canada should all have considerable capacity in terms of staff resources. OSFI's budget for monitoring the financial industry, a largely analytical set of activities, was over $90 million in 2011. Furthermore, the policy advice and support offered to finance by the Bank of Canada and OSFI seem particularly valuable in that staff are encouraged to see themselves as serious researchers (bank staff are notable for publishing their own research findings). Likewise, several survey projects have illustrated that policy staff in central agencies have considerably more analytical capacity, in terms of their training, education, time, and research competencies, to engage in more sophisticated policy analysis than other government agencies (see, e.g., Wellstead, Steadman, and Lindquist 2009). These kinds of cognitive capacities for policy analysis seem to be much higher in the larger, more formalized policy shops that exist in the federal government's central agencies.

There is, however, considerable reason to question the provinces' analytical capacity, which is particularly relevant here given their large role in finance and climate change adaptation. It is probably the case that provinces have a more direct role in managing climate change than the federal government, because they have a greater role in managing and funding infrastructure, the generation of energy, and transportation. Given the more geographically resource-dependent orientation of their economies, the provinces also have more to worry about in light of the impact of changing climate on their economies. From an analytical capacity perspective, however, as one recent study concluded:

> Provincial and territorial analysts, like their federal counterparts, are highly educated ... But they do not tend to have a great deal of formal training in policy analysis and mainly work in small units deeply embedded in provincial and territorial ministries ... They lack substantive knowledge in the areas in which they work and of formal policy analytical techniques and tend to bring only process-related knowledge to the table. They also tend to work on a relatively small number of issue areas, often on a "firefighting" basis ... [They] can be thought of as working in an interactive "client-advice" style somewhat removed from the traditional "rational style" promoted by ... policy schools. (Howlett and Newman 2010)

This general pattern is likely to be pronounced in finance. Even though provincial finance ministries are large and well staffed, their mandates are much narrower than those of their federal counterpart, and they are not supported by the high-quality satellite agencies that serve the federal government. Provincial securities regulators, for example, in some instances are "shell" organizations with little permanent staff and analytical capacity. Moreover, there is no equivalent to the Bank of Canada offering its own broad-reaching analysis of finance and economic challenges. In fact, the survey data collected for a SSHRC CEI project on the capacity of Canadian policy makers surrounding climate change underscores these claims.* As illustrated in Table 7.2, suspicion about differences in the training and education of officials in the two orders of government is clear. Generally, provincial officials are not as well educated, are less likely to have training in the social and natural sciences or policy analysis, and are more likely to have a training background in business administration.

There also appear to be statistically significant differences in the basic organization of policy analytical work at the federal and provincial levels (Table 7.3). Generally, provincial policy analysts are more likely to see their role as involving negotiation with stakeholders and short-term "firefighting," and they are less likely to use evidence-based approaches. Even though provincial officials are more heavily engaged in policy process activities, there is more scope for actual policy research at the federal level—something that officials will frequently comment on themselves.

---

* The survey was directed to federal and provincial policy analysts and administrators. Aside from examining the officials' knowledge of climate change adaptation challenges, it sought information on their research experience, competencies, educational backgrounds, and most interestingly, the organization of their policy-related research activities in government. Six hundred thirty-six officials completed the survey.

Table 7.2   Educational Differences in the Public Service, by Level of Government

	Non-Finance-Related Agencies		Finance-Related Agencies	
	Provincial (%)	*Federal (%)*	*Provincial (%)*	*Federal (%)*
Level of Education				
High school	2.41	0	6.38	0
College—Tech school	10.69	0.85	6.38	0
University	33.10	27.12	27.66	11.11
Graduate/professional	53.79	72.03	59.57	88.89
Type of Education				
Business or administration	12.42	5.95	25	26
Computing science	0.67	2.16	0	0
Engineering	7.76	3.24	2.41	6.67
Natural sciences	24.61	35.14	1.2	0
Social sciences	12.2	21.62	16.87	33.33
Number of Post-Secondary Policy-Specific Courses Undertaken				
None	35.32	45.71	34.88	0
One	13.19	8.57	11.63	0
Two	16.6	7.62	6.98	33.33
Three or more	34.89	38.1	46.51	66.66

Provincial policy staff often complain that federal offices have more time and staff resources for policy work. Furthermore, although many of the variations are small, there are statistically significant differences in the types of research tools the two groups report using (Table 7.4), and there are significant differences in key sources of information on which they rely in their policy deliberations. It is interesting to note, for example, that federal officials are more likely to rely on academic research, reports from foreign governments, and scientific findings in their analyses, while provincial officials are particularly reliant on reports from consultants and personal opinion.

This general evidence supports previous survey projects' claims that analytical capacity is likely much higher in central federal agencies, but once we focus on a

Table 7.3   Organization of Policy Work, by Level of Government

	Provincial	Federal
Differences in Types of Analytical Policy Work Conducted		
Appraise policy options	2.95	2.56
Brief high-level decision makers	2.16	1.78
Conduct scientific research	1.85	2.63
Consult with decision makers	3.16	2.93
Consult with the public	2.19	1.77
Evaluate policy processes	2.74	2.15
Evaluate policy results and outcomes	2.65	2.4
Identify policy issues	3.12	2.86
Identify policy options	2.99	2.7
Implement/deliver policies/programs	2.72	2.44
Negotiate with central agencies	2.11	1.62
Negotiate with program managers	2.46	2.27
Negotiate with stakeholders on policy	2.11	1.89
Differences in Timelines of Tasks		
Tasks demand immediate action (firefighting)	3.24	2.89
Short-term tasks (resolved in 1 month)	3.41	3.19

Note: Numbers reflect mean use rating per group on a 1 to 5 scale, where 1 = never and 5 = daily.

specific issue—climate change adaptation—the results are more complicated from an analytical capacity perspective. The starkest findings in this survey relate to the gap between finance officials and non-finance officials on awareness of/engagement in/concern about climate change adaptation issues. For example, while finance officials are more confident than other officials that their agencies *could* deal with adaptation questions, they tend to see the issue as being less important to themselves and to their agency (Table 7.5). Furthermore, their knowledge of climate change issues is lower, and they are more skeptical about climate change knowledge and are less positive about the extent to which finance organizations are dealing with that knowledge.

Table 7.4 Evidence and Analytical Tools Used, by Level of Government

	Provincial	*Federal*
Support for Evidence-Based Approaches among Users		
Required to use evidence-informed method	3.52	3.85
Provided with tools to implement method	3.18	3.47
Encouraged by managers to use method	3.45	3.75
Differences in Types of Analytical Tools Used for Policy Analysis		
Bayesian methods	0.96	1.23
Checklists	1.05	1.12
Cost-benefit analysis	1.26	1.44
Cost-effectiveness analysis	1.29	1.46
Cross-impact analysis	1.19	1.39
Decision analysis	1.18	1.32
Economic impact analysis	1.36	1.51
Financial analysis	1.33	1.55
Multicriteria analysis	1.34	1.48
Policy exercises	1.23	1.40
Preference scales	1.36	1.57
Problem mapping tools	1.34	1.48
Process influence diagrams	1.40	1.55
Ranking/dominance analysis	1.34	1.48
Social impact analysis	1.38	1.56

Note: Numbers reflect mean use rating per group on a 1 to 5 scale, where 1 = never and 5 = daily.

When examining the information sources used by officials in their policy work, there are interesting differences between non-finance and finance officials. Non-finance officials are far more likely to use scientific findings and academic research in their analysis, and finance officials rely more heavily on personal experience, opinions, and reports from industry (Table 7.6). Perhaps most importantly, while

Table 7.5   Climate Change Attitudes, Orientations, and Information Sources, by Type of Organization

	Non-Finance	Finance
Level of Concern about Climate Change		
How concerned are you personally about climate change?	3.998	3.542
How concerned is your department or agency about climate change?	3.845	2.97
Compared with other issues that your department or agency deals with, how much of a priority are issues related to adaptation to climate change?	3.16	2.239
Overall, how would you rate your department's or agency's capacity to deal with adaptation to climate change?	2.287	2.594
How relevant are issues related to climate change adaptation to your daily work?	3.37	2.015
How relevant are issues related to climate change adaptation to the mission of your department or agency?	3.796	2.478
How relevant are issues related to climate change adaptation to the daily operations of your department or agency?	3.236	2.212
Does your department's or agency's work help to increase capacity to adapt to climate change?	3.824	2.507
Familiarity with and Attitudes toward Climate Change		
I understand the concept of adaptation to climate change.	4.27	3.64
I understand the key issues surrounding adaptation to climate change.	4.05	3.34
Information regarding adaptation to climate change is readily available to me.	3.76	3.25
The body of knowledge regarding adaptation to climate change is growing.	4.07	3.82
Climate change is affecting policy decisions in my organization.	3.53	2.58

Table 7.5 (continued)   Climate Change Attitudes, Orientations, and Information Sources, by Type of Organization

	Non-Finance	Finance
Information regarding adaptation to climate change is understood within my organization.	3.18	2.54
There is an increased desire for information regarding adaptation within my organization.	3.44	2.43
Within my organization there exists a general consensus regarding the need for adaptation.	3.39	2.41
My organization is more aware of adaptation to climate change issues than 3 years ago.	3.81	2.85
Mitigation should be considered part of a larger adaptation strategy.	3.92	3.25

Note: Numbers reflect mean use rating per group on a 1 to 5 scale, where 1 = not at all concerned or strongly disagree and 5 = very concerned or strongly agree.

Table 7.6   Types of Information Sources Used in Policy Work

	Non-Finance	Finance
Academic research	3.24	2.73
Newspapers and news magazines	2.89	3.66
Personal experience	3.50	3.94
Personal opinion	3.02	3.39
Reports from industry	2.56	2.96
Scientific findings	3.12	1.78
Workshops	3.58	2.34

Note: Numbers reflect mean use rating per group on a 1 to 5 scale, where 1 = never and 5 = daily.

70 percent of all non-finance officials report having some direct involvement in climate change–related policy work, only 17 percent of finance officials report the same.

These data tend to confirm the general sense that analytical capacity is higher in the finance sector at the federal level and lower in the provinces. This alone suggests that effective climate change adaptation will require new mechanisms for conveying federal expertise to provincial and local officials. However, in the finance sector very little of that "high" federal capacity is actively engaged in climate change–related policy work. The data seem to suggest that finance officials, more commonly trained in business administration with little connection to the natural sciences, tend to be skeptical of the importance of adaptation as a major policy concern for their offices.

Much like the problem of assessing the integration of governance arrangements, it seems reasonable to suggest here that analytical capacity in finance, although generally high, will be lower on issues that are well outside of existing competencies, such as issues that require more scientific knowledge about likely climate impacts. As a result, there may be a need for more collaborative information- and expertise-sharing arrangements, not only across jurisdictions but also across policy domains.

Conclusions: Implications for Multilevel Governance

What then can be said about policy capacity in the finance sector relating to climate change and the impact of multilevel governance? In a multilevel governance setting, effective policy capacity, supportive of the learning required to meet the analytical challenges posed by climate change adaptation, requires first that there be sufficient analytical capacities within government to assess those challenges, and second that governance arrangements create both an "appetite" for that analysis as well as mechanisms for sharing information among relevant agencies. These conditions do not appear to exist in the Canadian case. Climate change issues cross jurisdictional boundaries and require significant expertise from all agencies. On the surface it appears that provincial authorities lack the same quality of advice that federal officials may receive, and that there are not effective lines of communication among governments on this issue. Finance officials, who have a relatively central role to play in planning and funding adaptation strategies, illustrate this general pattern, and even federal finance officials, working in a far more conducive environment than their provincial counterparts, seem to be disinterested or disengaged on climate change issues. They simply do not see climate change adaptation as a particularly pressing concern for their agencies. While other federal agencies have contributed significant resources to climate change issues, there is little specific demand in finance for collaboration on those ideas.

The structures of multilevel governance inherent in Canadian federalism interact with this particular issue in ways about which we should be concerned. Although Hollander (2009) is probably right in stating that the overlapping jurisdictions and increased points of entry mean that multilevel governance settings could be more responsive to societal concerns about the environment, those points of entry must be matched with systems inside government for sharing knowledge and expertise in policy analytical work. Otherwise, the information and ideas that might be useful in climate change adaptation are unlikely to get to where they may be needed.

In the absence of clearer mandates to assess climate change issues and communicative and coordinating mechanisms across governments to share that information, governance arrangements to address adaptation are poor, even though analytical capacity might in theory be high. Responses to climate change are likely "structurally impaired" (Table 7.1), meaning that considerable interest in adaptation throughout government will produce incoherent and ineffective policy responses. As Canada's environment commissioner noted in his 2010 report, the real problem with climate change adaptation is that no matter how much government departments talk about adaptation strategies or how many isolated programs are discussed and developed to deal with challenges, in the absence of a clear, coordinating *national* strategy, Canadian officials "do not have the capacity to address the scale, magnitude, and long-term effort required to respond to the impacts of climate change in Canada" (Canada, Office of the Auditor General 2010: sec. 3.47).

From a practitioner's perspective there are clear lessons to be learned. The complex properties of an issue like climate change adaptation require that we think more about policy capacity from the perspective of the advising and analyzing functions of public servants, something that has been sorely lost in the era of the new public management.

Governments must redouble their efforts to ensure that they have sufficient analytical resources to assess complex problems. For larger governments like the Canadian federal government, this seems to suggest the continued value of large policy shops that include wide ranges of expertise and staff with different backgrounds and different kinds of training. The federal finance department obviously has considerable analytical capacity, but it is unclear how it can assess scientific questions relating to climate change given the monolithic skills and background of its staff. Large, interdepartmental policy shops (such as the special climate change secretariats with which some jurisdictions have experimented) seem preferable. Shops like these can produce the kind of quality advising needed in this area.

For smaller governments lacking resources, the lesson is equally clear: governments must expand the mechanisms for communicating expertise and knowledge about certain policy problems across agencies and jurisdictions. Many of Canada's provinces and local urban governments are small and lack specialized staff and agencies to deal with problems like climate change adaptation. Given that deficit, the sharing of information from more specialized federal agencies is a necessity. As it stands, there has been no effort in Canada to create collaborative communication mechanisms to fill this gap in relation to climate change adaptation.

References

Anderson, George. 2008. The new focus on policy capacity in the federal government. *Canadian Public Administration* 39 (4) Winter: 469–488.

Bakvis, Herman. 2000. Rebuilding policy capacity in the era of the fiscal dividend: A report from Canada. *Governance* 13 (1) January: 71–103.

Bernier, Luc, and Michael Howlett. 2011. La capacité d'analyse des politiques au gouvernement du Québec: Résultats du sondage auprès de fonctionnaires québécois. *Canadian Public Administration* 54 (1): 143–152.

Canada. Office of the Auditor General. 2010. *Fall 2010 Report of the Commissioner of the Environment and Sustainable Development to the House of Commons.* Ottawa: Minister of Public Works and Government Services Canada. Available from http://www.oag-bvg.gc.ca/internet/docs/parl_cesd_201012_00_e.pdf.

Canada. Office of the Superintendent of Financial Institutions. 2008. *Plans and Priorities 2008–2011.* Available from http://www.osfi-bsif.gc.ca.

Canadian Policy Research Network. 2009. The future of policy capacity in Canada: Roundtable report. Available from http://www.cprn.org/documents/51380_EN.pdf.

Cohen, M., J. March, and J. Olsen. 1972. A garbage can model of organizational choice. *Administrative Science Quarterly* 17 (1): 1–25.

Coleman, William. 1996. *Financial Services, Globalisation and Domestic Policy Change.* London: Macmillan.

Etheridge, Lloyd S. 1981. Government learning: An overview. In *The Handbook of Political Behavior,* Vol. 2, edited by S.L. Long. New York: Pergamon, pp. 73–161.

Hall, Peter. 1993. Policy paradigms, social learning and the state. *Comparative Politics* 25 (3): 275–296.

Harris, Stephen. 2004. Financial services reform in Canada: Interests and the policy process. *Canadian Journal of Political Science* 37 (1) March: 161–184.

Harris, Stephen. 2010. The global financial meltdown and financial regulation: Shirking and learning—Canada in an international context. In *How Ottawa Spends 2010–2011,* edited by G. Bruce Doern and C. Stoney. Montreal and Kingston: McGill-Queen's University Press, pp. 68–86.

Hollander, Robyn. 2009. Rethinking overlap and duplication: Federalism and environmental assessment in Australia. *Publius* 40 (1): 136–170.

Holmes, M., and D. Shand. 1995. Management reform: Some practitioner perspectives on the past ten years. *Governance* 8: 551–578.

Hooghe, Liesbet, and Gary Marks. 2003. Unraveling the central state, but how? Types of multi-level governance. *American Political Science Review* 97 (2) May: 233–243.

Howlett, Michael, and Joshua Newman. 2010. Policy analysis and policy work in federal systems: Policy advice and its contribution to evidence-based policy-making in multi-level governance systems. *Politics and Society* 29: 123–136.

Lindblom, Charles. 1979. Still muddling, not yet through. *Public Administration Review* 39 (5): 517–529.

Oliphant, Samuel, and Michael Howlett. 2010. Assessing policy analytical capacity: Comparative insights from a study of the Canadian environmental policy advice system. *Journal of Comparative Policy Analysis* 12 (4): 439–445.

Peters, B. Guy. 1996. *The Policy Capacity of Government.* Research Paper No. 18. Canadian Centre for Management Development.

Preston, Benjamin L., Richard M. Westaway, and Emma J. Yuen. 2010. Climate adaptation planning in practice: An evaluation of adaptation plans from three developed nations. *Mitigation and Adaptation Strategies for Global Change.* 16 (4): 407–438.

Rose, Richard. 1988. Comparative policy analysis: The program approach. In *Comparing Pluralist Democracies,* edited by M. Dogan. Boulder, CO: Westview Press, pp. 219–241.

Sabatier, Paul. 1987. Knowledge, policy-oriented learning, and policy change. *Knowledge: Creation, Diffusion, Utilization* 8: 649–692.

Scharpf, Fritz W. 1997. Introduction: The problem solving capacity of multi-level governance. *Journal of European Public Policy* 4 (4) December: 520–538.

Schmidt, Vivien A. 2008. Discursive institutionalism: The explanatory power of ideas and discourse. *Annual Review of Political Science* 11: 303–326.

Wellstead, A., R.C. Steadman, and E.A. Lindquist. 2009. The nature of regional policy work in Canada's federal public service. *Canadian Political Science Review* 3 (1): 1–23.

Williams, Russell Alan. 2004. Mergers if necessary, but not necessarily mergers: Competition and consolidation at Canada's "big banks." In *The Real Worlds of Canadian Politics, Cases in Process and Public Policy*, 4th ed., edited by Robert Campbell, Leslie Pal, and Michael Howlett. Toronto: Broadview Press, pp. 155–214.

Williams, Russell Alan. 2009. Exogenous shocks in subsystem adjustment and policy change: The credit crunch and Canadian banking regulation. *Journal of Public Policy* 29 (1): 29–53.

Williams, Russell Alan. 2012. The limits of policy analytical capacity—Canadian financial regulatory reform. *International Journal of Public Sector Management*. Forthcoming.

Chapter 8

Government Fragmentation and Emergency Planning: Findings from the 2009 Red River Flood and Its Aftermath

Nicholas Bauroth

Contents

Introduction

On 28 March 2009, the Red River crested at nearly 41 feet, more than 20 feet above the official flood level (Nowatzki 2009). The surging waters threatened to overwhelm the cities of Fargo and Moorhead, which were protected by an ad hoc collection of temporary and permanent dikes. In the preceding weeks, city officials had called upon residents to volunteer for sandbagging while the governors of Minnesota and North Dakota mobilized their national guards. Thousands responded, working diligently to save their communities. These efforts ultimately proved successful, though not without cost. Damages ran into the hundreds of millions of dollars with at least three deaths attributed to the flood (Kolpack and Suhr 2010). At one point, the Federal Emergency Management Agency (FEMA) suggested evacuating Fargo. "We are not going to abandon our city," responded Fargo Mayor Dennis Walaker. "We've invested too much in this process to walk away from it" (Nowatzki 2009, 1).

The Red River basin of Canada and the United States experienced extensive flooding in 2009. Cities throughout Minnesota, North Dakota, and Manitoba, Canada, watched as the river rose to near unprecedented levels. Even though 2009 was an extreme situation, the Red River has surpassed flood levels every year since 1993. Spring flooding is expected to continue into the foreseeable future. In response, the states of Minnesota and North Dakota, as well as their numerous local governments, developed a regional plan for flood control. This plan would involve the construction of a massive system of diversion channels and dikes using federal, state, and local funds.

Initially, local actors were united on policy, but this consensus soon wavered. By 2011, the city of Fargo found itself pitted against downstream communities, as well as farmers and other landowners directly affected by the new infrastructure.

In contrast, the Canadian province of Manitoba already had an established flood control plan involving both local and provincial actors. The centerpiece of this plan was the Red River Floodway, developed in response to the flood of 1950. However, even though it was still effective in 2009, there were signs that the floodway had reached the limits of its capacity. Consequently, federal and provincial officials expanded the size of the floodway to better protect Winnipeg and other communities.

In this era of decentralization and devolution, nations such as the United States and Canada have transferred much of the responsibility for service provision from the federal governments to, first, the provinces/states and then, finally, to their local governments (Jeffery and Wincott 2006). As governmental fragmentation becomes a universal feature of federalism, the question arises as to whether regional matters can still be settled fairly and effectively. This study considers the development of regional policy within highly fragmented systems of governance. Specifically, it examines whether the local governments within North Dakota and Minnesota are capable of establishing a flood diversion around the city of Fargo. Toward that end, this study analyzes the aftermath of the Red River flood of 2009 and contrasts the experiences of Fargo, North Dakota, to those of Winnipeg, Manitoba, Canada, where the tradition of governmental centralization is much stronger.

Case Study 1: Planning for the North Dakota Diversion

The Red River basin is a collection of streams and tributaries spread across eastern North Dakota, northwestern Minnesota, and southern Manitoba, Canada. The topography of this region is generally quite flat, which allows for widespread flooding after a rapid spring thaw. This flatness makes it difficult to implement traditional flood control techniques on a large scale, such as dams and reservoirs. The center of the basin is the Red River, which runs along the North Dakota–Minnesota border into Canada. It should be noted that the Red River flows south to north.

Table 8.1 examines the Red River counties of North Dakota and Minnesota in terms of population and number of local governments. As can be seen, North Dakota is a rural state with a small population and slow growth between 2000 and 2008 (U.S. Bureau of the Census 2009a). However, the six counties along the North Dakotan side of the Red River are more urban and experienced rapid population growth in recent years. Conversely, Minnesota is a relatively urban state with a large population and steady growth. The six counties along the eastern side of the Red River are more rural than the rest of the state and had a slower population growth rate.

Whereas North Dakota stagnated over the previous decade, Cass County saw its population increase by 13.6 percent (U.S. Bureau of the Census 2009a). Consequently, Cass County, which includes the city of Fargo, now holds 23 percent of the state's population. In addition, the size of the Fargo–Moorhead metropolitan area's economy was recently pegged at $8.1 billion, or one-fourth of North Dakota's total economy (Springer 2010a). This area also provides more than one-fifth of the state's revenues from sales and income taxes.

Clay County, located just across the river from Cass County, also exceeds its state's growth rate (U.S. Bureau of the Census 2009b). However, Clay County contains just two percent of the state population. The fortunes of Cass County matter greatly to North Dakota, but Minnesota is perhaps less concerned about Clay County.

Table 8.1 also shows that Minnesota and North Dakota have very fragmented systems of governance. Minnesota was home to 3,482 local governments in 2002, while North Dakota reported 2,735 units (U.S. Bureau of the Census 2005). This fragmentation is reflected across the Red River counties. The six Red River counties of North Dakota had 494 local governments while their Minnesota counterparts had 330. It should be noted that local governments in the United States are ultimately "creatures of the state" and thereby owe their powers and very existence to their state government. However, Minnesota and North Dakota, like most states, allow considerable leeway to local governments in regard to local concerns.

Table 8.1 Indicators for North Dakota and Minnesota

	North Dakota	North Dakota Red River Counties	Cass County, North Dakota	Minnesota	Minnesota Red River Counties	Clay County, Minnesota
Population in 2008	641,481	248,956	148,956 (23.22%)	5,220,393	113,316	113,316 (2.2%)
Population growth, 2000–2008	–0.10%	5.20%	13.6%	6.10%	0.63%	8.90%
Percent urban 2000	55.90%	73.63%	86.55%	70.9%	48.68%	70.08%
Median household income in 2007	$43,936		$44,747	$55,664		$50,506
Total local governments in 2002	2,735	494	124	3,482	330	53
Cities in 2002	360	81	26	854	63	11

Sources: U.S. Bureau of the Census. 2005. 2002 Census of Governments: Finances of Special Districts. Washington, DC: Government Printing Office; U.S. Bureau of the Census. 2009a. Quick facts: North Dakota. Available from http://quickfacts.census.gov; and U.S. Bureau of the Census. 2009b. Quick facts: Minnesota. Available from http://quick-facts.census.gov. Retrieved 20 November 2009. With permission.

Governmental fragmentation in the Red River basin is expected to have a strong impact upon regional policy, though the direction is difficult to predict. One strain of urban scholarship views the metropolitan area as an interdependent economic, political, and social community (Foster 1997). This strain, known as the reform or consolidation approach, asserts that subdividing the community results in greater inefficiencies, gross inequities, and a predilection for corruption. Consequently, the patchwork systems of municipalities and special districts operating within most metropolitan areas should be replaced by regional governments (Jones 1942; Hawley and Zimmer 1961). Reformers would argue for a single autonomous entity to oversee flood-fighting operations across the Red River basin.

In contrast, the public choice approach asserts that governmental fragmentation is a preferable condition. Metropolitan areas with a variety of small governments provide a better selection of services than areas with just a single government (Hirsch 1964; Hawkins 1976). Citizens who like the mixture of costs and services found within a particular jurisdiction can settle there. If the mixture is not to their liking, citizens can "vote with their feet" and move to another jurisdiction more suited to their tastes (Tiebout 1956). To survive, local governments must enter into a never-ending competition for citizen allegiances. This competition results in greater efficiency and responsiveness across the metropolitan area. Thus, public choice scholars would call for cooperation among local governments across the basin to produce a viable plan.

Choosing a Plan

As the Red River subsided, the affected governments began to work on a regional solution. Because any solution would be contingent upon federal aid, they delegated a central role to the U.S. Army Corps of Engineers. The corps had a long history of working on matters related to flood control, water safety, and environmental remediation in the Upper Midwest (U.S. Army Corp of Engineers 2008). With this acknowledged expertise, the corps took responsibility for pricing the various flood-fighting plans. Final selection would be left, however, to the governments of North Dakota and Minnesota.

Given the number of local governments within the basin, there was some fear that the process would either be overwhelmed by the many competing voices or be curtailed as the state governments imposed their own solution. Instead, the city of Fargo, the city of Moorhead, Cass County, and Clay County formed the Metropolitan Flood Management Committee to oversee the process, a development that the state governments endorsed (Schmidt 2010c). Made up of elected officials from the four participating governments, the committee generally focused upon the long-term interests of Fargo. The committee then established a subgroup to work directly with the Corps of Engineers, called the Metro Flood Management Work Group. The work group consisted of two Fargo city commissioners, three Moorhead city commissioners, two Clay County commissioners, three Cass

County commissioners, an official from the Buffalo Red River Watershed District, and a manager from the Southeast Cass Water Resource District (Olson 2009). The water district officials did not have a vote on the committee, but their participation in the work group was seen as providing representation for rural interests.

Given the desire to start construction by 2013, the planning process followed a tight schedule. The corps requested a letter from local officials by 15 April 2010 describing their preferred flood-fighting plan. The corps required a second letter by 15 July tabulating the finances behind any plan (Schmidt 2010c). The planning process was also designed for speed: as soon as the corps released its latest analysis, the work group would schedule public hearings and then make its recommendations to the committee as a whole. The four member governments of the committee would then vote separately on those recommendations, taking into consideration public input (Schmidt 2009c).

Initially, most actors assumed that U.S. Senator Byron Dorgan (D-ND), a member of the Senate Committee on Appropriations and chair of the Subcommittee on Energy and Water, would shepherd the plan through Congress. However, Senator Dorgan's announcement that he would not seek reelection put this element into doubt (Daum 2010), heightening the sense that the plan had a limited window of opportunity.

While the region waited for the process to unfold, the city of Fargo secured its own share of the expected expenses. On 30 June 2009, 91 percent of Fargo voters approved a half-cent sales tax to pay for a still-to-be-determined flood plan (Schmidt 2009b). This tax was expected to raise $200 million over its 20-year lifetime.

On 20 October 2009, the U.S. Army Corps of Engineers presented its cost–benefit analysis of 11 flood-fighting options to the work group (Schmidt 2009d). Corp officials noted that the federal government would cover up to 65 percent of all costs on an option as long as its yearly benefit-to-cost ratio was greater than 1. Six options met this criterion. The corps recommended that the region pursue the Minnesota diversion option, which involved the construction of a 25-mile channel around Moorhead for $871 million (Schmidt 2010b). This diversion would provide protection from a "once-every-100-years" flood, though not a "once-every-125-years" flood as occurred in 2009.

Despite the corps' recommendation, the work group expressed greater interest in the North Dakota diversion. Under this option, participating governments would spend $1.3 billion on a 36-mile channel around Fargo, thereby protecting the city from a "once-every-500-years" flood (Kolpack 2010). Unfortunately, the corps' initial benefit-to-cost estimates for it were less than 1. Given the implications for federal funding, the corps did a second feasibility study in which economic development was given greater weight. The new study reported that although the Minnesota diversion would give the "biggest bang for the buck," the North Dakota diversion now had a recalibrated score of 1.29, making it eligible for federal funds (Schmidt 2010a).

As the work group deliberated, other local actors attempted to exercise influence. Officials from the city of Dilworth argued against the Minnesota diversion, claiming the planned half-mile-wide channel cut too close to their city. Not only would such a channel prevent further development on the town's eastside, but it would also force the Burlington Northern rail yard to relocate (Springer 2010a). City officials implied that environmental remediation for the rail yard would cost millions of dollars and delay the project. The mayor of Dilworth also claimed that the diversion could have a detrimental effect upon the Buffalo Aquifer, which supplied drinking water throughout the area (Schmidt 2010d).

West Fargo officials accepted the concept of a North Dakota diversion, even though this meant incorporating the existing Sheyenne diversion into the system (Schmidt 2009c). City officials believed the proposed diversion would allow for greater development in areas currently relegated for flood protection (Nowatzki 2009). They expressed disappointment, however, at being excluded from the work group.

Whereas initial estimates by the Corps of Engineers indicated that a diversion would add only one or two inches to flood crests downstream from Fargo, a more complete study indicated that the effect could be ten inches or more (Fargo Forum editorial 2010). This would greatly increase the likelihood of flooding in the northern cities of Hendrum, Georgetown, and Perley (Nowatzki 2010a). Not surprisingly, downstream officials were unhappy with this new assessment. Downstream farmers also expressed their concerns about its potential impact upon their crops.

Meanwhile, farmers closer to Fargo and Moorhead demanded further information on a policy requiring the purchase of thousands of acres of land (Roepke 2009). Maps provided by the corps indicated that the North Dakota diversion would affect at least 141 rural landowners across Cass County (Nowatzki 2010c). These landowners began organizing themselves in anticipation of further action by the corps.

"There's a lot of fear, a lot of volatility," said the manager of the Wild Rice Watershed District about the farmers' predicament. "We really want the cities to get their protection ... but we're worried and we need a seat at the table on this" (Davey 2009, 1).

Reacting to complaints by farmers and other property owners, U.S. Representative Collin Peterson (D-MN) declared that any plan dependent upon a Minnesota diversion would have trouble winning congressional approval (Olson 2009). Agreeing with this assessment, Minnesota Governor Tim Pawlenty added his support for the North Dakota diversion (Olson 2009).

Despite these attempts to influence planning, the key actor on the work group remained the city of Fargo, which favored the North Dakota diversion. Mayor Walaker wanted a plan that would protect Fargo from at least a "once-every-250-year" flood, such as found in Grand Forks (McEwen 2009). He urged the Fargo–Moorhead business community to lobby the state governments for better flood protection, emphasizing the economic costs of disaster (McEwen 2010). Walaker also announced that the city would institute its own flood mitigation plan if the Minnesota diversion was chosen. This fall-back plan would involve the construction of dikes and a series of diversion ditches on the south side of the city (Frank 2010).

On 18 March 2010, the Metro Flood Study Group voted to recommend the North Dakota diversion to the Metropolitan Flood Management Committee (Schmidt 2010f). This recommendation was summarily approved by the Fargo City Commission, the Moorhead City Council, and the Cass and Clay County commissions. In April, the Corps of Engineers agreed to pursue this option (Fargo Forum staff 2010).

Having selected a plan, the region's focus shifted to financing. Assuming congressional approval, the North Dakota diversion would receive $565 million in federal aid. Minnesota would contribute $100 million while North Dakota covered the remaining $730 million (Schmidt 2010e). North Dakota Governor John Hoeven said the state would provide $365 million, leaving local governments responsible for the rest.

To secure its share of the costs, Cass County placed a sales tax increase on the ballot. This measure was approved on 2 November 2010 by a vote of 64 percent to 36 percent (Nowatzki 2010b). Notably, a majority of voters living outside the proposed diversion channel did not favor the tax. However, overwhelming support in Fargo and West Fargo negated this opposition.

The 2010 general elections complicated matters further when a number of long-entrenched federal and state actors either retired or lost altogether. Governor Hoeven replaced Dorgan in the U.S. Senate, allowing for continuity in terms of flood policy. However, whereas Dorgan was a senior senator in a body controlled by his party, Hoeven entered as a freshman member of the minority. In Minnesota, Governor Pawlenty declined to run for reelection.

The Consensus Falters

On 18 November 2010, the Corps of Engineers released further information regarding the North Dakota diversion (Shaffer 2010). Previously, downstream communities had expressed their concerns that the diversion would push floodwaters north, creating high river levels beyond Fargo. The corps sought to alleviate such a situation with storage cells south of Fargo, which would keep excess water in temporary pools on an indeterminate number of acres. While minimizing the downstream effect, these storage cells would greatly impact the upstream cities of Oxbow and Hickson (Nowatzki 2010c). Community leaders in these cities, each home to some 400 residents, quickly announced their opposition to this aspect of the plan.

West Fargo commissioners also expressed concerns about the corps' revisions, arguing that the diversion should be moved further west to allow for additional property development within city limits (Daum 2011). West Fargo Mayor Rich Mattern warned that the city might revoke its support if this shift was not made (Reuer 2011).

On 30 March 2011, the Corps of Engineers revealed that the proposed storage cells would add at least three feet to upstream water levels during a flood (Shaffer 2011). Consequently, every home in Oxbow and Hickson would have to be bought out. These and other expenses added $200 million to the estimated cost of the project (Shaffer 2011). In reaction, government officials from the upstream communities, property owners along the Red River, and other affected parties formed the MinnDak Upstream Coalition in hopes of uniting opposition to the diversion (Springer 2011). The Richland County Commission offered its support by passing an anti-diversion resolution (Fargo Forum staff 2011b). Commissioners of this downstream county of 16,000 people insisted that flood planning take the whole basin into consideration, not just Fargo.

Despite growing opposition, political support for the diversion remained strong. In April, the Cass County Commission, Fargo City Commission, Moorhead City Council, Clay County Board of Commissioners, the Buffalo–Red River Watershed District, and the Southeast Cass Water Resource District passed resolutions reaffirming their support of the North Dakota diversion (Fargo Forum staff 2011a).

Regional Governance

Working through a series of temporary cooperative agreements, local governments in Clay and Cass counties produced a preliminary flood plan. These agreements kept the process on schedule and its focus upon Fargo. However, implementation of this plan would require a permanent means of enforcing cooperation across multiple jurisdictions. Two approaches to this issue came to the forefront.

The first approach called on the federal government to create a public corporation to oversee the Red River basin because a single, all-powerful entity could impose a comprehensive solution across so many jurisdictions (Bismarck Tribune staff 2009). Supporters argued that such an entity would act boldly for the overall good of the region, rather than getting bogged down by the objections of local governments and interest groups. On 28 April 2009, the North Dakota state legislature passed a resolution urging Congress

> to establish the Red River Valley Authority as an agency or authorized board of the federal government for the purpose of the regulation and control of water quality of the Red River and regulation and control of the retention and flow of water, including retention by dams or retention ponds or other areas, and of drainage on the Red River. (North Dakota Senate Concurrent Resolution No. 4035 2009)

The authority would be run by nine officials selected by the governors of Minnesota, North Dakota, and South Dakota, and appointed by the President of the United States. All flood-fighting powers would be centralized within the authority, thereby eliminating potential rivalries with water districts and other traditional flood-fighting bodies. This approach was backed by the Fargo City Commission, which voted unanimously for an identical measure in anticipation of the state resolution (Schmidt 2009a).

Thus, the first reaction by those creating regional policy was to follow the reform perspective: a single autonomous government, in this case a public corporation, was seen as best suited to supply complicated services across the region.

Just how this public corporation would operate was never fully clarified, though supporters pointed to the Tennessee Valley Authority, or TVA, as the most appropriate model (Dalrymple 2009). Currently, the TVA manages a 40,000-square-mile watershed over seven states, determining water policies and running an extensive set of infrastructure. The TVA is overseen by a nine-member board of directors, who are nominated by the President and confirmed by the Senate (Tennessee Valley Authority 2010).

As time passed, though, concerns arose over local control. North Dakota State Senator Tom Fischer, a sponsor of the original senate resolution, wrote a letter to Senator Dorgan reversing his earlier support for a federal authority, saying it would just create "another layer of bureaucracy" (Springer 2010b, 1). Local observers also noted that after the year-long debate over national healthcare reform, "all things 'federal' have lost their cache" (Fargo Forum editorial 2010). The TVA was also denigrated as being an insidious form of "socialism" (Letter to the Editors 2010). Thus, the initial enthusiasm for a single, autonomous entity faded.

Governor Hoeven announced his preference for a compact between the local governments of North Dakota and Minnesota (Springer 2010b), arguing it would serve as an effective substitute for a federal authority. Governor Pawlenty agreed, asserting that, despite allegations to the contrary, local governments could come together and impose a regional solution. Fargo Mayor Walaker expressed reluctance at accepting a partnership among cities and local water boards to determine flood control. He noted that water boards had traditionally been dominated by farmers and other rural interests who gave little consideration to urban concerns (Springer 2010b). He did not, however, reject such partnerships outright.

After flirting with the idea of consolidation, the relevant actors came down in favor of a more public choice approach whereby the various entities within a fragmented environment would cooperate on an issue affecting them all. To achieve permanence, though, this cooperation required an accepted legal template. Fortunately, the state statutes of both Minnesota and North Dakota allow local governments to enter into agreements providing for the "cooperative administration" of a specific project (Metro Flood Diversion Project 2010). Known as "joint power agreements," these agreements do not require approval by the state legislatures or governor. Joint power agreements typically focus upon small-scale matters; they can oversee regional projects such as the proposed North Dakota diversion. Consequently, Fargo, Moorhead, Clay County, and Cass County entered into a series of negotiations on a legal framework for the construction, maintenance, and governance of diversion infrastructure.

So far, this study has focused upon the politics surrounding the proposed North Dakota diversion. To provide a contrasting approach, the analysis will now consider the Red River Floodway of Winnipeg, Manitoba. Although the floodway was constructed during a different period under an alternative form of federalism, the fact that infrastructure similar to the North Dakota diversion was actually built along the Red River will be useful in sorting through today's dynamics. More importantly, comparisons between the two cases provide some insight into the approaches taken by federal systems when confronted with a fragmented environment.

Case Study 2: The Red River Floodway of Winnipeg

The city of Winnipeg is protected from Red River overflow by a 30-mile diversion system known as the Red River Floodway. The floodway was built after severe flooding in 1950 forced more than 100,000 residents, or one-third of Winnipeg's population, to flee (Rannie 1980). Completed in 1968 at a cost of $63 million, the floodway has been used 27 times to alleviate the effects of flooding, reportedly saving the city $30 billion in damages (Farlinger Consulting Group 2010). Despite this record, the structure was nearly overwhelmed by the flood of 1997.

The 1997 flood was perhaps the most significant of the twentieth century (Shrubsole 2000). Thousands of people throughout the basin were forced from their homes, and entire cities, most notably Grand Forks, North Dakota, were inundated (International Joint Commission 2000). Even though Winnipeg endured little damage, the city and provincial leadership were forced to address two issues.

First, the flood flow actually "exceeded the reliable capacity of its flood protection system" (International Joint Commission 2000, 29). Had the Red River risen a little higher, the floodway would have been breached. Thus, the 1997 flood provided a "wake-up call for the city" regarding its supposedly impregnable infrastructure (International Joint Commission 2000, 29).

Second, upstream flooding was actually exacerbated by the floodway (International Joint Commission 2000). Floodway operations brought an additional 2 feet of water to upstream communities (Shrubsole 2000). In subsequent hearings, residents of these communities complained that their interests had become secondary to those of Winnipeg (Manitoba Clean Environment Commission 2005).

In reaction to the "flood of the century," the Manitoba Floodway Authority, in conjunction with the federal government, the Province of Manitoba, Winnipeg, and other cities, set about expanding the capacity of the floodway system. Work on this expansion began in 2005 and continues into 2012.

The Red River Floodway

Manitoba is a large province with a relatively small population, pegged at 1,148,401 in 2006. However, this population had grown by 2.6 percent over the previous five years (Statistics Canada 2007a). The city of Winnipeg is a dominating presence, with 60.5 percent of Manitoba's total population living within its borders, but there are other local governments as well. Statistics Canada (2007b) lists 9 cities, 118 rural municipalities, 52 towns, 20 villages, and 86 Indian reserves. These numbers indicate some degree of fragmentation, but local governance in Minnesota and North Dakota is significantly more fragmented.

Again, it should be noted that Winnipeg and other local governments in Canada are "creatures of the province," meaning that they have only those powers allotted to them by the laws of the province. However, within certain parameters, local governments have some ability to deal with local concerns.

Winnipeg is located on a low-lying plain where the Assiniboine River intersects the Red River, making the city vulnerable to flooding (Canadian Business Journal staff 2010). The most devastating flood came in 1950 when the Red River exceeded the flood stage by twelve feet (Rannie 1980). The province was unprepared as the Red River inundated 640 square miles of land, leading to the evacuation of dozens of communities. Had water levels risen another 1.3 feet, Winnipeg would have been overwhelmed. As it was, some 10,500 houses inside city limits were flooded, producing $100 million in damages.

Once the waters receded, city and provincial agencies sought to alleviate future flooding. Initially, a system of dikes was constructed, but this proved inadequate. In 1956, a provincial Royal Commission was appointed to review options, eventually settling upon a flood diversion plan (Rannie 1980).

Flood fighting in Canada had traditionally been considered a problem best addressed by the affected municipalities. However, the 1950 flood so overwhelmed Winnipeg's resources that the federal government felt obligated to get more involved (Rannie 1980). At first, the federal government would pay for only additional dikes and underwrite studies. It soon became clear, however, that Manitoba could not afford something like the floodway, which would cost $72 million to be paid off over 50 years (Passfield 2001). With annual provincial revenues of just $74 million, Manitoba needed substantial outside assistance. After the 1958 election of Duff Roblin as Premier of Manitoba, the federal government agreed to cover 60 percent of construction costs (Passfield 2001). Excavation began in 1962.

The floodway was designed to minimize the disruption to private property, but hundreds of plots still had to be seized by the province. The project came under criticism for these expropriations, as well as its expense, leading to its nickname "Duff's Ditch" (Suburban Emergency Management Project 2006). Despite these controversies, the floodway was completed in 1968.

Regional Governance

The creation of the Red River flood control system was a top-down affair led by the provincial government in conjunction with federal agencies. In 1950, the province established the Greater Winnipeg Dyking Board to build an initial network of dikes and pumping stations (Passfield 2001). As Winnipeg recovered, the federal Department of Resources and Development offered its recommendations, including a 17-mile-long diversion. The provincial government appointed the Royal Commission on Flood Cost–Benefits to consider these proposals. In 1958, the provincial government signed an agreement with the federal government to build the diversion. Initially, the project would be overseen by the provincial minister of agriculture and conservation. Direct oversight was eventually given to the Red River Floodway Advisory Board, an agency of the Department of Agriculture and Conservation (Passfield 2001).

Once completed, the floodway remained under the control of Manitoba conservation agencies. This changed after the 1997 flood when rural municipalities complained about floodway operations, leading to the creation of the Floodway Operation Review Committee. This committee recommended a greater role for local governments. Consequently, the Floodway Operation Advisory Board was created to counsel the Manitoba Water Stewardship, a Department of Conservation agency dedicated to running the floodway (Red River Floodway Operation Review Committee 1999). Advisory board appointees include representatives from the Manitoba Water Stewardship; the federal government; the Rural Municipalities of Macdonald, Morris and Ritchot; the City of Winnipeg; and the Selkirk and District Planning Board (Manitoba Water Stewardship 2010).

Floodway operations are ultimately controlled by provincial agencies, but local municipalities establish land-use statutes for private development along the flood plain (Shrubsole 2000). Thus, municipalities determine which properties require protection, yet their ability to enforce these statutes varies considerably.

Floodway Expansion

Once the 1997 flood receded, the governments of Canada and the United States had the International Joint Commission study flooding across the basin (International Joint Commission 2000). The Commission placed an emphasis on protecting population centers, a recommendation in line with what the political leadership of Winnipeg and Manitoba ultimately sought. In 2003, the federal and provincial governments announced plans to expand the Red River Floodway (Manitoba Clean Environment Commission 2005). Each government agreed to contribute $80 million toward an expected overall cost of $660 million. Notably, the federal share was set at 50 percent, instead of the 60 percent it contributed during the initial floodway construction (Winnipeg Free Press staff 2003).

The Manitoba government passed the *Floodway Authority Act of 2004*, establishing the Manitoba Floodway Authority as a Crown corporation (Manitoba Clean Environment Commission 2005). As such, the authority would have the power to expand the floodway, as well as gather any necessary licensing and regulatory approvals, while the Manitoba Water Stewardship would still operate the floodway.

In November 2004, a board of directors was named for the Manitoba Floodway Authority, consisting of such civil servants as the secretary to the Treasury Board, the secretary of the Community Economic Development Committee, and the deputy minister of Intergovernmental Affairs and Trade, Finance, Advanced Education and Training, and Water Stewardship (Manitoba Floodway Authority 2006).

The Floodway Expansion Project enlarges the floodway channel, excavates new embankments, and upgrades support infrastructure (Manitoba Floodway Authority 2006). Once completed, floodway capacity will be increased from 60,000 cubic feet of water per second to 140,000. Winnipeg will see its protection increased from a "1-in-90 level of probability" flood to a "1-in-700 level" flood (Manitoba Floodway Authority 2005).

Analysis

Federal governments across the world have experienced considerable decentralization since the 1980s, with power and resources shifting to their subnational entities (Rodden 2004). This decentralization has left local actors with greater control over the creation and implementation of public policy, particularly in the area of economic development (Feiock 2001). Conversely, local actors are better able to stymie policies that they deem detrimental to their long-term interests. Given this situation, two questions arise: (1) are local actors capable of coordinating regional policy with one another, particularly when this policy proves detrimental to some? and (2) what role, if any, should a national government play in balancing the various local interests to achieve regional goals? The examples explored here give some sense of the dynamics at play.

The circumstances surrounding the proposed North Dakota diversion share certain similarities with those associated with the Red River Floodway. These include (1) the most populous and economically important city in the region faced a near-existential threat; (2) this city was unable to resolve this threat by itself; and (3) resolution set the parameters for future regional development. However, the differences between the two cases are more revealing.

First, even though planning for the Red River Floodway was initiated by the Canadian government and the province of Manitoba in response to the 1950 flood, its post-1997 expansion came about after coordination between Canada and the United States as members of the International Joint Commission. In its report on Red River flooding (2000), the Commission emphasized the need to protect population centers, particularly those outside of the city of Winnipeg. This emphasis became a central theme of subsequent planning.

In contrast, planning for the North Dakota diversion has not had a significant international component. Protecting Fargo from future floods is seen by federal, state, and local officials as a domestic concern, with minimal regard given to its impact upon the boundary waters. By excluding international organizations, these officials ensured that fragmented governance would be a key feature of the unfolding process.

Second, construction of the Red River Floodway became possible only after the national government took the lead on policy and financing. The governments of Manitoba and Winnipeg were quickly reduced to subordinate roles. With the national government in charge, coordinating local and provincial actors in support of the plan proved uneventful.

In regard to the North Dakota diversion, the federal government provides considerable technical knowledge and expertise through the U.S. Army Corps of Engineers. Federal dollars will also serve as a crucial source of funding. However, policy will largely be determined by local governments, with some oversight by the states. These entities will also fund much of the diversion through their own resources. Although this arrangement has produced greater local control over the project, it has also allowed for the introduction of discordant politics.

Even though it may be tempting to disparage the disruptive influence of local actors, civil servants need to understand that the days of centralized planning for megaprojects such as the North Dakota diversion are quickly receding. To achieve anything substantial, bureaucrats must invent strategies for dealing with multiple local governments and constituencies. One such strategy can be found in North Dakota: the Corps of Engineers and other agencies incorporated a process that allowed for substantial input by the affected parties. Sometimes this input seemed to put the diversion in doubt. However, the Metropolitan Flood Management Committee kept the project moving forward through a series of votes by its member governments.

Third, the governing structure of the Red River Floodway largely follows the reform model whereby a single entity oversees operations. This entity, ultimately controlled by the provincial government, focuses exclusively upon its mission to protect Winnipeg, even if this proves detrimental to other communities. Although such a governing structure was typical for a 1960s project, its leadership seemed dated and out-of-touch when confronted by local complaints after the 1997 flood.

Supporters of the North Dakota diversion flirted with the idea of a single autonomous government to run operations but ultimately came down in favor of something more in line with the public choice approach. The largest local governments began negotiating with one another over a joint powers agreement to oversee the diversion. Thus, officials appointed by Fargo, Moorhead, Cass County, and Clay County will control the largest piece of flood-fighting infrastructure in the region. However, there are limits to local control: residents living beyond these entities will have little recourse when dealing with the diversion.

Finally, this study indicates that local actors in a fragmented environment are capable of creating and implementing regional policy. However, they are also capable of ruining consensus and producing a dead end in terms of policy. The debate over the North Dakota diversion will not be settled until Congress appropriates federal funding. Thus, on an ironic resolution, the federal government's decision to fund will ultimately end conflict between local governments.

References

Bismarck Tribune staff. 2009. Resolution seeks federal authority. *Bismarck Tribune*, 2 April. Available from http://bismarcktribune.com/news/state-and-regional/resolution-seeks-federal-authority/article_4b36b4fd-84ae-5b49-b1fb-e78be23abdfc.html. Retrieved 9 April 2010.

Canadian Business Journal staff. 2010. Manitoba Floodway Authority. *Canadian Business Journal*, 10 February. Available from http://www.cbj.ca/business_in_action/february_10/manitoba_floodway_authority.html. Retrieved 19 May 2011.

Dalrymple, Amy. 2009. Basin authority wouldn't be a first. *Fargo Forum,* 14 June.

Daum, Kristen. 2010. 3 down, 1 to go. *Fargo Forum,* 23 March: A1.

Daum, Kristen. 2011. WF to revisit support for diversion. *Fargo Forum,* 2 January: C1.

Davey, Monica. 2009. Red River flooding solution is a problem to some. *New York Times,* 29 December.

Fargo Forum editorial. 2010. Managing watershed not likely. *Fargo Forum*, 2 March: C2.

Fargo Forum staff. 2010. Corps to request approval of North Dakota Diversion. *Fargo Forum*, 2 April. Available from http://beta.inforum.com/event/article/id/274147/. Retrieved 5 May 2011.

Fargo Forum staff. 2011a. Local councils reaffirm support for ND diversion. *Fargo Forum*, 5 April: A1.

Fargo Forum staff. 2011b. Richland County opposes F-M diversion. *Fargo Forum*, 19 April: A6.

Farlinger Consulting Group. 2010. *Red River Floodway: Public Consultation on the Rules of Operation*. Manitoba: Westdal & Associates.

Feiock, Richard. 2001. A quasi-market framework for local economic development competition. *Journal of Urban Affairs* 24: 123–142.

Foster, Kathryn. 1997. *The Political Economy of Special-Purpose Government*. Washington, DC: Georgetown University Press.

Frank, Tracy. 2010. Walaker says Fargo will pursue South Side Flood Plan if smaller diversion chosen. *Fargo Forum,* 11 March.

Hawkins, Robert. 1976. *Self Government by District*. Stanford: Hoover Institution Press.

Hawley, Amos, and Basil Zimmer. 1961. Resistance to unification in a metropolitan community. In *Community Political Systems*, edited by Morris Janowitz. New York: Free Press. pp. 148–184.

Hirsch, Werner Z. 1964. Local versus area-wide urban government services. *National Tax Journal* 17: 331–339.

International Joint Commission. 2000. *Living with the Red: A Report to the Governments of Canada and the United States on Reducing Flood Impacts in the Red River Basin*. Washington, DC: International Joint Commission.

Jeffery, Charlie, and Daniel Wincott. 2006. Devolution in the United Kingdom: Statehood and citizenship in transition. *Publius: The Journal of Federalism* 36 (1): 3–18.

Jones, Victor. 1942. *Metropolitan Government*. Chicago: University of Chicago Press.

Kolpack, Jeff. 2010. Area officials debate flood projects. *Fargo Forum,* 1 February: C1.

Kolpack, Jeff, and Jim Suhr. 2010. F-M not alone in U.S. flooding. *Fargo Forum,* 6 March: A1.

Letter to the Editors. 2010. Opening to debate common good? *Fargo Forum,* 13 March.

Manitoba Clean Environment Commission. 2005. *Red River Floodway Expansion: Report on Public Hearing*. Winnipeg: Manitoba Clean Environment Commission.

Manitoba Floodway Authority. 2005. What is floodway expansion? Available from http://www.floodwayauthority.mb.ca/floodway_expansion.html. Retrieved 28 May 2011.

Manitoba Floodway Authority. 2006. *2006 Annual Report.* Winnipeg: Manitoba Floodway Authority.

Manitoba Water Stewardship. 2010. *A Public Review of the Rules of Operation for the Red River Floodway.* Winnipeg MB: Manitoba Water Stewardship.

McEwen, Craig. 2009. Fargo-Moorhead officials agree communities can't afford $2.5 billion disaster. *Fargo Forum,* 28 June.

McEwen, Craig. 2010. F-M businesses urged to support flood-fight plan. *Fargo Forum,* 12 March.

Metro Flood Diversion Project. 2010. Limited Joint Powers Agreement. Retrieved 24 February 2012. Available from http://www.fmdiversion.com/pdf/08%2012%202011%20-%20Limited%20Joint%20Powers%20Agreement.pdf.

North Dakota Senate Concurrent Resolution No. 4035. 2009. North Dakota State Legislature.

Nowatzki, Mike. 2009. Fargo defends decision not to evacuate. *Fargo Forum,* 30 March: C3.

Nowatzki, Mike. 2010a. Landowners organize to oppose diversion. *Fargo Forum,* 11 April: A1.

Nowatzki, Mike. 2010b. Cass approves diversion sales tax. *Fargo Forum,* 2 November: A1.

Nowatzki, Mike. 2010c. New plan is "scary" for those upstream. *Fargo Forum,* 20 November: A1.

Olson, Dave. 2009. Flood Management Work Group aims to find consensus. *Fargo Forum,* 24 October: A1.

Passfield, Robert W. 2001. "Duff's Ditch": The origins, construction, and impact of the Red River Floodway. *Manitoba History* 42 (Autumn/Winter).

Rannie, W.F. 1980. The Red River flood control system and recent flood events. *Water Resources Bulletin* 16 (2): 207–214.

Red River Floodway Operation Review Committee. 1999. *A Review of the Red River Floodway Operating Rules.* Winnipeg: Floodway Operation Review Committee.

Reuer, Wendy. 2011. WF gives diversion one more chance. *Fargo Forum,* 4 January: A1.

Rodden, Jonathan. 2004. Comparative federalism: On meaning and measurement. *Comparative Politics* 36 (4): 481–500.

Roepke, Dave. 2009. ND, Minn. Want Flood Force. *Fargo Forum,* 6 May: A1.

Schmidt, Helmut. 2009a. Fargo seeks Red River Valley Authority. *Fargo Forum,* 7 April: A1.

Schmidt, Helmut. 2009b. Fargo voters OK tax. *Fargo Forum,* 1 July: A1.

Schmidt, Helmut. 2009c. Dilworth, WF unhappy about being left out of diversion talks. *Fargo Forum,* 25 October: A1.

Schmidt, Helmut. 2009d. F-M group narrows flood fight options. *Fargo Forum,* 6 November: A1.

Schmidt, Helmut. 2010a. ND plans fill corps criteria, but Minn. option preferred. *Fargo Forum,* 2 February: A1.

Schmidt, Helmut. 2010b. Officials weigh how to pay for diversion project. *Fargo Forum,* 2 February: A4.

Schmidt, Helmut. 2010c. Flood work group digs into financing, ownership issues. *Fargo Forum,* 15 January. Available from http://dev3.inforum.com/event/article/id/265990/. Retrieved 5 May 2011.

Schmidt, Helmut. 2010d. No easy choices on flood control. *Fargo Forum,* 2 February: A1.

Schmidt, Helmut. 2010e. Fargo, Cass group to meet on sales tax. *Fargo Forum,* 30 March: A1.

Schmidt, Helmut. 2010f. ND diversion gets OK. *Fargo Forum,* 19 March, A1.

Shaffer, Heidi. 2010. New details of Fargo-Moorhead diversion shift more water upstream. *Fargo Forum,* 18 November.

Shaffer, Heidi. 2011. Diversion price tag rises. *Fargo Forum*, 31 March: A1.

Shrubsole, Dan. 2000. Flood management in Canada at the crossroads. *Environmental Hazards* 2: 63–75.

Springer, Patrick. 2010a. Mayor: Divert to ND. *Fargo Forum*, 19 February: A1.

Springer, Patrick. 2010b. Leaders endorsing ND, Minn. oversight. *Fargo Forum*, 1 March: A1.

Springer, Patrick. 2011. New diversion foes: MinnDak upstream coalition forms to try to stop project. *Fargo Forum*, 4 April: A1.

Statistics Canada. 2007a. *2006 Community Profiles*. Statistics Canada Catalogue no. 92-591-XWE. Ottawa. Released 13 March 2007.

Statistics Canada. 2007b. Winnipeg, Manitoba (Code4611040) (table). 2006 Community Profiles. *2006 Census*. Statistics Canada Catalogue no. 92-591-XWE. Ottawa. Released 13 March.

Suburban Emergency Management Project. 2006. *Duff's Daring Ditch: Canada's Unbridled Success in Building the Red River Floodway to Protect Winnipeg after the Great Flood of 1950*. Biot Report #392. Lisle, IL: Suburban Emergency Management Project.

Tennessee Valley Authority. 2010. TVA: Board of Directors. Available from http://www.tva.com/abouttva/board/index.htm. Retrieved 1 March 2010.

Tiebout, Charles. 1956. A pure theory of local expenditures. *Journal of Political Economy* 64 (5).

U.S. Army Corp of Engineers (St. Paul District). 2008. *Fargo-Moorhead Metropolitan Area Reconnaissance Study*. St. Paul, MN: U.S. Army Corps of Engineers.

U.S. Bureau of the Census. 2005. *2002 Census of Governments: Finances of Special Districts*. Washington, DC: Government Printing Office.

U.S. Bureau of the Census. 2009a. Quick facts: North Dakota. Available from http://quickfacts.census.gov. Retrieved 20 November 2007.

U.S. Bureau of the Census. 2009b. Quick facts: Minnesota. Available from http://quickfacts.census.gov. Retrieved 20 November 2007.

Winnipeg Free Press staff. 2003. Half-hearted help. *Winnipeg Free Press*, 1 April: A10.

Chapter 9

The Importance of Multilevel Governance Participation in the "Great Lakes Areas of Concern"

Thomas J. Greitens, J. Cherie Strachan, and Craig S. Welton

Contents

Introduction

This chapter examines the influence of multilevel governance actors on program success. As policy problems such as environmental pollution become more complex and cross more governmental boundaries, multilevel governance systems, in which local, subnational (e.g., American states and Canadian provinces), national, and international governments cooperate on solving problems, become more important. An especially vital part of such complex relationships is the role of local and subnational governments. The involvement (or lack of involvement) of these actors often has a direct impact on whether multilevel governance programs succeed or fail. Consequently, this study examines the role of these lower-level governmental actors in the "Great Lakes Areas of Concern" and whether their involvement led to successful program outcomes.

Subnational and local governmental actors are now vital components of public management because they help to decentralize decision making, marking a shift from the prototypical (perhaps even mythological) model of a centralized, national government issuing mandates with little or no input from affected parties. In the twenty-first century, governance now depends on a decentralized approach that emphasizes more intergovernmental involvement, intersectoral collaboration, and active participation from citizens. Decentralization has influenced both the study and practice of public management in positive and negative ways over the last 25 years. Perhaps on the negative side, public management has often been interpreted as validating the view that public programs should rely more on intersectoral partners such as private contractors to implement programs (Scott, Ball, and Dale 1997). On the positive side, however, public management has helped to reinterpret the importance of collaboration and the role of the public and lower orders of government in meeting the challenges of governance. Intergovernmental relationships that allow information to be shared and participants to work together to solve problems are arguably now a central component of good governance (Kettl 1997). A subtle shift has occurred such that the views of the public and other decentralized actors have become valued. Although the ultimate effect of this type of decentralized participation on policy is still debatable (for a more positive perspective see Frederickson 1997; Box 1998; Kovalick Jr. and Kelly 1998; Yang and Callahan 2007; O'Flynn 2010; and for a more negative perspective see Beierle and Konisky 2001; Wang 2001; Beierle and Cayford 2002), it has helped to reshape the role of citizens, subnational governments, and local governments from receivers of programs from the national government to active participants in the process of determining how best to implement those programs. Correspondingly, such a view has helped subnational and local governments to be more actively represented in multilevel governance efforts.

Environmental remediation efforts around the Great Lakes have depended on this new face of public management, with its emphasis on the involvement of multiple orders of government, collaboration between the public and private spheres, public participation, and decentralized decision making. The following sections outline those remediation efforts and examine whether or not differences in the participation of subnational (e.g., U.S. states or Canadian provinces) and local governments had any indirect influence on their success. Additionally, differences in the participation of subnational and local governments in Canada and the United States are analyzed to determine if significant variations in subnational and local government participation exist between these two countries.

Presentation of the Case: The Great Lakes Areas of Concern

Management of environmental concerns around the Great Lakes has always emphasized collaboration because Great Lakes ecosystems span multiple governmental jurisdictions. In 1901, the United States and Canada formed the International Joint Commission (IJC), which is a permanent, bi-national organization that exists to help resolve conflicts on water issues between the two countries (International Joint Commission 2006). Its governance is quasi-judicial and depends on active representation from governmental actors from both countries as well as academia (MacKenzie 1996). In 1972 and 1978, the IJC helped to negotiate the Great Lakes Water Quality Agreements; the IJC was also instrumental in the negotiation of amendments to the agreements in 1987 (International Joint Commission 2006).

The 1987 amendments remain particularly relevant as they specifically identified 43 Great Lakes Areas of Concern (GLAC or AOC in governmental documents) with impaired beneficial uses ranging from fishing to recreation to industry (Great Lakes Commission 2002) (see Table 9.1). Additionally, the 1987 amendments established a process for restoring these areas. Participants in each area of concern had to follow a three-stage remedial action plan (RAP) process to reach the ultimate goal of being "delisted" from the areas of concern. In stage one, the AOC had to identify both the scope and cause of environmental degradation that contributed to beneficial use impairment. In stage two, the AOC had to identify specific goals and recommend actions to help the restoration of beneficial uses and, ultimately, the protection of the ecosystem. These actions were then to be implemented in stage three, as were measures of restoration progress and ecosystem health. In each stage, the AOC had to complete an official report and submit it to the IJC for review. If the IJC approved, then the AOC could proceed to the next RAP stage. After IJC approval of stage three and implementation of the remediation strategy, the area would be "delisted" if the remediation goals identified in the RAP had been achieved. The decision to "delist" an AOC was (and remains) a collaborative effort dependent on national, subnational, and local governments as well as on various RAP participants and the IJC (MacKenzie 1996).

Table 9.1 The Great Lakes Areas of Concern (GLAC)

Canada	United States	Jointly Administered
Bay of Quinte	Ashtabula River, OH	Detroit River, MI
Collingwood Harbour	Black River, OH	Niagara River, NY
Hamilton Harbour	Buffalo River, NY	St. Clair River, MI
Jackfish Bay	Clinton River, MI	St. Lawrence River, NY
Nipigon Bay	Cuyahoga River, OH	St. Marys River, MI
Peninsula Harbour	Deer Lake, MI	
Port Hope	Eighteen Mile Creek, NY	
Severn Sound	Grand Calumet River, IN	
Spanish Harbour	Kalamazoo River, MI	
Thunder Bay	Lower Fox River/Green Bay, WI	
Toronto and Region		
Wheatley Harbour	Manistique River, MI	
	Maumee River, OH	
	Menominee River, WI	
	Milwaukee Estuary, WI	
	Muskegon Lake, MI	
	Oswego River/Harbor, NY	
	Presque Isle Bay, PA	
	River Raisin, MI	
	Rochester Embayment, NY	
	Rouge River, MI	
	Saginaw River and Bay, MI	
	Sheboygan River, WI	
	St. Louis River and Bay, MN/WI	
	Torch Lake, MI	
	Waukegan Harbor, IL	
	White Lake, MI	

Inherent in the RAP process was a reliance on ecosystem-based management, which tended to focus on multiple environmental dimensions (e.g., air, water, and soil were considered all at once) with interdisciplinary participants from the AOC (e.g., governments, industry, environmental groups, and the public) working together in order to implement a successful remediation strategy for the AOC's entire ecosystem (Great Lakes Water Quality Agreement 1994). Decisions were decentralized. Participants from national, subnational (e.g., U.S. state or Canadian provincial governments), and local governments; industry and environmental stakeholders; academia; and the public at large had to develop a deliberative process to allow for the eventual completion of all three RAP stages (and hopefully delisting from the GLAC). This entailed agreeing to a decision-making process, the goals and objectives to guide the process, and who should be involved in the process (Sproule-Jones 2002). As a result, from the beginning, the RAP strategy relied on the core tenets of public management—namely, collaboration, citizen participation, and decisions—coming from the bottom up rather than from the top down.* Almost all of the 43 areas of concern initiated the RAP process with impressive participation from governments, industry, environmental groups, academia, and the public in the late 1980s and early 1990s. Typically at the start of the process, each GLAC would form a public advisory committee (PAC) where the governments and all other stakeholders and citizens from an AOC would meet to deliberate on the issue and to formulate a strategy to complete an official RAP report that would then be sent to the IJC for approval. By 2011, however, only four areas of concern (one in the United States, three in Canada) had been delisted and only two additional areas of concern had submitted the preliminary stage three documents necessary for future delisting. Almost every area of concern had made some progress on remediation, but most seemed stuck in the first and second stages of the RAP process.

The reasons for this are many. Some of the AOCs faced such severe environmental degradation that only national governments could have successfully remediated the area, but national governments often lacked both the political will and the financial resources for such an effort (Rabe 1999). Some of the AOCs, especially many of those located in Michigan, had local governments that were given the opportunity to participate in decision making but declined or dropped out because of fears over possible financial obligations for remediation (MacKenzie 1996). Additionally, many PACs within an AOC failed due to questions of their legitimacy. In one case, outside academic interests and the subnational government controlled the PAC to such an extent that many local governments did not believe their input would be taken seriously (MacKenzie 1996).

A comprehensive analysis of participation in each AOC has never been done. Instead, scholars have usually focused on a few specific AOC cases. Typically, these

---

* Some of the communities involved in the Great Lakes Areas of Concern RAP process had an exclusive rather than inclusive process for citizen deliberation; that is, a small number of communities used multilevel government actors as gatekeepers for citizen deliberation. These actors specifically excluded some environmental groups and Aboriginal populations in a small number of communities and thus restricted citizen deliberation. Most analyses indicate, however, that the majority of communities involved in the Great Lakes Areas of Concern RAP process had an inclusive process for citizen deliberation. (See Sproule-Jones, 2002, for a more detailed discussion of this issue.)

cases have revealed the importance of local governmental and local stakeholder participation. For example, cases in the Oswego, New York, AOC reveal high levels of local government involvement, with local governments and business leaders using the RAP process to spearhead renewed economic development interests (New York Department of Environmental Conservation 2006). Other issues, such as levels of existing pollution and funding, perhaps explain more directly a successful delisting outcome, and the participation and buy-in of local governmental actors and other local participants in the PAC deliberative process must also be acknowledged as factors in the delisting of Oswego as an area of concern—the only American AOC to be delisted as of 2011.

Assessment of Participation in the Great Lakes Areas of Concern

The RAP process in the Great Lakes Areas of Concern is now over two decades old. During that time, the initial PAC of each AOC either transformed into a new organization representing the AOC, met on an infrequent basis, or simply stopped meeting after a stage one report had been completed. As a result, measuring participation levels of subnational and local governmental actors in the RAP process for a comprehensive analysis becomes problematic. The RAP documents are also of limited use because some RAP documents list all of the PAC representatives, but others do not. In addition, even in those RAP documents that list the representatives, specific information on participants is often not mentioned. For example, many RAP documents simply state that local governments participated, but they do not indicate which local governments were participants.

Consequently, we examined recent Great Lakes documents and Web sites to identify major partners and stakeholders listed by the agencies as important and active participants in the RAP process as of June 2011. The list of these major partners and stakeholders emerged from documents such as overviews of RAP implementation in the Great Lakes (Great Lakes Commission 2002) and the Great Lakes Areas of Concern Web sites from the U.S. Environmental Protection Agency (http://www.epa.gov/glnpo/aoc/) and Environment Canada (http://www.ec.gc.ca/raps-pas/). Such listings are admittedly imperfect. They may leave out important early participants in the RAP process in the late 1980s and early 1990s. The agencies may also make errors in constructing the lists for their documents and Web sites.

However, there are advantages to using the lists. First, the lists provide a snapshot of who the agencies think are the most important participants in the RAP process. Outdated participants or minor participants who do not influence the process substantially would presumably be excluded from such a public list. The listed participants should be those actors who have deliberated in the RAP process and who have become authentic, legitimate participants in the process over the years.

Second, the lists provide a degree of participant standardization not attainable from any other documents. As mentioned previously, some AOCs produce RAP documents that list participants, but others do not. Also, some AOCs stopped listing the participants after the RAP stage one document (typically formed in the late 1980s or early 1990s). RAP documents from the same AOC may not list participants who took part in subsequent RAP stages.

Therefore, we coded the listed partners and stakeholders (who we will now refer to as participants) for each AOC according to a simplified protocol (see Appendix) that grouped governmental actors into two categories. Direct actors were those governmental actors who represented their government directly during the process. Indirect actors were coalitions of different governmental actors who joined together to form one organization that then represented their interests during the process. For example, if an actor from the city of Windsor participated, then it was coded as a local government actor. But if the Southeast Michigan Council of Governments participated, then it was coded as an inter-local government coalition providing a type of indirect representation for all of its members.

Web sites for the actors were analyzed to determine the level of government actor and the type of coalition. If no information on the actor could be ascertained, or if the actor represented only non-government organizations, then the actor was classified as "other." From the United States, 616 stakeholders and partners were coded, and 210 stakeholders and partners from Canada were coded. For this analysis, these 826 actors are considered the major, active participants in the Great Lakes Areas of Concern.

These participants were coded to answer the following research questions about participation levels of subnational and local government actors in the RAP process. First, did more participation from subnational and local levels of government help to influence the RAP process in a positive way? Second, did more participation from subnational and local levels of government help to influence delisting actions in a positive way? Third, did more participation from subnational and local levels of government help to ensure that the original RAP public advisory committee (PAC) would survive into the 2000s? Fourth, did the United States and Canada exhibit any significant differences in the participation rates of their subnational and local levels of government during the RAP process? Although environmental outcomes are hard to link to participation (see Beierle and Cayford 2002), based on most of the existing literature on participation and deliberation, we would expect that more subnational and especially local governmental influence would result in the completion of more RAP stages, the achievement of delisting, and the survival of RAP PACs. Underlying all of these questions is also the issue of "direct influence" and "indirect influence." In other words, did the direct or indirect participation of governmental actors help to influence the RAP process, delisting actions, and RAP PAC survival? And, did differences exist in the use of direct and indirect influence in the United States and Canada?

To help answer these research questions we analyzed the composition of partici-pants for each AOC. We totaled all of the participants in the AOC and divided that number by the coded category totals mentioned above. That calculation resulted in interval level percentages that could be easily analyzed. Additionally, for a more comprehensive view of local governmental participation, we added the additional variable of "percentage of total local government actors." This variable represents the sum of all local governmental variables (city/town government actors, county government actors, and special district government actors).

It should be noted that this analysis is not deterministic; that is, we are not trying to explain all of the variables that influence the RAP process, delisting, and RAP PAC survival. Instead, this analysis attempts to determine if the issue of sub-national and local governmental participation is associated with the RAP process, delisting, and RAP PAC survival. By examining subnational and local government participation, this analysis hopes to determine whether it should be an issue for further study in order to make public management and deliberation/citizen partici-pation more effective in the future.

Results of the Assessment

Results for the first research question of whether more participation from subna-tional and local levels of government helped to influence the RAP process in a positive way are shown in Tables 9.2 through 9.4. As observed in Table 9.2, the percentage of local government actors typically increases as more RAP stages are achieved. This is especially true for the "total local government actor" variable. AOCs had total local government participation rates as low as 6.67 percent for RAP stage zero, 13.9 percent for RAP stage one, 20 percent for RAP stage two, and as high as 28.1 percent for RAP stage three. The largest change appears to be in those AOCs that reached RAP stage three. For those AOCs, 18.1 percent of their participants were city/town government actors compared to 6.67 percent for AOCs in RAP stage zero. The percentage of subnational government actors also increased as more RAP stages were reached. Because achieving more RAP stages indicates that the remediation strategy is being developed and implemented, the average per-centage participation rates indicate that higher RAP stages are typically associated with higher levels of subnational and local governmental participation.

Of note is the dominance of national governmental participation in those AOCs that did not achieve any RAP stage (i.e., RAP stage zero). For those AOCs, the national government comprised 71.7 percent of the participants as opposed to just 19.8 percent of participants in those AOCs that achieved RAP stage three. Additionally, the dominance of direct participation rather than indirect participa-tion suggests that most governments still preferred to participate directly in the RAP process as opposed to having an umbrella organization indirectly represent their interests.

Table 9.2 Average Composition Percentages for Major Participants Involved in the Remedial Action Plan (RAP) Process in Each Great Lakes Area of Concern, by RAP Stage Achieved

	RAP Stage			
	0	**1**	**2**	**3**
Direct Influence				
Percent of city/town government actors	6.67	9.30	9.00	18.1
Percent of county government actors	0	2.34	4.53	3.91
Percent of special district government actors	0	2.28	6.47	6.14
Percent of subnational government actors	13.3	17.1	18.6	20.3
Percent of national government actors	71.7	16.2	22.2	19.8
Percent of tribal government actors	0	0.620	0.700	0
Percent total local government actors	6.67	13.9	20.0	28.1
Indirect Influence				
Percent of inter-local government coalitions	0	1.42	0.580	0
Percent of intergovernmental coalitions	0	3.24	2.40	0.880
Percent of international coalitions	8.33	4.48	1.91	0.880
Percent of intersectoral coalitions	0	15.7	4.37	1.08
Totals				
Total direct percent	91.7	47.8	61.5	68.1
Total indirect percent	8.3	24.9	9.26	2.83
N	3	19	15	6

Table 9.3 uses ANOVA to determine if there are statistically significant differences in participation based on RAP stage. The results indicate that the observed differences were generally not statistically significant. However, differences in national government actors, intersectoral coalitions, and total and indirect participation were significant. Table 9.4 shows a post hoc ANOVA analysis using the Bonferroni procedure that allows for a determination of which categories were statistically different. Table 9.4 reveals that most statistically significant differences occurred between those AOCs in RAP stage zero and those AOCs in the other

Table 9.3   ANOVA Results for Average Composition Percentages for Major Participants Involved in the Remedial Action Plan (RAP) Process in Each Great Lakes Area of Concern, by RAP Stage Achieved

	F	Significance
Direct Influence		
Percent of city/town government actors	0.718	0.547
Percent of county government actors	0.875	0.462
Percent of special district government actors	3.39	0.270
Percent of subnational government actors	0.173	0.914
Percent of national government actors[a]	11.6	0.000
Percent of tribal government actors	0.449	0.719
Percent total local government actors	1.812	0.161
Indirect Influence		
Percent of inter-local government coalitions	0.388	0.762
Percent of intergovernmental coalitions	0.697	0.559
Percent of international coalitions	1.20	0.324
Percent of intersectoral coalitions[a]	6.38	0.001
Totals		
Total direct percent[a]	4.54	0.008
Total indirect percent[a]	5.51	0.003

[a] <0.10.

RAP stages. These specific differences seem to confirm the idea that participation by government was different for AOCs in RAP stage zero as opposed to AOCs that reached higher RAP stages.

Results for the second research question of whether more subnational and local government participation resulted in delisting are presented in Tables 9.5 and 9.6. Once again, results in Table 9.5 seem to indicate not only a greater percentage of subnational and local government participation for those AOCs that were delisted, but also an increase in direct participation rates for those delisted AOCs. Because there are only two categories ("no delisting" or "delisting") for the second research question, a *t*-test was used to show significant differences between the variables. The *t*-test revealed significant differences for total local government actors, total direct

Table 9.4 ANOVA Post Hoc Comparison (Bonferroni Correction) for Average Composition Percentages for Major Participants Involved in the Remedial Action Plan (RAP) Process in Each Great Lakes Area of Concern, by RAP Stage Achieved (Only Statistically Significant Results Shown)

	Difference between Groups	Mean Difference	Significance
Direct Influence			
Percent of city/town government actors	—	—	—
Percent of county government actors	—	—	—
Percent of special district government actors	RAP stages 1 and 2	−0.04196	0.080
Percent of subnational government actors	—	—	—
Percent of national government actors	RAP stages 0 and 1	0.5550	0.000
	RAP stages 0 and 2	0.4951	0.000
	RAP stages 0 and 3	0.5191	0.000
Percent of tribal government actors	—	—	—
Percent total local government actors	—	—	—
Indirect Influence			
Percent of inter-local government coalitions	—	—	—
Percent of intergovernmental coalitions	—	—	—
Percent of international coalitions	—	—	—
Percent of intersectoral coalitions	RAP stages 0 and 1	−0.1572	0.076
	RAP stages 1 and 2	0.1135	0.010
	RAP stages 1 and 3	0.1465	0.015
Totals			
Total direct percent	RAP stages 0 and 1	0.4388	0.012
Total indirect percent	RAP stages 1 and 2	0.1561	0.018
	RAP stages 1 and 3	0.2203	0.012

Table 9.5   Average Composition Percentages for Major Participants Involved in Remedial Action Plan (RAP) Process in Each Great Lakes Area of Concern, by Delisted Outcome (as of June 2011)

	No Delisting	Delisting Achieved
Direct Influence		
Percent of city/town government actors	9.18	20.6
Percent of county government actors	2.99	4.84
Percent of special district government actors	4.01	5.18
Percent of subnational government actors	17.1	25.1
Percent of national government actors	22.4	25.1
Percent of tribal government actors	5.70	0
Percent total local government actors	16.2	30.6
Indirect Influence		
Percent of inter-local government coalitions	0.910	0
Percent of intergovernmental coalitions	2.55	0.810
Percent of international coalitions	3.61	0.810
Percent of intersectoral coalitions	9.34	1.61
Totals		
Total direct percent	56.2	80.8
Total indirect percent	16.4	3.23
N	39	4

participation, and total indirect participation. Thus, those delisted AOCs were different in terms of participation from AOCs that were not delisted. The delisted AOCs had a greater percentage of participating local government actors and also relied more on direct governmental representation in the participation endeavor.

Results for the third research question on whether more participation from subnational and local levels of government helps to ensure that the original RAP public advisory committee (PAC) would survive into the 2000s are presented in Tables 9.7 and 9.8. Table 9.7 indicates that slightly more local government actors

Table 9.6 Differences in Major Participants Based on Delisting Outcome (as of June 2011) (Equality of Variances Assumed)

	t	Significance
Direct Influence		
Percent of city/town government actors	−1.549	0.129
Percent of county government actors	−0.663	0.511
Percent of special district government actors	−0.436	0.665
Percent of subnational government actors	−1.060	0.295
Percent of national government actors	−0.254	0.801
Percent of tribal government actors	0.727	0.472
Percent total local government actors[a]	−1.723	0.092
Indirect Influence		
Percent of inter-local government coalitions	0.514	0.610
Percent of intergovernmental coalitions	0.724	0.473
Percent of international coalitions	0.775	0.443
Percent of intersectoral coalitions	1.303	0.200
Totals		
Total direct percent[a]	−2.043	0.048
Total indirect percent[a]	1.558	0.127

[a] <0.10.

were participating in those AOCs whose RAP PAC survived in some capacity into the 2000s. For example, in those AOCs whose RAP PAC disbanded, the total percentage of local government actors was 11.4 percent, whereas in those AOCs with surviving RAP PACs, the total percentage of local government actors was 18.7 percent. The biggest difference, however, was for subnational government actors, who comprised 5.62 percent of the stakeholders and partners in those AOCs whose RAP PAC failed, and 20.2 percent of the stakeholders and partners in those AOCs that survived. Table 9.8 shows the *t*-test results and indicates that statistically significant differences only existed for the subnational government actors and the international coalitions. The international coalition finding is somewhat confounding. Tables 9.7 and 9.8 seem to indicate that when more international coalitions are identified as partners and stakeholders, the RAP PAC is more likely to be absent.

Table 9.7 Average Composition Percentages for Major Participants Involved in the Remedial Action Plan (RAP) Process in Each Great Lakes Area of Concern, by Original RAP Public Advisory Committee (PAC) Presence in 2011 (as of June 2011)

	Original RAP PAC Absent	Original RAP Present or Transformed
Direct Influence		
Percent of city/town government actors	4.84	11.3
Percent of county government actors	4.40	2.92
Percent of special district government actors	2.15	4.50
Percent of subnational government actors	5.62	20.2
Percent of national government actors	33.7	20.5
Percent of tribal government actors	0.390	0.550
Percent total local government actors	11.4	18.7
Indirect Influence		
Percent of inter-local government coalitions	0	0.990
Percent of intergovernmental coalitions	3.04	2.26
Percent of international coalitions	9.50	2.15
Percent of intersectoral coalitions	6.93	8.95
Totals		
Total direct percent	51.1	59.9
Total indirect percent	19.5	14.4
N	7	36

Table 9.8   Differences in Major Participants Based on 2011 RAP Public Advisory Committee (PAC) Presence in June 2011 (Equality of Variances Assumed)

	t	Significance
Direct Influence		
Percent of city/town government actors	−1.100	0.278
Percent of county government actors	0.677	0.502
Percent of special district government actors	−1.126	0.267
Percent of subnational government actors[a]	−2.589	0.013
Percent of national government actors	1.609	0.115
Percent of tribal government actors	−0.255	0.800
Percent total local government actors	−1.088	0.283
Indirect Influence		
Percent of inter-local government coalitions	−0.709	0.482
Percent of intergovernmental coalitions	0.409	0.685
Percent of international coalitions[a]	2.797	0.008
Percent of intersectoral coalitions	−0.425	0.673
Totals		
Total direct percent	−0.897	0.375
Total indirect percent	0.751	0.457

[a] <0.10.

The final research question examined U.S. and Canadian differences in the composition of governmental partners and stakeholders during the RAP process. Results are presented in Tables 9.9 through 9.11. Results indicate that Canada and the United States are statistically different in their use of direct and indirect participation, with Canada typically using more direct participation as opposed to the United States. For example, Table 9.9 shows that 78.5 percent of Canadian partners and stakeholders were direct government actors, while in the United States that number was at 49 percent. Table 9.10 reveals this difference as statistically significant, and Table 9.11 shows that the difference is between the United States and Canada (and not between the United States and the jointly administered areas).

Table 9.9   Average Composition Percentages for Major Participants Involved in Remedial Action Plan (RAP) Process in Each Great Lakes Area of Concern, by Country

	Joint Canada/ United States	United States	Canada
Direct Influence			
Percent of city/town government actors	13.6	7.08	15.7
Percent of county government actors	4.10	4.43	0
Percent of special district government actors	3.77	3.87	4.82
Percent of subnational government actors	19.2	13.7	26.2
Percent of national government actors	17.8	19.5	31.4
Percent of tribal government actors	1.05	0.450	0.440
Percent total local government actors	21.5	15.4	20.5
Indirect Influence			
Percent of inter-local government coalitions	0	1.37	0
Percent of intergovernmental coalitions	3.01	3.38	0
Percent of international coalitions	4.63	4.65	0
Percent of intersectoral coalitions	6.89	12.5	0.88
Totals			
Total direct percent	59.5	49.0	78.5
Total indirect percent	14.5	21.9	0.880
N	5	26	12

Table 9.10 ANOVA Results for Average Composition Percentages for Major Participants Involved in the Remedial Action Plan (RAP) Process, by Country of Origin (United States, Canada, Joint)

	F	Significance
Direct Influence		
Percent of city/town government actors	1.715	0.1930
Percent of county government actors[a]	3.296	0.0470
Percent of special district government actors	0.152	0.859
Percent of subnational government actors	3.442	0.0420
Percent of national government actors	1.641	0.206
Percent of tribal government actors	0.350	0.707
Percent total local government actors	0.560	0.575
Indirect Influence		
Percent of inter-local government coalitions	0.850	0.435
Percent of intergovernmental coalitions[a]	2.448	0.0990
Percent of international coalitions	2.088	0.137
Percent of intersectoral coalitions[a]	5.240	0.010
Totals		
Total direct percent[a]	8.613	0.001
Total indirect percent[a]	9.505	0.000

[a] <0.10.

Lessons Learned

Our results indicate that those AOCs with the best outcomes (e.g., RAP stage two or three achieved; delisting achieved; RAP PAC survival into the 2000s) typically had subnational and local governments comprising close to or over 20 percent of their partners and stakeholders. This is in contrast to AOCs with the worst outcomes (e.g., RAP stage zero; no delisting; RAP PAC absent in 2000) whose subnational and local governments typically comprised less than 20 percent of their partners and stakeholders. The AOCs with the worst outcomes also shared a trait of having national government actors dominate the composition of partners and stakeholders. In these AOCs, national government actors comprised over 20 percent of their

Table 9.11   ANOVA Post Hoc Comparison (Bonferroni Correction) for Average Composition Percentages for Major Participants Involved in the Remedial Action Plan (RAP) Process in Each Great Lakes Area of Concern, by Country of Origin (United States, Canada, Joint) (Only Statistically Significant Results Shown)

	Difference between Groups	Mean Difference	Significance
Direct Influence			
Percent of city/town government actors	—	—	—
Percent of county government actors	United States and Canada	0.04434	0.047
Percent of special district government actors	—	—	—
Percent of subnational government actors	United States and Canada	−0.12505	0.038
Percent of national government actors	—	—	—
Percent of tribal government actors	—	—	—
Percent total local government actors	—	—	—
Indirect Influence			
Percent of inter-local government coalitions	—	—	—
Percent of intergovernmental coalitions	United States and Canada	−0.03375	0.100
Percent of international coalitions	—	—	—
Percent of intersectoral coalitions	United States and Canada	−0.11653	0.008
Totals			
Total direct percent	United States and Canada	−0.29532	0.001
Total indirect percent	United States and Canada	0.21048	0.000

partners and stakeholders (with percentages for AOCs in RAP stage zero reaching as high as 71.7 percent).

International differences were minor. Generally, the United States did not rely as much as Canada on direct government actors. Instead, in the United States, indirect representation of government actors through another organization (identified as a coalition in this chapter) was approximately 20 percent. The effectiveness of indirect representation is still open to debate and beyond the scope of this analysis, but as of 2011 Canada had more delisted AOCs than the United States.

The results of this research seem to indicate a basic framework for effective participation: when possible, subnational and local government actors need to be directly involved in the participation effort, and they need to comprise a large percentage of the participants. When these subnational and local governments are actively involved, the propensity for program success increases. This reflects the strength of bottom-up policy making. Solving the complex public problems currently facing all levels of government, from localities through nation states, requires a collective effort from all levels of multilevel governance systems. Top-heavy policy solutions created and implemented by national governments and international bodies are unlikely to be successful for several reasons.

First, policy solutions developed from the top down do not include insights from those who must comply with their implementation. Even though experts understand technical aspects of public problems, they often cannot provide pragmatic advice on how well a policy will be received in a particular setting or how local variation in circumstances may affect its impact. But when deliberation over policy alternatives includes diverse groups of citizens and multilevel governance actors who are actually affected by the policy problem, a more nuanced understanding of the problem and solution will emerge.

Second, when citizens and lower-level governments are not included in collective decision making about issues that affect them, policy decisions from national governments and international organizations can unknowingly threaten values, identities, or traditions of a community. In such a case, citizens and lower-level governments may exhibit purposeful noncompliance, passive disinterest, or outright rejection of the policy solution which ultimately causes the policy to fail.

Finally and perhaps most importantly, top-heavy policy solutions fail to help citizens and lower-level governments grapple with their own priorities. Most complex problems are hard to resolve precisely because solutions often bring our shared, underlying values into conflict. In short, there is no single "correct" way to resolve most public concerns, and the appropriate solution will depend on how those involved decide to weight their own competing values. Thus participation in public deliberation by citizens and lower-level governments provides an important opportunity for social learning. Through discussion, the tensions among competing values are made clear, which forces citizens and lower-level governments to develop their own priorities and to make hard choices about what they are willing and unwilling to sacrifice.

In the United States, most participation efforts have not traditionally focused on the importance of participation from lower-level government actors such as subnational and local governments. Instead, most of the focus remains on increasing the public's participation. Although increasing public participation obviously remains important, our results suggest that subnational and local governments are integral to the success of such an effort. In the Great Lakes Areas of Concern in the 1990s, many local governments seemed to abandon the participation effort due to unfounded fears over financial obligations or because they viewed the process as illegitimate (MacKenzie 1996). Twenty years later, those areas are still floundering, stuck in the lower RAP stages with little hope of a delisting action in the immediate future. Our results indicate that the successful AOCs relied more heavily on direct subnational and local government participation rather than on national governments to control the process or indirect government coalitions to influence the process. Consequently, the successful implementation of projects via deliberation/participation depends on these lower levels of government. They are perhaps the most necessary component for a successful implementation of a program via deliberation/participation.

Recommendations for Multilevel Management

Few studies have considered the influence of multilevel actors, such as subnational and local governments, on deliberation, despite the fact that decentralized participation is important for the future of public management because top-heavy policy solutions are often ineffective. Public managers in national governments and international organizations understand the technical aspects of policy problems, but they often cannot provide effective input on implementation problems that may plague policy solutions "on the ground." Failure to obtain decentralized input, especially from citizens, often results in policy failure (Roberts 2008).

Given the growing recognition that average citizens and lower orders of government must play a role in resolving seemingly intransigent policy issues, we recommend that multilevel managers focus more on integrating decentralized participation from citizens and lower orders of government into public policy. As illustrated by this analysis, when those multilevel government actors are present, effective policy solutions occur. From a policy perspective, this is positive news for multilevel public managers. But this type of participation also has positive benefits for citizens in that many avenues of citizen participation can be funneled through local government participation in multilevel governance systems. And when citizens have a greater voice in policy, they develop civic identity and skills through direct, face-to-face experiences in deliberative settings which eventually help to enhance the value of democracy (Boyte 2011).

Future Considerations

This analysis has limitations. We analyzed only the presence or absence of multilevel government actors in citizen deliberations regarding the Great Lakes Areas of Concern (GLAC). We urge future scholars to examine the roles played by these multilevel government actors in these deliberations. In particular, future studies could examine whether or not local levels of government do a better job of facilitating citizen participation in multilevel governance systems. Local levels of government may be able to break the propensity of some governments to restrict citizen involvement in public policy. For instance, a very small number of government actors apparently restricted certain citizens and groups from participating in GLAC citizen deliberations (Sproule-Jones 2002). In some ways, this type of restrictive action is not surprising given the traditional, bureaucratic role of managers in multilevel government. Courting citizen deliberation is often at odds with notions of traditional Weberian bureaucracy. As explained by Max Weber:

> Bureaucracy is the means of transforming social action into rationally organized action. Therefore, as an instrument of rationally organizing authority relations, bureaucracy was and is a power instrument of the first order for one who controls the bureaucratic apparatus. Under otherwise equal conditions, rationally organized and directed action (*Gesellschaftshandeln*) is superior to every kind of collective behavior (*Massenhandeln*) and also social action (*Gemeinschaftshandeln*) opposing it. Where administration has been completely bureaucratized, the resulting system of domination is practically indestructible. (Weber 1922 [1968], 987)

This suggests that public managers may not have the incentive to "share" decision-making power with citizens. Consequently, we urge future scholars to examine deliberation in two ways: first, from the perspective of the citizen; second, from the perspective of the local government public manager, because the real impact of citizen deliberation will only be realized when both citizens and public managers value it. And that change may end up being the responsibility of local government actors in multilevel governance systems.

References

Beierle, Thomas C., and Jerry Cayford. 2002. *Democracy in Practice: Public Participation in Environmental Decisions*. Washington, DC: Resources for the Future Press.

Beierle, Thomas C., and David M. Konisky. 2001. What are we gaining from stakeholder involvement? Observations from environmental planning in the Great Lakes. *Environment and Planning C: Government and Policy* 19 (4): 515–527.

Box, Richard C. 1998. *Citizen Governance: Leading American Communities into the 21st Century.* Thousand Oaks, CA: Sage.

Boyte, Harry C. 2011. *We the People Politics: The Populist Promise of Deliberative Work.* Dayton, OH: The Kettering Foundation.

Frederickson, H. George. 1997. *The Spirit of Public Administration.* San Francisco, CA: Jossey-Bass.

Great Lakes Commission. 2002. *An Overview of U.S. Great Lakes Areas of Concern: Summaries of the 31 U.S. and Binational Areas of Concern, Including the Status of Remedial Action Plans, Scheduled Meetings, Progress and Achievements, Beneficial Use Impairments, Research, Publications, Community Involvement, and Partner Agencies and Organizations.* Ann Arbor, MI: Great Lakes Commission.

Great Lakes Water Quality Agreement. 1994. *Great Lakes Water Quality Agreement, Annex 2 (2a).* Windsor: International Joint Commission.

International Joint Commission. 2006. *13th Biennial Report on Great Lakes Water Quality.* Washington, DC: International Joint Commission.

Kettl, Donald F. 1997. The global revolution in public management: Driving themes, missing links. *Journal of Policy Analysis and Management* 16 (3): 446–462.

Kovalick Jr., Walter W., and Margaret M. Kelly. 1998. The EPA seeks its voice and role with citizens: Evolutionary engagement. In *Government Is Us: Public Administration in an Anti-Government Era,* edited by Cheryl S. King and Camilla Stivers. Thousand Oaks, CA: Sage, pp. 122–139.

MacKenzie, Susan H. 1996. *Integrated Resource Planning and Management: The Ecosystem Approach in the Great Lakes Basin.* Washington, DC: Island Press.

New York State. Department of Environmental Conservation. 2006. *Oswego River Remedial Action Plan State 3-Delisting.* Albany, NY: New York State Department of Environmental Conservation, Division of Water.

O'Flynn, Ian. 2010. Deliberative democracy, the public interest and the consociational model. *Political Studies* 58 (3): 572–589.

Rabe, Barry G. 1999. Sustainability in a regional context: The case of the Great Lakes Basin. In *Toward Sustainable Communities: Transition and Transformations in Environmental Policy,* edited by Daniel A. Mazmanian and Michael E. Kraft. Cambridge, MA: MIT Press, pp. 247–281.

Roberts, Nancy C. 2008. *The Age of Direct Citizen Participation.* Armonk, NY: M.E. Sharpe.

Scott, Graham, Ian Ball, and Tony Dale. 1997. New Zealand's public sector management reform: Implications for the United States. *Journal of Policy Analysis and Management* 16 (3): 357–381.

Sproule-Jones, Mark. 2002. Institutional experiments in the restoration of the North American Great Lakes environment. *Canadian Journal of Political Science* 35 (4): 835–857.

Wang, Xiaohu. 2001. Assessing public participation in U.S. cities. *Public Performance & Management Review* 24 (4): 322–336.

Weber, Max. 1922 [1968]. *Economy and Society.* Translated by Guenther Roth and Claus Wittich. Berkeley, CA: University of California Press. (Original work published 1922.)

Yang, Kaifeng, and Kathe Callahan. 2007. Citizen involvement efforts and bureaucratic responsiveness: Participatory values, stakeholder pressures, and administrative practicality. *Public Administration Review* 67 (2): 249–264.

Appendix

Coding protocol for remedial action plan (RAP) participants identified by the U.S. Environmental Protection Agency or Environment Canada as being "partners" or "stakeholders" in each Great Lakes Area of Concern.

Direct Actors

A. Governmental actors represent the entire government, their agency, their department or their program. One government can have multiple actors present. Elected policy makers and bureaucrats are both considered governmental actors.

1. City/Town Governmental Actor
   • If the participant represented a government/agency/department/program in a municipality, village, township, or town
2. County Government Actor
   • If the participant represented a county government/agency/department/program in the United States or corresponding subdivision in Canada
3. Special District Government Actor
   • If the participant represented a single purpose government/agency/department/program
4. Sub-national Government Actor
   • If the participant represented an American state government/agency/department/program or a Canadian province government/agency/department/program
5. National Government Actor
   • If the participant represented the American national government/agency/department/program or the Canadian national government/agency/department/program
6. Tribal Government Actor
   • If the participant represented a Tribal government/agency/department/program
7. Other Actors
   • If the participant represented industry, business, environmental groups, academia, or just themselves as a citizen participant

Indirect Actors

B. Coalition actors represent governments working with other types of organizations under one umbrella organization.

8. Inter-local Government Coalitions
   • If the participant was an organization representing the interests of many governments/agencies/departments/programs from municipalities, villages, townships, or towns

9. Intergovernmental Coalitions
    - If the participant was an organization representing the interests of different levels of governments in America or Canada (any combination of local, county, special district, subnational and national governments)
10. International Coalitions
    - If the participant was an organization representing the interests of different levels of governments in America and Canada (any combination of local, county, special district, subnational, and national governments) or any other international country or international organization
11. Intersectoral Coalitions
    - If the participant was an organization representing the interests of different orders of governments in America or Canada (any combination of local, county, special district, subnational, and national governments) and any actor from the private, non-profit or academic sectors

CONCLUSION: CONTESTING MULTILEVEL PUBLIC MANAGEMENT

III

Chapter 10

Recasting and Reframing a Polymorphous Concept: A Sober Second Look at Multilevel Governance

Christian Rouillard and Geneviève Nadeau

Contents

Introduction

The preceding chapters aimed at examining how to "make multilevel public management work." The rationale for this intellectual endeavor can be framed as twofold: (1) as a call for a better conceptual understanding of multilevel governance (MLG) as an analytical tool; and (2) as an invitation to normatively operationalize MLG in response to the pragmatic imperatives of efficiency, efficacy, and accountability.

Each of the chapters has animated, from a distinct perspective, the conversation about the current challenges of coordination that arise from increasing fragmentation, shifting responsibilities, new loci of power, and multiple points of decision making.

To date, a large proportion of the empirical work on MLG has been articulated in and around the environmental policy sector, where the characteristics of MLG might be more easily distinguished (e.g., implosion of traditional policy frontiers) (Eckerberg and Joas 2004). In their interesting contribution to this collection, Greitens, Strachan, and Welton highlight that the environmental remediation efforts in the Great Lakes Areas of Concern "depended on this new face of public management that relied on the involvement of multiple levels of government, collaboration between the public and private spheres, public participation, and decentralized decision making." (pp. 160–161).

In this regard, a major contribution of this edited book is its offering of a broader scope of comprehensive case studies including, but not limited to, environmental issues. Whether economic development policy governance within a multilayered institutional system (Conteh), financial regulation in the European Union (McKeen-Edwards), the policy capacity of the Canadian finance sector with respect to climate change adaptation (Williams), the introduction of fiscal federalism in Italian jurisdiction (Mussari and Giordano), institutional innovation based on horizontal coordination and consensus (Scotti), collaborative asymmetry for central–regional government relations (Cepiku), or the politics of securities markets supervision and regulation in Canada (Roberge), this collection of essays offers rich empirical insights for numerous fields and themes of public policy and public management.

To the same extent, this book tackles core issues that are currently challenging public administration, such as co-production of service delivery by different types and levels of actors (Conteh), coordination between departments to address emerging major issues that test conventional institutional capacities (Williams), intergovernmental accountability (Mussari and Giordano), the role of local and subnational governments (Greitens, Strachan, and Welton), and decentralized emergency planning (Bauroth), to name a few. It also offers a comprehensive overview of the constellation of issues and perspectives related to the use of MLG, enabling the reader to see points of convergence and divergence within the important body of work initially stimulated by, but no longer limited to, the experience of the European Union (EU).

Yet it seems that the use of MLG as a descriptive or analytical concept necessarily comes with a relative ambiguity and a certain uneasiness. Some of the chapters seemingly understand MLG as a synonym for federalism and decentralization, while others mobilize the term to describe dynamics of participation and collaboration. Consequently, it is challenging to draw from these contributions a coherent sense of MLG as a truly distinctive notion. In one of the chapters, moreover, the absence of MLG illustrates the difficulty and perhaps even impossibility of differentiating an analysis based on MLG from a more traditional analysis that builds upon numerous levels of regulation and/or issues of representativeness and consultation. This is quite possibly an illustration of the inherent limits of the MLG concept as it currently stands, not only in this book, but also throughout the relevant literature.

Therefore, a theoretical synthesis is required in order to examine briefly whether, beyond an actualization of the classic themes of public management (accountability, autonomy, decentralization, etc.), the MLG construct has a specific theoretical added value and if so, how it could best foster new and innovative analysis for the joint fields of political science and public administration. In this chapter, after putting the emergence of MLG as a concept in its historical and ideational context,* a comprehensive definition of this notion is laid out before questioning its relevance both as an analytical tool and as a normative concept.

Multilevel Governance as a Historically Situated Construct

Different "islands of theorizing" (Hooghe and Marks 2003) form the landscape of MLG. However, the contextualization of this concept is particularly inseparable from the development of "European Union studies," which look at the EU as a governance system that constitutes "a unique set of multi-level and regulatory institutions, as well as a hybrid mix of state and non-state actors in a nonhierarchical system of network governance" (Kohler-Koch and Rittberger 2006, 42).

Since the creation of the EU in 1957, diverse theoretical approaches have tried to conceptualize the fragmentation of power and the decentralization of authority (Jordan 2001). This necessitated a shift away from the study of the national and supranational levels associated with the ideal type of sovereign state, as articulated since the seventeenth century, and thus from the traditional dichotomies in policy studies (e.g., domestic/international policies, comparative politics/international relations) (Bache and Flinders 2004a; Piattoni 2009).

---

* For a more exhaustive contextualization, see Bache and Flinders (2004a, 1–3).

During the 1980s, some scholars pointed to the ineffectiveness of classic theoretical approaches, such as intergovernmentalism, neofunctionalism, and supranationalism, in capturing the nature, extent, and implications of the mutations associated with a multiplication of the levels of political mobilization within the EU, until then dominated by the field of international relations. In their view, new theoretical tools were required (see Bache and Flinders 2004b; Piattoni 2009; Littoz-Monnet 2010). Therefore,

> The point of departure for [the] ... [MLG] approach is the existence of overlapping competencies among multiple levels of governments and the interaction of political actors across these levels. (...) Instead of the two level game assumptions adopted by state-centrists, MLG theorists posit a set of overarching, multi-level policy networks. The structure of political control is variable, not constant, across policy areas. (Marks et al. 1996, 41 in Jordan 2001, 199)

A set of other economic and sociopolitical factors seem to have contributed, in an incremental fashion, to the attractiveness of the concept of MLG. Conteh, in his analysis of the governance of innovation systems in a multilayered institutional context, underlines notably the joint impact of globalization, shifts in the political culture, regionalism, and civic engagement on the public management climate. To this list could be added other classic and significant trends, such as decentralization, horizontality, networks, the hollowing out of the state, continuous budget cuts in public spending, and increasing professionalism at the infranational level (Peters and Pierre 2001).

In that regard, the MLG concept appeared well suited to facilitate an alternative understanding of the uncertain and unpredictable patterns of this new governance landscape, especially as far as coordination issues were concerned (Hooghe and Marks 2002; Bache and Flinders 2004a), to the point that MLG became "an established theory of EU policy making" (Bache and Flinders 2004b, 197). In 2001, EU President Romano Prodi took up the expression in his call for more effective MLG in Europe (Hooghe and Marks 2003).

Although the emergence of the notion of MLG appears to have taken place in a coherent political and theoretical setting, its contours still seem vague today, almost 20 years after its first use. To some extent, the collection of essays in this book illustrates the relative conceptual and ontological stretching that seems to plague the concept, regardless of the inherent merits of their analyses. The authors who made the effort to situate the concept of MLG gave it different, if not opposing, meanings. While some authors refer to autonomy and partnerships that would supersede hierarchy, others speak of vertical coordination. Thus, before moving forward to examine the range of MLG as an analytical tool and a normative concept, a conceptual clarification, albeit a tentative one, appears unavoidable.

Toward a Conceptual Clarification of Multilevel Governance?

As is the case with the concept of governance, many definitions of MLG coexist. The initial definition proposed by Marks (1993, 392 in Hooghe and Marks 2003, 234) is one of a "system of continuous negotiation among nested governments at several territorial tiers—supranational, national, regional and local." This definition echoes Mussari and Giordano's discussion of MLG as a "shared rule among diverse levels of government" (p. 30). While such a definition is more oriented toward the informal, shifting dynamics of MLG, other definitions, such as Jessop's, are geared toward the "institutionalization of reflexive self-organization among multiple stakeholders across several scales of state territorial organization" (2004, 57). In almost all tentative definitions in the literature, however, the reference to MLG seems to underlie four common assessments and assumptions.

First, as Piattoni (2009) has emphasized, MLG voluntarily confuses analytical distinctions that have been, to date, central to the reflection on the modern (European) state and to the field of international relations—namely, those between center and periphery, between state and society, and between domestic and international levels. Therefore, the identification of territorial levels embedded in decision making becomes more difficult in the context of complex and overlapping networks. Moreover, according to Peters and Pierre, MLG "makes no normative prejudgments about a logical order between different institutional tiers" (2004, 77).

Second, the concept of MLG highlights the undefined, complex, and highly contextual institutional relations between different intra- and (increasingly) extragovernmental actors, networks, and levels (Bache and Flinders 2004b; Peters and Pierre 2004). MLG can therefore be understood as a specific pattern of power relations, where the presumed loosening of regulatory frameworks favors the strategic and autonomous behavior of non-governmental actors (Bache and Flinders 2004b; Peters and Pierre 2004).

Third, and echoing this second dimension, the new political order is assumed to be negotiated rather than predefined legally by constitutions and by other conventional juridical frameworks (Bache and Flinders 2004b; Peters and Pierre 2004).

Fourth, the role of the state is transformed while state actors are developing new strategies for coordination, direction, and networking to protect and, in some cases, improve its autonomy (Bache and Flinders 2004b). In this regard, the nature of democratic accountability is somehow challenged. As will be discussed further, this question seems to have been rarely addressed in the literature on MLG.

In light of these dimensions, and for the purpose of this discussion, we will retain Peters and Pierre's definition, in which MLG "refers to negotiated, nonhierarchical exchanges between institutions at the transnational, national, regional and local levels (...) [and] to a vertical 'layering' of governance processes at these different levels" (2001, 131).

Does this resemble the informal yet fundamental side of federalism, especially when driven by network analysis? Let us take a closer look.

Old Wine in a New Bottle: Federalism with a Discursive Turn?

In a noted conceptual effort, Hooghe and Marks (1996, 2001) elaborated two ideal types of MLG. Type I is to "establish a stable division of labor between a limited number of levels of government with general jurisdiction over a given territory or a given set of issues and mutually exclusive membership" (Piattoni 2009, 170). Thus, it reminds us of traditional federal systems and could be embedded more formally in a set of values related to community and representative democracy.* This similitude between MLG and federalism is omnipresent in the book, which can be at least partly explained by the fact that most of the chapters explore Canadian cases, thus situated in a federal context. Consequently, the conceptual boundary between MLG and federalism appears somewhat blurred, particularly in the chapters by Bauroth, Mussari and Giordano, Greitens and colleagues, Roberge, and Williams. This blurring also exists, to a lesser extent, with the concepts of devolution, subsidiarity, and decentralization. For example, Williams' comprehensive study of the policy capacity of the Canadian finance sector vis-à-vis climate change adaptation illustrates this conceptual closeness when it refers to "structures of multilevel governance inherent in Canadian federalism" (p. 136).

Different works in the literature have already questioned the articulation of the concepts of federalism and MLG. Wasn't federalism precisely focused on the distribution of power among diverse orders of government and on the interactions between these orders (Hooghe and Marks 2003)? According to some, one of the pertinent distinctions is that MLG refers to overlapping jurisdictional levels, while federalism refers to levels defined more formally (Bache and Flinders 2004a). Yet most people familiar with the study of federalism would find it hard to accept this rigid dichotomy as a clear and satisfactory distinction for MLG. According to Peters and Pierre (2004), MLG is also meant to go beyond the sole thesis of federalism in mutation because the emerging processes that it addresses, while not always escaping standard institutional constraints, are not systematically attached to them, and rely more on informal negotiation, flexibility, and vagueness.

Other viewpoints include Stein and Turkewitsch's proposal (2010, 3) to extend the concept of federalism to include MLG's key lines and thus reflect federalism more accurately in a global era, ultimately speaking in terms of "networked federalism," which does very little to clarify things. Peters and Pierre (2001, 75) suggest that the MLG concept distinguishes itself from federalism's "institutional layering"

---

* Type II, which does not seem to have much relevance as a contemporary phenomenon, is understood as a somewhat anarchic and shifting layering of jurisdictions (Piattoni 2009).

by providing a more comprehensive illustration of "intergovernmental relations in which subnational authorities engage in direct exchange with supranational or global institutions" (2001, 75). In this regard, networks appear to be central to the analysis of these exchanges, just as interest groups were for liberal pluralism in the 1950s and 1960s (Piattoni 2009).

In light of this overview, the definition of what MLG *is* appears somewhat clearer, and so is the understanding of what MLG *isn't*. For example, it is not a deepening of the traditional assumptions of the field of intergovernmental relations. It is not the organization of different governance processes into a hierarchy (Peters and Pierre 2004). Nonetheless, these few elements of definition leave some important gray areas regarding what the concept covers and what it does not. Did Orwell (1946, in Bache and Flinders 2004b) not warn us against the use, often with some teleological purpose, of conceptual imprecision in political language?

This partial assessment raises major questions. For example, what might be the ontological and epistemological contributions of an analysis that does not acknowledge similar work undertaken on federalism at the very core of the same issues (jurisdictional politics, coordination, collaboration, harmonization, etc.) in previous years and even decades? Is MLG policy analysis trying to catch up to new and complex sociopolitical realities or is it instead a way of framing these sociopolitical realities—that is, a different process of reification that marginalizes the state as a unit of analysis and an empirical object? These central questions call for a deeper examination of the added value of the concept, notably as an analytical tool.

Multilevel Governance as Analytical Tool: Reification of the Decision-Making Process?

Numerous works have highlighted some of MLG's theoretical contributions to the understanding of contemporary and emerging political dynamics, especially in the context of the European Union. Among them are the identification of new research themes (Armstrong and Bulmer 1998 in Jordan 2001), a facilitation of the meshing of European studies with other subdisciplines (Jordan 2001), an actualization of the henceforth mutual dependencies characteristic of institutional exchanges (Jessop 2004; Rhodes 1997 in Peters and Pierre 2004), and a better appreciation of the variations in patterns of participation and influence (Bache and Flinders 2004b). From a public administration perspective, one of the contributions of MLG would be to explain how the autonomy of the state's executive powers is increasingly undermined (Jordan 2001), notably by forcing the analyst to account for the dynamics of fragmentation of authority, decentralization, and supranationalization (Bauroth, this volume; Stubbs 2005). Overall, according to Peters and Pierre, this notion "challenges much of our traditional understanding of how the state operates, what determines its capacities, what its contingencies are, and ultimately of the organization of democratic and accountable government" (2001, 131).

The previous chapters contribute to putting some of these key elements in perspective. Yet the added value of the concept for causal explanation and interpretation remains unclear. Fifteen years ago, Smith raised an essential question that draws us beyond these general considerations:

> Described at such a high level of generality, multi-level governance no doubt helps us get an initial analytical grip on a "nobody in charge world" (Stoker 1995, p. 3). However, as soon as one attempts to discern the political consequences of this situation in specific areas, doubts flood in about what it helps to study and what it actually aims to explain. (Smith 1997, 112)

Thus it would be useful to determine if the contribution of the concept resides in the novelty of the phenomenon described or in the originality of the perspective raised.

Novelty

Would the value of MLG as an analytical framework be found in the novelty of its proposed perspectives? On the one hand, Peters and Pierre underline that the described phenomenon might not be as new or emergent as it appears, because

> On closer inspection, it becomes clear that for the most part intergovernmental relations in most advanced states have always been characterized by two concurrent types of exchanges; a formal, constitutionally defined exchange and an informal, contextually defined exchange. Most intergovernmental relations probably require both of these exchanges to operate efficiently. (Peters and Pierre 2004, 89)

On the other hand, Jordan (2001) suggests not only that the "multilevel governance" expression dates back to the 1980s, but also that the perspective it underlies is far from new. As early as the 1950s and 1960s, students of local government were dedicated, especially in the United States and in Western Europe, to the understanding of the dynamics of polycentric governance, as well as to its articulation within various levels of rule (Hooghe and Marks 2003). Moreover, dynamics of MLG would have been significant in Europe 20 to 30 years before the Single European Act (1987), swinging between periods of supranationalism and intergovernmentalism (Hooghe and Marks 2003). In this regard, MLG essentially appears as a postmodernist reconfiguration of largely preexisting theoretical notions (Jordan 2001).

If we admit that these perspectives and phenomena are not new, we must ask why the proponents of MLG neglect to acknowledge and integrate earlier work related to these questions, especially—but not exclusively—regarding informal exchanges between different orders of government. As illustrated by Cepiku's interesting chapter on central–regional government relations in Italy, federalism, be it asymmetrical or not, remains relevant for many discussions and analyses often hidden under the MLG umbrella. The novelty of MLG as a concept, or its relative distinction from federalism, lies in its emphasis on horizontal processes and consensual relations, whereas federalism is restricted to vertical processes and hierarchical relations. In many ways, MLG (flexible and informal) is to federalism (rigid and formal) what management is supposed to be to administration. But that may be precisely the problem: MLG's novelty comes from its being distinct from a very limited and narrow understanding of the previous term of reference, more so than from being truly distinct from all that federalism had to offer for analytical work and empirical research.

Originality

Alternatively, does the value of MLG rest in the originality of the tools it provides to better understand in all their complexity integration and institutional change, two major markers among others of the theoretical debate (Littoz-Monnet 2010)?

In light of the existing literature, it seems that the answer is no. Some of the main advocates of the concept of MLG agree on this:

> We make no claim to originality. The types we describe are distilled from research in local government, federalism, European integration, international relations, and public policy. Type I and Type II governance arise—under different guises and with different labels—as fundamental alternatives in each of these fields. (Hooghe and Marks 2003, 241)

So, as Hamlet would say, there's the rub. While its lack of distinctive content may have prevented MLG from being assessed critically by some scholars, the concept has been criticized in the literature. Some of the most salient criticisms are the following: inadequate acknowledgement of the multisectorial dimension of the European Union (Jordan 2001); excessive emphasis on the implementation phase and insufficient differentiation of all phases of the policy process (Jordan 2001); inappropriate dismissal of the nation–state in regard to the real interactional dynamics and processes among collective actors (Jordan 2001; Welch and Kennedy-Pipe 2004 in Bache and Flinders 2004b); unwarranted emphasis on the mobilization of new actors, while neglecting the impacts and influences of such mobilization on policy outcomes (Bache and Flinders 2004b); lack of significant difference or contribution when compared with other dominant approaches (Littoz-Monnet 2010); paradoxical focus on government, rather than on governance (Littoz-Monnet 2010); substantive ambiguity linked to the important number of trends indistinctly included in the concept (e.g., denationalization of the state, reintroduction of functional and territorial powers, internationalization of policy regimes, etc.) and lack of appreciation for counter-trends (increased role of the state in metagovernance)

(Jessop 2004); inadequate assumptions about the aconflictual nature of the negotiation process (Peters and Pierre 2004); stato-centric naturalization of the state–
society frontier (Jessop 2004); disproportionate focus on problem-solving successes,
at the expense of understanding governance failures (Jessop 2004); and anachronic
normative assumptions regarding the type of government resources and contemporary forms of democratic systems (Jessop 2004).

In addition, authors such as Stubbs question the reification of the *levels* at the
core of MLG-centered approaches and suggest that rather than being given, such
geographic scales are shifting and dynamic social and political constructs, whose
evolution and contingency must be critically examined through a perspective on
the *politics of scale* (2005, 76). For authors such as Jessop (2004), it is only the
inclusion of both non-state and state actors, as well as territorial and functional
issues, that distinguish MLG from widespread intergovernmentalism. This distinction sometimes appears confused in the preceding chapters, as evidenced, for
example, by the comprehensive and thorough analysis of Italian fiscal federalism
developed by Mussari and Giordano.

Peters and Pierre suggest that because of the realities of governance, such as the
difficult definition of common goals by means other than coercion or centralization, "the outcomes of multi-level governance processes are likely to be either conflicts that have to be resolved in other venues, or 'pork-barrel' agreements that give
everybody something and do not necessarily resolve the fundamental policy problems that produced the need for the bargaining in the first place" (2004, 86–87).

However, because the outcomes of the policy process in MLG settings have yet
to be explored, 20 years after the coining of the concept, there is no detailed and
comprehensive understanding of these issues. Littoz-Monnet (2010) even suggests
that the fundamental objective of understanding how governance's transformations are shaped by the interactions among different levels of actors (infranational,
national, supranational) has been completely abandoned. Moreover, major methodological questions concerning the appropriate strategies to better understand
those transformations and identify other types of factors have, so far, remained
unaddressed (Bache and Flinders 2004b).

At this point, the applicability of MLG to a very broad scope of situations could
be considered either a strength or a weakness of the concept (Bache and Flinders
2004b; Peters and Pierre 2004). Couldn't any complex problem with multiple dimensions be labeled, from now on, as a MLG phenomenon (Peters and Pierre 2004)?

It is also worth noting that MLG's relative deficiency as an explanatory or inter-
pretative framework echoes the preoccupation of Conteh who, in his chapter, states
that "there is not enough attention given to how different political systems actually
adapt their institutional and policy designs to operate effectively in the emergent
complexity of multilevel governance systems design" (p. 96).

The gap between the description of the characteristics of a given phenomenon (or a set of mixed elements conceptualized as a sole phenomenon) and the
explanation or interpretation of this phenomenon constitutes a major source of

the criticisms of MLG approaches: "MLG provides an appealing picture of what the EU looks like but is weak at explaining which levels are the most important and why, and what actually motivated the experiment in governance in the first place" (Jordan 2001, 194).

The rich narrative and strong historical nature of Bauroth's paper on floods in Michigan and Manitoba, Canada, might be representative of this mostly descriptive trend. Yet, the balance between description and analysis is evidently not static, as illustrated by Williams' contribution, which aims to portray MLG as an explanation for the institutional limits of Canada's financial policy capacity to deal with climate change, albeit arguably at the expense of the conceptual vagueness that plagues MLG to this day.

In light of these elements, it might be more appropriate to speak of MLG as a convincing description of the ongoing phenomena or as "an organizing perspective" (Bache and Flinders 2004b, 203) that serves as a counterweight to a state-centered perspective, rather than an analytical framework of the governance process that integrates causal explanations or provides interpretive tools (Jordan 2001; Olsson 2003; Bache and Flinders 2004b; Jessop 2004; Peters and Pierre 2004). In this regard, Jordan (2001, 201) wondered if MLG would be a promising "framing metaphor" as opposed to a conceptual tool. This is possibly how one might best understand Greitens and colleagues' use of MLG to report on the "importance of participation from lower level government actors such as subnational and local governments" (pp. 177–178).

This relative blurring between description and explanation is a reminder of the nature of pluralist approaches, which paradoxically did resolve fundamental questions regarding the structure of power relations (Stubbs 2005), as well as the criticisms they faced many years and, indeed, decades ago (Peters and Pierre 2004). As such, the destructive power of the MLG concept as initially sketched by Marks (1996) and, more notably, its actor-centeredness may be more significant than its constructive power to facilitate an understanding of what happens regarding the *policy* (e.g., policy arrangements), the *polity* (e.g., state structures), and the *politics* (e.g., political mobilization) (Piattoni 2009).

It seems that the stage is (still) set for a deep(er) reflection on the specific ontology of MLG and its theoretical relevance, as well as on its epistemology and its empirical range, notably compared to other existing concepts (Piattoni 2009). Such examination would benefit from an empirical evaluation at the core of a "thick description" (Geertz 1973 in Smith 1997, 720) and from a true theoretical articulation that goes beyond relatively ad hoc repetitions of some key elements (Smith 1997; Jessop 2004; Kohler-Koch and Rittberger 2006). For Bache and Flinders (2004b), a real concept that moves beyond the traditional realms of discussion for MLG (e.g., Europe, environmental policies) will help to clarify whether we are in a situation of conceptual stretching, where the broadening of the concept to cover more elements has led to a distortion of its substance, or whether the content of the concept might be effectively extended to other new empirical cases.

If the case has not been convincing regarding the potential of the concept of MLG as an analytical framework, perhaps MLG could be considered instead as a normative notion? The next section will explore this possibility.

Multilevel Governance as a Normative Concept: Perspectives on Democracy, Legitimacy, and Accountability

Ideas, like human beings and objects, can have great powers of seduction. Behind the discussions of the potential of the concept for theoretical analysis, MLG (as a theoretical approach and as a mode of organization) seems to spark a real normative enthusiasm among some scholars, who perceive it as "a normatively superior mode of allocating authority" (Bache and Flinders 2004b, 195). For Marks and Hooghe, for example,

> A common element across these literatures is that the dispersion of gov-ernance across multiple jurisdictions is both more efficient than and normatively superior to the central state monopoly. Most important is the claim that governance must operate at multiple scales in order to capture variations in the territorial reach of policy externalities. Because externalities arising from the provision of public goods vary immensely (…) so should the scale of governance. (Marks and Hooghe 2004, 16)

Some contributions in this collection inherently embrace the assumptions of the desirability of MLG as a model of governance, most notably by prescribing winning conditions for its effective implementation (e.g., Greitens, Strachan, and Welton). Conteh, for example, suggests that "the governance of innovation systems requires a governance architecture that transcends and integrates the various levels of government as well as institutionalizes a network governance framework. In this regard, public management is about multi-sector and multi-actor engagement energized by global forces" (p. 89).

Stubbs (2005, 69) qualifies as "premature normativism" such a trend to (try to) evaluate normatively the merits of MLG in terms of efficiency or responsiveness, rather than to (try to) understand first its inner workings. For Stubbs, to suggest that "there is no agreement about how multi-level governance should be organized" (Hooghe and Marks 2004, 16 in Stubbs 2005, 69) is to naturalize a set of judgments and assumptions on the nature of this new form of governance, on what it should become, and on the sole necessity of such a consensus for its implementation.

Having said that, is there a way to go beyond the dichotomy of state-centered versus society-centered approaches, which seems to be a perennial feature of the governance literature, including that of MLG? This may possibly occur by stressing processes instead of institutions and actors, while still including them in the analysis. To that extent, governance, including MLG, can be understood as *a dynamic and multidimensional process through which collective actors in the public, private, and voluntary (third) sectors construct, deconstruct, and reconstruct the configuration of their interactions, including the sharing of common, but always fragile and temporary, (strategic or operational) goals, through the selection and implementation of instruments for public action. The problem-solving capacity (resources and constraints) is asymmetrically fragmented among collective actors, whose autonomy fluctuates depending on the issues, challenges, technical devices, and policy sectors. The state remains a key player in the governance process, due to its exclusive authority (capacity and legitimacy) to aggregate diverse sociopolitical goals, as well as to implement the administrative means to govern.*

Simply put, only the state can find a relative point of equilibrium between unlimited and conflicting demands, through (more or less) coherent policy statements. Yet the state is not just a referee or a broker, but a stakeholder as well. Therefore, in the end, the notion of governance is not meant to express the presumed transformation of the bureaucratic welfare state to a more horizontal strategic state or, in other words, from autocratic government to shared governance, *but rather the passage from one configuration of complex interactions among collective actors, be they multilevel or not, to another.*

Obviously, this chapter does not aim to settle whether or not MLG constitutes "a more desirable approach to intergovernmental decision-making" (Stein and Turkewitsch 2010, 6), but rather to examine, in the next section, how this normativity seems to have affected the treatment (or the non-treatment) of fundamental democratic issues, namely those of legitimacy and accountability, for the study of political science and public administration.

Multilevel Governance, Legitimacy, and Accountability

The basis on which governance and, more specifically, MLG rest appears distinct from that on which the traditional conception of representative democracy was established and, incidentally, can hardly be compared with the latter (Jachtenfuchs 1997 in Piattoni 2009). Nonetheless, among the aspects that raise significant questions are those related to the positioning, on an equal footing, of actors and jurisdictions with a general (e.g., infranational governments) versus a specific (e.g., interest groups) mandate. Considering those actors as capable of demonstrating that they can intervene to the same degree for the sake of the common good not only raises legitimacy issues (Jobert and Muller 1987 in Smith 1997), but it also reveals some important transformations in terms of public philosophies. For example, when authors highlight the major institutional role of "local private and public research firms" in the new governance architecture, the silent disappearance of the nation-state as a key actor, to the point that it becomes unclear what is "public" anymore (in the sense of *public management*), underscores a political and philosophical posture that cannot be kept implicit.

On the democratic level, significant tensions exist between the partnership and deliberative dimensions of MLG, and the intrinsic dimensions of representative authority (Eckerberg and Joas 2004; Peters and Pierre 2004), especially when MLG operates in a framework exempt from democratic rules to better adapt to these new realities. Peters and Pierre thus raise a major issue of accountability: "But is multi-level governance the outcome of political deliberation, and how do we hold multi-level governance to political account? Has problem-solving capacity (Scharpf 1997) and outcomes taken precedence over democratic input and accountability?" (2004, 85).

The complete omission of this "crisis of accountability" in the MLG-related literature constitutes a crucial problem (Stubbs 2005). Furthermore, how could one dissociate MLG from the trends of globalization, decentralization, deregulation, and agencification, which shape the contemporary political landscape, notably by eroding the basis of modern political authority (Peters and Pierre 2004)? For Stubbs, "insofar as neo-liberalization represents a 'form of social rule' (Graefe 2004), the silence regarding this phenomenon in the multi-level governance literature is astonishing and deeply problematic because it ignores the complex ways in which pressures from above and below the Nation-state can themselves contribute to neo-liberalization and new forms of social rule" (2005, 72).

Admittedly, discussing these issues necessitates making explicit some normative assumptions about the definition of democracy that is in play, but it is still possible to explore the potential mechanisms required to adapt political responsibility to emerging models of MLG. Would it be the extension of representative democracy to new levels of governance? Or would it be the creation of new control systems inspired by self-governance (Bache and Flinders 2004b)?

Those issues converge toward the central problem of legitimacy. In her contribution, McKeen-Edwards proposes an interesting articulation of the questions of legitimacy and democratic accountability in EU governance, although without linking it explicitly to intrinsic characteristics of MLG. And yet, while electoral legitimacy henceforth appears insufficient to ensure the accountability of new types and levels of actors involved in political decisions and interventions embedded in largely fragmented processes and structures (Bache and Flinders 2004b), how can MLG be said to constitute an added value for—or at least not a plague on—the democratic level? The question of legitimacy goes, in this context, way beyond the sole managerial dimension of efficiency, especially when keeping in mind that "participation" does not equate with "influence" in any political process, including those labeled as "governance." It thus appears risky to promptly eliminate from the MLG analysis nation–state institutions that, so far, have played the role of democratic safeguards in terms of political control and accountability.

Lessons Learned: Beware of Conceptual Stretching, Theoretical Plasticity, and Reification

Along with Peters and Pierre, one can wonder if the concept of MLG constitutes "a 'Faustian bargain' in which core values of democratic government are traded for accommodation, consensus and the purported efficiency in governance" (2004, 85). In this context, the devil, or at least those benefiting strategically from this trade-off, would be the actors who are advantaged by informal negotiation processes among orders of government over legal and constraining procedural frameworks that grant some power to the less powerful (Peters and Pierre 2004). The use of one given concept over another does make a difference, even if those concepts are not necessarily mutually exclusive: one will place the emphasis on different elements or suggest a different relational dynamic between similar elements, leading the research in a different direction. Reification of the topic—that is, making the object of study analytically real and empirically concrete—is but one of many consequences. The relative vagueness of MLG, including its ambiguous kinship with federalism, also illustrates some conceptual stretching (Collier and Mahon 1993)—that is, when the cumulative distortion of a concept applied to different cases and situations renders it vague to the point of lacking any distinctive and specific features.

Given that these questions have been relatively (Bache and Flinders 2004b), if not largely (Peters and Pierre 2004), absent from the scholarship on MLG, one wonders whether the proponents of a research agenda on MLG would even find it necessary, or at least preferable, to integrate and deepen them. Such an attentive examination appears especially important in a context where the extent of the transformations and, more particularly, of the political impacts of the MLG model for contemporary democratic governance are yet to be known and understood. Conceptual stretching should not lead to theoretical plasticity—that is, when analysis seems to be (or is in fact) built in an ad hoc fashion on iconoclastic elements of different theoretical traditions, oftentimes lacking rigor and cohesiveness.

Finally, labeling is always a difficult and, at times, sterile thing to do. But it is also important in order to make sense of the academic literature in any field, or on any topic, as well as to understand the current state of research. Labeling and its corollary, classification, are needed to distinguish true contributions to knowledge from rhetorical innovation.

Concluding Remarks: One Step Forward or Two Steps Back?

This edited book aimed to present a collection of scholarly work based on North American and EU case studies on "how to make MLG work." This concluding chapter began by identifying two facets to the issue in question: whether it is "making MLG work" as an analytical and theoretical tool or as a governance model. After reviewing the historical and theoretical context of the emergence of the MLG concept, this chapter explored its internal coherence and added value, on both analytical and normative levels, taking into account the analyses of the preceding chapters, as well as the relevant literature. It briefly highlighted, among other things, the discomforts, paradoxes, and conceptual issues and challenges that are associated with this concept. The need for a renewal of the MLG concept remains an open question. Nonetheless, interesting avenues have been identified in the literature, which can facilitate reflection on these matters. Some aspects of the MLG-related scholarship appear largely overtheorized, at the expense of empirical validations among diverse sectors and levels of policy (Jordan 2001), while other major political issues associated with MLG seem confined to a blind spot in the literature on these questions. Even though the transition from description to (1) a theorization subject to (2) empirical analysis seems difficult (Piattoni 2009) because of the scope of the relevant literature, it should not impede this intellectual enterprise. It appears essential to locate MLG research in a broader set of deep and ongoing global transformations, both sociocultural and politico-economic, to understand what, exactly, is at stake (Jessop 2004). It is only in this way that we will be able to clarify how, for example, the concept of MLG offers an added value over those of federalism and decentralization when it comes to developing a comprehensive understanding of such major phenomena.

Beyond these criticisms, however, the attractiveness of the MLG concept will ensure that the theorization of MLG continues to occupy a place of choice in the contemporary academic tradition, even if it fails to provide a richer understanding of the dynamics between the different "levels" of policy (Littoz-Monnet 2010). Thereby, we echo Jordan, who suggests that

> The "governance turn" (…) reluctance to ask "big" questions about the governance of the EU is partly also a symptom of post-modernism's attention to local dynamics and differences in perspective, and its dislike of grand narratives and overarching explanatory frameworks (…) For this reason MLG will probably survive as a useful descriptive picture of the EU even though it fails to reach the standards of a comprehensive theory of integration. (Jordan 2001, 205)

Continuing in the current direction of an essentially technical theorization or description of a given mode of coordination without consistently exploring the fundamental epistemological, theoretical, and political issues raised by the reification of a loose concept such as MLG would be tantamount to renouncing the study of key questions that arguably constitute the essence of our respective disciplines.

Those few elements of reflections suggest that the theoretical and epistemological discussion of MLG as a normative concept is far from being settled or even truly initiated. If this concept presents some interesting dimensions, it also carries its own limitations. These limits deserve to be better understood in order to avoid the mirage of "institutional invention" (Smith 1997, 114). It is by rising to such challenges that the discussion of MLG will truly be embedded in the cornerstones of political science and public administration, as rigorous, innovative, and coherent intellectual ventures. The time has come.

References

Bache, I., and M. Flinders, eds. 2004a. Themes and issues in multi-level governance. In *Multi-Level Governance*, edited by I. Bache and M. Flinders. Oxford: Oxford University Press, pp. 1–7.

Bache, I., and M. Flinders, eds. 2004b. Conclusions and implications. In *Multi-Level Governance*, edited by I. Bache and M. Flinders. Oxford: Oxford University Press, pp. 194–229.

Collier, D., and J.A. Mahon, Jr. 1993. Conceptual "stretching" revisited: Adapting categories in comparative analysis. *American Political Science Review* 87 (4): 845–855.

Eckerberg, K., and M. Joas. 2004. Multi-level environmental governance: A concept under stress? *Local Environment* 9 (5): 405–412.

Hooghe, L., ed. 1996. *Cohesion Policy and European Integration. Building Multi-Level Governance*. Oxford: Clarendon Press.

Hooghe, L., and G. Marks. 2001. *Multi-Level Governance and European Integration*. Lanham, MD: Rowman & Littlefield.

Hooghe, L., and G. Marks. 2002. Types of multi-level governance. *Les Cahiers Européens de Sciences Po.* 03/2002, 30p.

Hooghe, L., and G. Marks. 2003. Unraveling the central state, but how? Types of multi-level governance. *American Political Science Review* 97 (2): 233–243.

Jessop, B. 2004. Multilevel governance and multilevel metagovernance. Changes in the EU as integral moments in the transformation and reorientation of contemporary statehood. In *Multi-Level Governance*, edited by I. Bache and M. Flinders. Oxford: Oxford University Press, pp. 49–74.

Jordan, A. 2001. The European Union: An evolving system of multi-level governance...or government? *Policy & Politics* 29 (2): 193–208.

Kohler-Koch, B., and B. Rittberger. 2006. Review article: The "Governance Turn" in EU studies. *Journal of Common Market Studies* 44: 27–49.

Littoz-Monnet, A. 2010. Dynamic multi-level governance—Bringing the study of multi-level interactions into the theorising of European integration. *European Integration Online Papers* 14: article 01.

Olsson, J. 2003. Democracy paradoxes in multi-level governance: Theorizing on structural fund system research. *Journal of European Public Policy* 10 (2): 283–300.

Peters, B. Guy, and Jon Pierre, 2001. Developments in intergovernmental relations: Towards multi-level governance. *Policy & Politics* 29 (2): 131–135.

Peters, B. Guy, and Jon Pierre. 2004. Multi-level governance and democracy: A Faustian bargain? In *Multi-Level Governance*, edited by I. Bache and M. Flinders. Oxford: Oxford University Press, pp. 75–89.

Piattoni, Simona. 2009. Multi-level governance: A historical and conceptual analysis. *Journal of European Integration* 31 (2): 163–180.

Smith, A. 1997. Studying multi-level governance—Examples from French translations of the structural funds. *Public Administration* 75 (Winter): 711–729.

Stein, M., and L. Turkewitsch. 2010. Multilevel governance and federalism: Closely linked or incompatible concepts? *Participation* 34 (2): 3–5.

Stubbs, P. 2005. Stretching concepts too far? Multi-level governance, policy transfer and the politics of scale in South East Europe. *Southeast European Politics* VI (2): 66–87.

Index

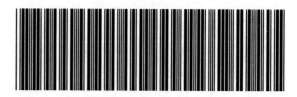